OUT OF THE GHETTO?
The Catholic Community in Modern Scotland

Edited by
RAYMOND BOYLE
and
PETER LYNCH

JOHN DONALD PUBLISHERS LTD
EDINBURGH

For Noelle (RB)
and
James and Margaret Lynch (PL)

ISBN 0 85976 487 7

British Library Cataloguing in Publication Data
A catalogue record for this book is available from the British Library.

Typeset by WestKey Limited, Falmouth, Cornwall
Printed and bound in Great Britain by Bell & Bain Ltd., Glasgow

PREFACE

The origins of this book arise from a conference held at Stirling University in January 1997. What we wanted to achieve at this one-day event was to examine the multi-faceted and complex relationship between Catholicism, Catholics, the Catholic Church and aspects of Scottish society. It had struck us that, though historians had examined the experience of Catholics of Irish origin in Scotland, there existed little work which attempted to locate the impact and influence of Catholicism on contemporary Scottish culture and identity.

Such a wide-ranging aspiration is, of course, not going to be achieved in this volume. However, it is a start and opens up many lines for future enquiry. As is often the case, it is perhaps useful to state what this book is *not* about. It is not specifically about the Catholic Church; rather it is an attempt to locate the contemporary interplay between that institution and others in Scottish society. It wants to look at the extent to which it is still viable (or indeed helpful), as it appears to have been in the past, to talk about some sort of Catholic ghetto mentality in Scottish society. Or is it now possible to claim that the influence of Scottish Catholicism pervades all aspects of the country's political and cultural life, and that the metaphor of the ghetto is no longer either appropriate or accurate?

The editors would like to thank the contributors for their hard work in preparing drafts, responding to suggestions and, in one case, dealing with the vagaries of the Islands' postal service. Without them, it would have been a very thin book indeed. We would also like to thank the University of Stirling and Stirling Media Research Institute for their support in the completion of this volume, as well as family and colleagues who had to put up with us while we worked on it.

Raymond Boyle and Peter Lynch
University of Stirling

CONTRIBUTORS

Raymond Boyle is a member of the Stirling Media Research Institute at the University of Stirling and an assistant editor of *Media, Culture and Society*.

Joseph Bradley is a researcher and author of *Sport, Culture, Politics and Scottish Society: Irish Immigrants and the Gaelic Athletic Association* (John Donald, 1998).

Ray Burnett is a freelance writer and producer.

Peter Lynch is a lecturer in the Department of Politics, University of Stirling and author of *Minority Nationalism and European Integration* (University of Wales, 1996).

David McCrone is Professor in the Department of Sociology, University of Edinburgh and co-author of *Politics and Society in Scotland* (Macmillan, 1996).

Patrick Reilly recently retired as Professor of English Literature at the University of Glasgow.

Michael Rosie is a postgraduate student in the Department of Sociology, University of Edinburgh.

Cliff Williamson is a postgraduate student in the Department of History, University of Strathclyde.

CONTENTS

1

INTRODUCTION:
CATHOLICISM AND SCOTTISH SOCIETY

Raymond Boyle and Peter Lynch

Introduction

Though Scotland boasts a significant higher education sector of universities and colleges and considerable numbers of academics and students studying Scottish culture, history and politics, many aspects of Scottish life and society remain obscured from view. Major fields of study such as politics, the media and religion remain relatively under-researched and most areas of academic and social interest in Scotland are plagued by serious gaps and limited coverage. Part of the explanation for this situation lies in the fact that Scotland has a lot of history and its academics are spread thinly across it, in addition to being engaged in a wide variety of international research that does not feature Scotland at all.

The gaps might seem unsurprising for a small country with extensive global interests and links: and therefore concerned with the outside world rather than just the small, domestic arena. Yet Scotland has a vigorous community of historians, journalists and writers in addition to a well-educated public which regularly digests Scottish writing of both the factual and fictional variety. Newspaper consumption in Scotland is strong and the media does address a wide range of Scottish issues. In addition, Scottish affairs have become a prominent part of public life in recent times and Scotland has become increasingly conscious of its national identity and history: a situation evident through a popular willingness to identify as Scottish rather than British in opinion polls,[1] and in the constitutional debate over the last decade which found expression in the referendum of 11th September 1997. These developments and realities make some of the gaps in academic knowledge of

Scottish history and society even more glaring: a gap this book attempts to bridge.

Because of these gaps, many aspects of modern Scottish society remain hidden and subject to informed guesswork by academics and commentators which can create the equivalent of urban myths. Good examples of the phenomena are the myth that Catholics are not supportive of constitutional change because they fear for their position in a Presbyterian Scotland and are also deeply suspicious of the Scottish National Party. Both of these myths, which spring up on occasions such as the Monklands East by-election in 1994, are challenged by the contents of this book through the work of David McCrone and Michael Rosie. This book is therefore intended as an exercise in peeling back some of the more hidden layers of Scottish society and debating and examining some Scottish myths and viewpoints through fresh material and perspectives.

One of the difficulties in examining the development of the Catholic community is the dearth of existing literature to build upon. Notable works concerned with or touching on the Catholic community such as David McRoberts' *Modern Scottish Catholicism*, Tom Gallagher's *Glasgow: The Uneasy Peace* and Tom Devine's *St. Mary's Hamilton* study have managed to penetrate some aspects of the Catholic experience in Scotland, yet so much more remains to be done. One of the problems the editors faced in putting together this book was the lack of researchers available to focus on the many aspects of Scottish Catholicism such as gender and the role of women, the role of Catholics in party politics, young people and youth culture and analysis of the differential experiences of ordinary Catholics in Scottish society. Indeed while much of this book focuses on the contemporary, certain areas, such as the role and influence of Catholicism in the Western Isles, suffer from such a lack of rigorous examination, that Ray Burnett's chapter – of necessity – attempts to locate current influences on Catholics in the Isles by providing a degree of historical perspective through much needed original research. The study of the Catholic community in Scotland, and indeed Scottish society generally, therefore still has many gaps to fill despite our best efforts.

An aspect of this book which may immediately strike the reader on examining the contents page is the extent to which question marks pepper some of the chapter titles. In many ways this signifies the extent to which this book marks an ongoing process of examination, and also suggests that what follows will raise as many questions as it answers. While it is the aim of the book to stimulate debate, it is also hoped that some answers are provided and in so doing, a clearer picture of the complex position of Catholicism in contemporary Scottish politics and culture begins to emerge. This picture is not merely important in relation to the specific position of Catholics in Scotland – we are not trying to 'ghettoise' the study of the Catholic community by any means – but also is intended to contribute to a greater understanding of Scottish society.

It is perhaps useful to emphasise the importance of the Scottish context within which the work that follows is placed. To put it bluntly, while the Catholic Church may be universal, the role, position, importance and profile of the Catholic Church in Scotland differ significantly from its English counterpart. As we write, *The Herald* of the 18 February 1998 has on the masthead of its front page a picture of columnist Michael Fry beside a heading informing us that on page 17 we will find, 'A Protestant who thinks Catholics are right about their schools'. It is hard to imagine a similar heading being carried by an equivalent English/UK broadsheet newspaper, such is the continued and heightened position of the Catholic Church within both the Scottish media community and public discourse in this country. Context is everything.

The different Scottish context is evident in the extent to which Catholic-Irish values have permeated the culture of a city such as Liverpool, while these same values have been viewed by some as divisive in a city such as Glasgow demonstrate differences in context and labelling. In Liverpool, the influences of Irish Catholicism have become interwoven into an internal resilient city identity which has in part been constructed as a reaction to the actual and perceived hostility of 'official England'. The Irish Catholic experience in Glasgow, while initially bearing strong similarities to those immigrants who arrived in Liverpool, has been different due to the differing economic, political and religious context within which Glasgow and Scottish society has developed.

The Catholic Community

The Catholic community of Scotland has its origins in the survival of the Catholic tradition post-Reformation as well as periods of immigration which brought the Irish, Italians, Lithuanians and Poles into Scotland. Whilst Catholics of Irish origins tend to be the largest segment of the Catholic community and are concentrated around central Scotland, and particularly in the West, there are Catholic communities in the Highlands and Islands and the North East. The overall size of the Catholic community has been put at 725,685, through figures produced by the Catholic Church,[2] though the annual mass attendance survey determined that 248,935 Catholics attended mass at the 1995 survey.[3] The number of Catholics has fallen in Scotland over the last twenty years or so (the Church claimed 817,000 adherents in 1972),[4] but then the Scottish population has also fallen through emigration and the different religious beliefs of immigrants have also had an effect on the religious make-up of Scottish society.

One important question to consider is whether there actually is a 'distinct' Catholic community in Scotland. Arguments in favour of its existence would point to the shared religious experience of Catholics; their distinctive socialisation through Church, family and school, which has produced certain attitudes and values; and their position as a socio-economic or indeed ethnic minority in some parts of Scotland. However, on the other hand, the position of Catholics has changed so much in twentieth century Scotland that large numbers of Catholics have as many attributes in common with other religious or non-religious groups as they do with each other. The Catholic community itself is also quite heterogeneous and can be subdivided into active and lapsed Catholics, those of different ethnic origins, social class and education. Social change in Scotland has therefore contributed to the development of a much more internally differentiated Catholic community than previously existed and integrated Catholics into most aspects of Scottish life and society.

A key argument found in most of the chapters of this book is that Catholics have experienced levels of social and economic change which have led to their integration and acceptance into Scottish society, something which was not always the case in the past. For the purposes of the argument about social change in this book, we use the idea of the ghetto as a starting point to chart the progress of a largely immigrant community which moved into central Scotland in the nineteenth century. The concept of the ghetto is a familiar one for ethnic and religious minorities and it is used here to denote a period when the social interactions and living patterns of the Catholic community were fairly homogenous, with Catholics and the 'Irish' residing in identifiably Catholic districts and towns, often created through sectarian employment practices, and very much part of the industrial working class. We are not suggesting that all

Catholics lived in the ghetto or experienced discrimination in employment or housing by any means, because the Catholic experience of Scotland in the nineteenth and early twentieth century was also varied and subject to very different types of responses from sections of Scottish society. However, what we want to emphasise is that the Catholic community has become increasingly socially mobile and integrated into Scottish society, thus leaving the ghetto behind them.

Part of the explanation for the integration of Catholics into Scottish society revolves around shared experiences. The Catholic community has experienced major events and social changes on the same plane as non-Catholics in twentieth century Scotland, such as the First and Second World Wars, the construction of the post-war welfare state and the expansion of higher education.[5] The population changes associated with urban redevelopment, the New Towns, deindustrialisation, the growth of a service economy and changing patterns of housing ownership have all contributed to socio-economic changes which have integrated ordinary Catholics through breaking-up some of the older, Catholic communities in West-Central Scotland and dispersing them to new areas.[6]

One of the key things to remember about Scottish society over the last ten or twenty years is that it has changed to such a degree that we could talk about Scotland having experienced a social transformation. A country in which the public sector was the dominant housing tenure until the late 1980s is now one dominated by home ownership. For example, owner occupiers comprised 33 per cent of housing tenure levels in 1974 whilst the public sector accounted for 54 per cent. By 1995, the figures had almost completely reversed, with owner occupiers now dominating housing with 58 per cent and the public sector comprising only 31 per cent.[7] Changes in housing tenure within the Catholic community are difficult to discern, but it would be remarkable if Catholics were immune to the trends in home ownership evident over the last decade.

Changes in economic structure and employment patterns have also contributed to social mobility within the Catholic community and a movement away from its earlier position as a relatively poor, immigrant community in industrial Scotland. For example, though employment in Scotland in 1974 was previously dominated by manufacturing (32.4 per cent), distribution, hotels and catering (11.6 per cent), professional and scientific services (15.5 per cent) and other industries and services (26.9 per cent), patterns of employment in

1995 clearly show the development of a service economy, in which
manufacturing accounts for only 9.7 per cent of employment, compared to 16.9 per cent for finance and business services, 26.6 per cent
for distribution, hotels and catering, and 30.3 per cent for education,
health and social services.[8]

The Catholic community has not been immune to the social
changes examined above, which have resulted in extensive employment changes, new skills, expanded educational levels and opportunities, new housing patterns, etc., impacting on a formerly
industrialised Catholic working class and helping to create a new
Catholic middle class. It can also be argued that social change has
also impacted upon the Catholic community by making it less Catholic and more secular: a general trend in Scottish society in the last
forty years. The levels of Catholic marriages peaked in the years
between 1961–1970 at 16.5 per cent of all marriages and experienced
a constant decline between 1985 to 1995 from 13.2 per cent to 9.6 per
cent. Church of Scotland marriages also declined in the post-war
period, with civil marriages now accounting for 46.4 per cent of all
marriages in Scotland.[9]

Catholics and Political Behaviour

The role and involvement of the Catholic community are a keen
focus of this book, with three separate chapters examining different
aspects of Catholic political behaviour. There is clearly much to be
done in this area, through both contemporary and historical research, though the chapters presented here represent original contributions to an understanding of Catholics in Scottish politics. There
are three areas of interest in examining the political behaviour of
Scottish Catholics, focusing on the electoral behaviour and socio-
political attitudes of Catholic voters; the form and content of Catholic
political behaviour in terms of Catholic political action and involvement in political parties and movements; and the involvement of
Catholics and the Church in the policy process in Scotland, through
consultation, representation and lobbying activities.

One of the main problems in examining the political participation
of Scottish Catholics has been the tendency to focus on the role of
Catholics in party politics, whilst neglecting other areas. This book
adopts a broad approach and definition to political behaviour and
action which eschews a narrow approach to politics which focuses
solely on party politics. Thus political parties are merely one actor in

the Church-state-society triangular relationship, alongside a range of social movements, pressure groups, religious institutions, government agencies and individuals. As will become clear from the chapters in this book, the authors are concerned with examining these latter aspects of political involvement rather than the party sphere, as so much of the action and behaviour of politics takes place outside the parties themselves and is often obscured from public view in government organisations, local authorities and the hierarchy of the Catholic Church.

Issues of Representation

While there is a concern with examining the political behaviour of the Catholic community, we also want to explore the wider political impact of Catholicism in Scottish society. By politics in this instance we look beyond orthodox politics to focus on issues relating to the organisation of power in society in the domains of the media and culture. To this end, we view the issue of representation as being crucial in understanding the mechanisms through which certain values, groups and ideas become normalised or indeed marginalised by society. Popular culture in all its various forms becomes an important site in which many of these battles are waged. Cultural forms such as sport, writing and the media are constantly reflecting and at times shaping public attitudes while also giving (and at times denying) a voice to sections of society.[10] Often these forms impose narratives on events and in so doing make sense of them for wider audiences and publics. Values and attitudes are often projected onto cultural forms reflecting the status (or lack of) a community may have in the wider society and above all representations can play a crucial role in the construction of wider collective identities.

Thus any examination of the role and position of Catholicism in contemporary Scotland must consider both popular culture and increasingly the central role that the media play in this aspect of cultural life. We are not arguing for a media-centric approach to understanding the position and influence of the media in modern society, rather suggesting that the media at times are both constrained by wider economic and political pressures while in other circumstances can challenge some of the dominant assumptions of society. In other words, changes in the range and quality of representations of aspects of Catholicism in popular media culture can often reflect wider economic and political change. However, it should also be noted that positive media representations are in themselves no guarantee of economic or political change, or indeed do they necessarily signify an overnight sea change in deeply-rooted attitudes.

The section on representations in this book marks an attempt to examine some of these aspects as they relate to Catholic identity in Scotland. It is a far from comprehensive examination, however what does emerge is the importance of the social and economic context in shaping the contours of the media and popular culture in Scotland. Despite the impact of economic globalisation we are not witnessing the withering away of local cultural difference. The media in Scotland are, of course, subject to wider global pressures, yet their concerns remain those rooted in talking to a Scottish marketplace about Scottish concerns. While they may be doing this increasingly for purely commercial reasons, globalisation has not seen a simplistic erosion of national cultural identities. It may change them and interact with them but, as Schlesinger has noted, it isn't simply a case of either/or.[11]

We still experience rigid definitions of categories of identity. For some in Scottish society to carry a Catholic identity is to be associated with an Irish identity. While some groups may be happy to assert this as their collective identity (chapter 5), others feel that this misrepresents sections of the Catholic community in Scotland (chapter 8). This of course is one of the challenges faced by the media in a democratic culture, how to reflect the diversity of experience and identities which exists within seemingly coherent 'communities' which in reality are of course diverse and multi-faceted. As Schlesinger has pointed out:

> National cultures are not simple repositories of shared symbols to which the entire population stands in identical relation. Rather, they are to be approached as sites of contestation in which competition over definitions takes place. . . . It may also reproduce distinctions between 'us' and 'them' at the intra-national level, in line with the internal structure of social divisions and relations of power and domination.[12]

So while we talk of the 'Catholic community' in Scotland and argue that it displays certain characteristics, we must also be aware of the complexities which exist within this community and which in many ways have never substantially been addressed by academics and journalists alike.

A Church in Crisis?

Analysis of the Catholic community must also involve consideration of the position of the Catholic Church in Scotland. Whilst the Church has become a well-established institution in Scotland, it faces a number of contemporary challenges to its position which can present a picture of a Church in crisis. The scandals over Bishop Wright, alleged abuses in Catholic nursing homes and sexual abuse by priests, have all cast a shadow over the Church. However, the manner in which the Church has sought to deal with these issues has often exacerbated the problem and occasionally given the Church the image of a secretive organisation which puts its own interests above those of the victims of abuse. Similarly, the Church faces a number of challenges which result from developments within its membership and changing attitudes within society. Celibacy, women priests, the conservative attitude towards moral and social issues and the role of the Church's membership in a deeply hierarchical organisation all present current and future difficulties for the Church to manage, aside from occasional scandals or recurrent debates over Catholic education.

What follows, we hope, marks an intervention in an ongoing public debate about the position and impact of the Catholic community on Scottish cultural and political life. To this end, we have not set out to impose particular strictures on the authors' varying, and at times contradictory positions and viewpoints. While some articles more than others draw on historical antecedents to legitimise their arguments, most focus specifically on the contemporary and bear the academic imprint of that broadest of churches: the social sciences.

NOTES

1. J. Brand, L. Bennie and J. Mitchell, *How Scotland Votes* (Manchester, 1997).
2. *Catholic Directory for Scotland* (Glasgow, 1996), p. 551.
3. *Ibid.*
4. *Catholic Directory for Scotland* (Glasgow, 1974), p. 415.
5. T. Fitzpatrick, *Catholic Secondary Education in South-West Scotland Before 1972* (Aberdeen, 1986), p. xii.
6. For analysis of these developments see M. Keating and R. Boyle, *Remaking Urban Scotland* (Edinburgh, 1986).
7. *Regional Statistics 1975–80* (London, 1980), p. 82; and *Regional Trends 32* (London, 1997), p. 83.

8. *Regional Statistics 1975–80* (London, 1980), p. 118; and *Regional Trends 32* (London, 1997), p. 69.
9. Registrar General for Scotland, *Annual Report 1995* (Edinburgh, 1996), p. 124.
10. Studies into the relationship between Catholicism and football in Scottish society has become increasingly common over the last number of years. Chapter 5 documents some of the main research in this area. In addition for a comparative dimension see R. Boyle, *Football and Cultural Identity in Glasgow and Liverpool*, unpublished Ph.D. thesis, University of Stirling, 1995.
11. P. Schlesinger, *Media, State and Nation* (London, 1991).
12. *Ibid.*, p. 174.

2

'AN ANTIDOTE TO COMMUNISM': CATHOLIC
SOCIAL ACTION IN GLASGOW, 1931–39

Cliff Williamson

This chapter adopts an historical approach to the study of Catholic political activism in Scotland. Rather than examining the sphere of party politics, Williamson concentrates on an analysis of distinctive Catholic political organisations in the Archdiocese of Glasgow in the 1930s to determine their varied attempts to play a political role on behalf of the Church and Catholic community. His stated intention is to put the Catholic back into the Catholic community and political action. Williamson also places Catholic political action within the broader context of Catholic social ideas and the necessity of combating the influence of the far left in relation to working-class politics.

Introduction

The Catholic community in Scotland has often been viewed as a secluded and insular 'Ghetto Community', unwilling and unable to join the mass of Scots in improving their country. The purpose of this chapter is to hold up this view to scrutiny and challenge the idea that Scottish Catholics were a marginal community cut off from the rest of Scotland. The majority of work in this chapter is based on primary sources from my own research, in which I have endeavoured to correct some of the imbalances which have been endemic in the study of the Catholic community in Scotland. An understanding of the development of Catholicism in modern Scotland requires an awareness of two key points. The first point is to stress that most initiatives in the modern development of the Catholic community in the West of Scotland has been inspired by the European dimension. The senior laity as well as the clergy were well aware of the changing priorities of the Catholic Church in continental Europe and followed these developments with interest. The second point to be highlighted is the nature and dynamics of Catholic social action. There has been a tendency to devalue the overtly 'Catholic' aspects of the social and political behaviour of the Catholic community in the West of Scotland, in order to focus on the interaction between the Catholic community and the Labour Party in particular. This focus has concealed the myriad of organisations and activities that were at heart inspired by religious commitment not tactical political choice.

Catholicism is not simply a means of identification, a tag to separate one section of the community from others for the convenience of social scientists and historians. It brings with it a 'world view' and series of obligations that go to the core of individual identity. My purpose here is simply to put the 'Catholic' back into the Catholic community, so that when we look at the development of a community defined to a large extent by their religiosity that religion is included in the discussion. This chapter is not and does not seek to be a comprehensive assessment of the Catholic community in Scotland. Its focus is narrower and therefore more specific in its interpretation. I have chosen to look at an organisation that has been well covered in the literature on Scottish Catholicism, though from a different angle than that which will be attempted here. As pointed out previously, historical writing on this subject has stressed the party political dimension to Catholicism in Scotland. The Catholic Union of the Archdiocese of Glasgow, which is discussed below, certainly had a political role through its contacts and influence, not just with Glasgow politicians but also with national and international politicians. However, in adopting such a narrow definition of political action to focus solely on party politics, we miss the whole point of Catholic social action which was aimed at the rejuvenation of the Catholic Church and its message.

We also miss how Catholic Action built up the confidence of the Catholic Community in the West of Scotland to assert their identity as Catholics and as part of Scotland. For this book which questions the idea of the 'Ghetto mentality' through observing the social action of the Catholic community, we can gain an idea of how far the Catholic community has travelled since the early part of this century: from the racial and political periphery to the position of being regarded as a legitimate part of the country and not strangers in a strange land. The Catholic journey has involved a number of stages. This chapter deals with the crucial intermediate stage of development: the period between the wars. It is perhaps more descriptive than full-blooded interpretation, though this is for the simple reason that there is value in opening up the subject and making it a source of debate. Therefore, there is limited space to deal exhaustively with the nuances of the apostolic vision of Pope Pius IX or his successors. The same limits apply to the Catholic Union in this chapter, which requires an exhaustive monograph in itself. Thus, I have chosen to look at one aspect of Catholic social action in a set time period and argue that it represents a profound and meaningful insight into the workings of the Catholic community, both in Scotland and throughout the Catholic world.

Social Catholicism and Catholic Action

A key part of this chapter involves an understanding of the concepts of 'social Catholicism' and 'Catholic action'. In order to do this we have to look beyond the immediate context of Scotland and examine issues which the Catholic Church was beginning to address in the latter part of the 19th century and the early years of the 20th century. In doing this we can open up a further issue for discussion: the relationship between Scottish Catholics and the European Catholic Church. My reason for opening up this theme is to stress the European dimension of the Catholic Church in its operation in Scotland. The traditional emphasis in academic scholarship and indeed in almost all writing in relation to Scotland has been to compare Scotland and England. However, here we have a unique opportunity to examine the experience of Scotland as measured against the developments in Catholicism in Europe. Indeed, it will be argued that instead of looking South, the Catholic Church in Scotland was looking East to the continent.

The idea of 'Catholic Action' was promoted by the Papacy during the last decades of the 19th Century. It had the simple function of binding the laity and clergy of the Catholic Church closer together. The idea was to create an auxiliary group under the direction of the clergy to assist in the work of the church. The way in which this was to be achieved, and also the nature of the message itself, developed gradually over a period of half a century but did not represent a clear process of development and evolution. It was to emerge through various swings and deviations as the political and social environment interacted with the institutional development of the Catholic Church. Two trends can be detected during this period. First, a clear reassertion of the primacy of the Vatican and second, a gradual intellectual shift within the doctrine and ethos of Catholicism.

The first trend of greater centralism in the Church was something of a paradox in what was an age of nationalism and of liberalism (1848–1914) which comprised a wave of state building in Europe. The 19th and 20th centuries had been marked with a process of building and strengthening the central state and the authority of national state institutions. The majority of the nations of Europe developed parliamentary governments and bureaucracies that were specifically, though not exclusively based, on the dominant national and ethnic groups. From the hodge-podge of multi-ethnic or dynastic states emerged nation states which still dominate the continent of Europe. Germany, Italy, Belgium, Holland, and Belgium with latterly Poland, Austria and the Czech-Slovak states all emerged from the wreckage of the Hapsburg and Ottoman Empires. As this process took place, the Catholic Church to a great extent moved in the opposite direction.

The national ecclesiastical hierarchies that had formed a deep bond with the dynasties of Catholic Europe abruptly found themselves on the outside of political and social influence as, one by one, the monarchies either disappeared or put the Church at arm's length. Although in some cases the national hierarchies resisted the embrace of the Vatican (most famously in Germany), the vulnerable position of the Church in many countries left them without any option, even in countries with small Catholic populations who had been left, relatively, to their own devices such as in Scotland and England. The restructuring of the Catholic Church in the second half of the 19th century, under the pontificates of Pius IX and Leo XIII, saw many of the areas where the church had been officially designated as a 'mission', restored to the full status of a national hierarchy, which brought them into the mainstream of European Catholicism.[1] The English hierarchy was restored in 1850 and the Scottish hierarchy in 1878. Thus, by the beginning of the 20th century, the Catholic Church was a more solidly centralised institution with the national hierarchies subservient to the Vatican in which the Papacy had acquired an intellectual veneer to justify such Ultramontanism.[2]

It was in Rome that the Catholic Church re-established its pre-eminence over the national churches by both structural and doctrinal means. The Pontificate of Pius IX between 1846 and 1878 introduced a series of innovations in doctrine and dogma that served to justify the centralism of the church.[3] The first was the Syllabus of Errors in

1864 followed in 1869/80 by the First Vatican Council, which resolved under the Constitutional document 'Pastor Aeternus' the primacy of the Papacy and the Vatican. The Syllabus of Errors attacked the foundations of Liberalism and Nationalism and proclaimed that it was an error for the Pontiff, 'to reconcile himself to, and agree with progress, liberalism, and civilisation as lately introduced.'[4] The Errors were the benchmark of the response of the Catholic Church to the state of Europe in the last decades of the century, coupled with the structural changes and culminating in the 'Dogmatic Constitution of the Catholic Faith', part of which comprised 'Pastor Aeternus', in addition to the controversial 'Dogma of Papal Infallibility' promulgated at the third session of the Vatican Council in 1870. No document in the recent history of the Catholic Church has been a greater source of dispute and misrepresentation than the idea of Papal infallibility. The Pope, as Bishop of Rome and the successor of St. Peter, in theory represented the unbroken line that stretched back to biblical times and the apostles as the Pastor and doctor of the Church who spoke in terms of faith and morals as *ex Cathedra* in effect with the authority of God. It is only within the narrow terms of 'faith and morals' that the Pope spoke with ultimate authority.

In reorganising the Church, the Papacy recovered much of its lost authority and stressed the unity and universality of the Catholic faith. This is not to say that the national hierarchies had no autonomy, quite the reverse. There was to be no standardised pattern of action in dealing with broader political and social issues faced by national churches, though the Vatican certainly made its views clear on the main issues of the day. In 1870, following the defeat of the Second Empire in France, the recently unified Italian State recovered the Papal States and Rome from French control. The Papacy condemned this action and refused to recognise the legitimacy of the new Italian State, an estrangement which was to last until 1929. In Germany, the new Empire launched an all-out assault on the Catholic Church – the Kulturkampf – that placed severe restrictions on the Church. The response of the Church was to be conciliatory and within a decade the prohibitions were lifted. Under Pius IX's successor, Leo XIII, the most important unresolved issue was addressed, the position of France and the new Third Republic. Leo XII called for French Catholics to rally around the State. However, this proposal was not a success with the French Right, which persisted in its opposition to the Republic and the Republicans accelerated the separation of Church and State with further secular laws on divorce at the start of the twentieth century.

Social Catholicism and Scottish Catholicism

The big issues of state power and the constitutional position of Catholics were to some extent alien to Catholics in Scotland as well as throughout the United Kingdom. The 1829 Catholic Emancipation Act had removed the biggest obstacles to participation and involvement by Catholics in British public life. The issue of the constitutional status of Ireland also tended to conceal the more mundane and ordinary political issues that faced Catholics in their everyday life, such as economic status and political organisation. This situation led to a general lack of attention on the way in which the 'Irish' dealt with the important domestic issues which confronted them more substantially than the issue of Irish home rule could ever have done.

On the continent, where Catholics formed large political parties and Trade Unions, the issue of Church and state was clearer where the concerns of Catholics met with the broader constitutional issues of the day. The Catholics of Scotland and Britain had to deal with a very different environment in order to give voice to their concerns and defend their interests. In the absence of national political institutions, Catholics had to deal with politics in a local and parochial manner. Added to this problem was the important issue of organising their own communities and giving a lead and direction to the way in which Catholics addressed their own circumstances. The theme of Catholic Action in the period under discussion was one of consolidation: consolidation of the Church's organisation and consolidation of the economic and social position of the Catholic community. Only through this initial stage could Catholics understand the environment they were living in and the options for development and advancement.

Social Catholicism differed in its objectives from Political Catholicism in that it was directed at the internal relationships within the Catholic community. It has to be borne in mind that the socio-economic situation at the start of the twentieth century was quite unlike anything before encountered. The whole of the previous century had seen a massive structural change in Europe, with the majority of the population shifting from rural to urban areas and patterns of life which had remained untouched by centuries were changed in the matter of a few years. The Catholic Church, like all churches, had been a rural phenomenon. The drift to the towns took many out of the orbit of the clergy and into the dangerous secular world of the large towns and cities of industrial Europe. In common with many other denominations, the Catholic Church experienced a crisis in how to deal with the new political and social structures of the continent. The problem was telescoped for the Catholic Church as it was seen as a particular obstacle to the ambitions of Liberals and nationalists.

For the Catholic Church the initial response to the new environment in which it found itself was to denounce modernity. However, this response only served to put the Church into greater conflict and isolation. For instance, it left the German, Italian and French Catholics high and dry against the anti-Catholic instincts of Republicanism in France and authoritarianism in Germany and Italy. The Church encouraged detachment and isolation from these new structures, which promoted a 'ghetto Catholicism' in which Catholics were encouraged to forge their own institutions and organisation which stressed Catholic autonomy from political institutions. In Scotland, this approach only served to keep the 'Irish' Catholic Community at arm's length from the rest of the country, though this should be balanced by recognising the desire of the majority Protestant communities and, it has to be said indigenous Catholics in Scotland, to do exactly the same. The Catholic Irish were seen as an alien influence on Scotland. The Education (Scotland) Act of 1872 forced Catholics to fund and support their own schools. Coupled with this policy were the various residency qualifications of the Poor Law which excluded newly arrived Catholics, whose tenure in work had expired, from poor relief.

Rerum Novarum

The key event in the development of social Catholicism was the promulgation of the Encyclical 'Rerum novarum' in May 1891. The Encyclical written by Pope Leo XIII put forward Catholic ideas on the social order and responses to the threat of socialism. In particular, it addressed the position of the working classes in modern society. 'By degrees it has come to pass that working men have been given over, isolated and defenceless, to the callousness of employers and the greed of unrestrained competition:'[5] a form of class analysis that would not look out of place in a communist or socialist pamphlet. The papacy viewed the methods and the solutions proposed by the left as just as bad as the shortcomings of Capitalism: 'their proposals are so clearly futile for all practical purposes, that if they were carried out the working man himself would be among the first to suffer.'[6] Leo denounced the socialists for the whipping up of envy towards the rich and private property. Socialism also brought the spectre of the state further into the lives of ordinary people. What, therefore, was the solution? There was no physical solution, no policy or ideas to ameliorate the position of the poorest in the communities *per se*, though there were those in the Church who sought to promote a different organisation of society and a return to rural values and organisation. The Church argued that the reason for the unequal situation in Capitalist society was based on the ethos which governed Capitalism, Liberalism and Socialism: that of individuality and class consciousness which were seen to promote avarice and greed in equal measures.

As a response, the Church promoted ideas that it believed would introduce a common series of values, by which a new social system could exist in peace and tranquility as 'no practical solution of this question will ever be found without the assistance of religion and the church.'[7] The Church stressed that its first principle 'when we undertake to alleviate the conditions of the masses, must be the inviolability of private property.'[8] This issue went to the heart of the experience of the Catholic Church during the French Revolution in 1789 and the unification of Italy half a century later, where Church lands and property itself became a means of political struggle.[9] The solution was to be based on Christian values: 'If Christian precepts prevail the two classes will not only be united in bonds of friendship but also in those of brotherly love.'[10] This notion, in genesis, was the idea of communitarianism that was to shape the great Christian Democratic movements of Europe in the twentieth century. Leo XIII urged action by the whole of the Church to promote the Christian values and to participate in the development of a new Christian politics.

The solution may have been undefined or lacking in concrete ideas, but the overwhelming message of the Encyclical was to promote Catholic Action through using all the institutions and arenas of political debate to spread the word of social Catholicism. In essence, it took the Church from a basically abstentionist and ambivalent attitude to political action into a determinedly pro-active stance. Under Pius IX, the Church had been antagonistic and aloof from the politics of Europe, it saw the developments of Capitalism and of Liberalism as transient and ephemeral, just as the Reformation had been centuries earlier. Socialism was a greater danger, as it made its appeal directly to the masses not elites. Therefore, through its espousal of social Catholicism, the Church found a means to combat the influence of secular political ideologies by encouraging participation but not commitment to the new organisation of society based on class.

The point of this initial preamble is to set the religious and political context in which Scottish Catholics had to operate as members of a universal Church. A number of conclusions can be drawn from these early remarks. Firstly, the religious environment was more firmly under the direct influence of the Vatican than previously, with structural and intellectual changes adding both positive and negative elements to the context of Scottish Catholicism. The Vatican offered clearer direction than before in the priorities of the Catholic Church as a universal and as a local Church. The pattern of activity was to be determined not at a central level but through a consideration of local and national religious and political priorities. Secondly, the promulgation of the encyclical 'Rerum Novarum' offered an intellectual solution to the problems highlighted by the emergence of Liberalism, Capitalism and Socialism. It also pointed to the value of Catholic Unity in pursuing greater political and social influence. In Scotland, this meant that a structure had to be found to rally the disparate Catholic community, focus the attention of the community on individual issues which the Church saw as crucial and seek to carve out an identity in the hostile climate of Presbyterian Scotland. The following sections will focus on the efforts of the Catholic Church in Scotland to put these goals into practice.

The Catholic Union of the Archdiocese of Glasgow

From 1885 until the start of the Second World War, the Catholic Union of the Archdiocese of Glasgow (CUAG) was recognised as the senior Catholic Lay organisation in the Archdiocese of Glasgow, 'a zealous watchdog over Catholic interests', as Archbishop Macintosh described it.[11] As an officially-sanctioned body, the CUAG was able to gain access to the Catholic laity in a manner second only to the clergy. The reach of the Catholic Union stretched from the organisation and mobilisation of the Catholic vote in elections to the Poor Law authorities and the School Boards in and around the city of Glasgow, to providing the main forum of discussion within the Catholic community. It was an organisation that drew together the cream of the Archdiocesan professional class and gave them the chance to help to co-ordinate their efforts in the service of the Church and the betterment of the Catholic community. Part of its effort was in providing a political and social focus for the defence of Catholic interests but also to promote the idea of good citizenship amongst the Catholic population at a time in which they were singled out for vilification and ostracism by sections of the indigenous Presbyterian community.

Through the Catholic Union of the Archdiocese of Glasgow it is possible to chart the various stages of development of the Catholic population in Scotland and the development of Catholic Action. From 1891 until 1939 the Papacy remodelled its approach and prescriptions to the rise of Liberalism, which constituted a particular intellectual and economic challenge to the Catholic Church, and to the increasingly polarised politics of the 1920s and 1930s. Developments within the CUAG mirrored the changes of strategy and approach of the Vatican. For our purposes, the important aspect of the Catholic Union is that it keyed into the major European developments in Catholicism, despite the fact that the Catholic population of Scotland was a small percentage of the population of a small country. This reading of the Catholic history of Scotland has been much neglected. Whilst Scottish Catholicism was small or peripheral to the larger Catholic states of the continent, it was as much a part of European history as the diplomatic or political intrigues of the time and Scottish Catholics played their part in the focusing of the message of the Pontiff.

The Catholic Union was formed in 1885 as a direct result of the intervention of the Archbishop of Glasgow, the Reverend Charles Eyre. The new Archbishop was a highly motivated man who, in addition to helping develop the CUAG, was responsible for a major expansion of religious and devotional orders in the city and environs, as well as a major programme of church building. The impact of Eyre is more impressive when you consider that the Catholic community bore the weight of local rates but also had to provide for their own schools as until 1918 the Education Scotland Act prevented the raising of rates for the building and maintenance of Catholic Schools. The Catholic Union had a strong continental feel to it. It was in the first instance a body formed in the 1880s by the slew of academic and aristocratic converts who came over from the Church of England. It was not to shake off its aristocratic and elitist background and reflected a strongly paternalistic trend in Catholicism not just noticeable in the United Kingdom but also elsewhere. The success and endurance of the Catholic Union in Glasgow was due to the fact that it was able to survive, evolve and flourish as other older Catholic bodies became redundant.

The Constitution of the CUAG stressed the defensive role of the organisation through stating its purpose as 'the protection and advancement of Catholic interests, congregational and general.'[12] Protection was very much the watchword in the Catholic lexicon, reflected in the ethos of the Church since the Reformation: basically paternalistic and conservative. In the world of secular politics, the Catholic Union was seen as a bulwark against the encroachment of atheistic ideas and also as a mechanism to maintain a Christian ethic in the emerging institutions of liberal society. It was formed, apart from its social and cultural objectives, as the main voice of the Catholic community in local government. From 1885 until 1929 the Catholic Union stood candidates for election to the School Boards, which did not have control over Catholic schools but had responsibility for local rates collected from Catholics and Protestants alike.

Historically, education has been the principal focus of Catholic action and energy, not just in Scotland but in Europe. A trend in Catholic politics throughout the nineteenth century was the growing emphasis on the influence of children and their welfare. Education and schooling were a key battlefield between the Church and state, through competition for the control of young minds and attempts to influence their formative development. The separation between Church and state was a trend which Catholics strove to oppose. This breach was perhaps most noticeable in France. The history of France from before the revolution in 1789 had 'enlightenment ideas' at its heart. Such ideas involved a crucial emphasis on education and learning as the dynamo of society, as part of the process of eliminating superstition and, by extension, the influence of the Church. Continental ideas about education and its impact on Catholic politics mixed with local circumstances. The British education system had a strong religious element and, from 1871 until 1903, provision was a key issue in government. Leaving the influence of English educational politics with its mix of Anglicanism, non-conformity and Catholicism to one side, Scottish education politics was less complicated but no less fractious. It is important to realise that until relatively recently all education had a strong religious dimension. Today, the debate on Catholic Schools revolves around the maintenance of a small religious element in education. In the past, the debate on education was between Protestant education and Catholic education, though both emphasised the centrality of religion in the formative years of the child and the influence into later life as a form of social engineering. The Catholic Union had to operate with an understanding of the general European environment and the way in which it was manifested in Scotland. Catholics on School Boards were concerned with the maintenance of good accounting but also with resisting the slow encroachment of the state on separate Catholic education, and by state they meant a Protestant State.

Education provided the main raison d'etre for the Catholic Union. It was to contest all of the elections to the local School Boards from 1885 until they were abolished in 1930 following the Local Government (Scotland) Act. The Catholic representatives formed a formidable block on local boards and were backed up by a well-organised local political machine. In the Poor Law Boards, Catholic representatives were less numerous but again they took their work very seriously. In contrast the Corporation of Glasgow and the other Burgh councils had no direct Catholic representation. At School Board level and at Poor Law Council elections the CUAG stood in direct opposition to the Progressives and the Labour Party. The relative failure of the Labour and Independent Labour Parties to make an electoral impact serves as a reminder that voting behaviour can be compartmentalised and that the reflection of identity changes with the given context. Catholics had free reign to vote in Corporation elections to reflect their class identity but in the competitive elections for the School and Parish Boards, the 'Irish' working classes chose to emphasise their religious solidarity. This duality or multiplicity of identities is crucial to understanding the various aspects of Catholic life up until 1939. It reflects the way in which the Catholic community chose to represent itself and explains the failure to carry religious conviction into the party political sphere.

Anti-communism and Catholic Action

The threat or perceived threat of the Communist Party and its fellow travellers was a powerful dynamic in the action and activity of the Catholic Union. The collectivist and anti-property elements of communism and socialism had been condemned as far back as 1891 by Pope Leo XIII in the celebrated encyclical 'Rerum Novarum'. After the end of the First World War the minor threat of Marxist Communism had been transformed by the Russian Revolution in 1917 and the temporary revolutions in Germany and Hungary, which had given heart to the Communist Parties of Western Europe. The Catholic Church viewed the nature of the struggle with the Communists as a simple one between God and the anti-God doctrines of the Bolsheviks. The socialists in the Labour Party were seen to be bad enough but both the British Communist Party and the Independent Labour Party were effectively beyond redemption.

The approach of the Catholic Union to the threat of the Communist Party was unusual and contradictory. On the one hand, the Catholic Union unambiguously attacked the Communist Party and its methods but, on the other hand, the CUAG was to ape the Communist efforts to organise the unemployed and disaffected through a highly effective form of social action. Again the context of the time is important and two issues predominate. Firstly, the domestic circumstances of the time. Secondly, the evolution of Catholic Social action. The interaction of both is crucial to understand the response towards the Communist bogey and ideals of Catholic Unity. Since the end of the First World War, the British economy had been in a persistent downturn. Although the British Empire remained all-powerful, the domestic economy which had been mobilised to fight the German empire with full employment and the employment of women was providing a false picture of economic health. The symbol of British financial and economic ascendency – the Gold Standard – had been abandoned in 1929 after a five year struggle which had put irresistible pressure on the ailing institutions of the economy. Along with it went some faith in the institutions of political democracy, as mass unemployment hit hard in areas of the country where social and class structures were based on the hierarchy of the workplace. In some respects the collapse of the industrial economy acted as a bonus for Catholics, as it brought an end to many exclusively Protestant skilled enterprises and contributed to the erosion of sectarian practices in the labour market.

The scramble for work and the bitterness associated with mass unemployment was compounded by a divided and partial social security system. Part of the Ramsay MacDonald National government package on abandoning the Gold Standard involved a harsh cut in National Assistance and Public Assistance. At this time it must be remembered that the Poor Law was still in effect, though it was not as punitive as it had previously been. The Poor Law was the main source of welfare for the uninsured workforce. National Insurance was controlled by local agencies – the Public Assistance Boards – and contributions were collected by local insurance firms.

Many Catholics contributed through organisations such as the Ancient Order of Hibernians, but the scheme provided for the insurer alone, not the family of the contributor, and there were few organisations to guide the ordinary citizen through the maze of agencies and means tests.

Added to this difficult economic situation was a heightened atmosphere of sectarian division. Much has been written about the impact of the Church of Scotland and the Scottish Protestant League during this period. In 1923, the General Assembly of the Church of Scotland commissioned a report into the Irish in Scotland: 'The menace of the Irish race to our Scottish Nationality.' It was to call for the ending of immigration from the Irish Free State and the eventual repatriation of the Irish living in Scotland. The Kirk was fearful of the eventual take-over of Scotland by the Catholic Irish, ending the Presbyterian tradition in one of the cradles of the Reformation as well as diluting the quality of the 'race stock' of Scotland. The intention of the report was to 'secure to future generations the traditions, ideals, and faith of a great people unspoiled and inviolate.'[13] The impact of the report was probably felt greatest within the upper echelons of the Church of Scotland. It was a self-serving document giving vent to the growing frustrations of the Kirk in Scotland as the nature of Scotland became less uniform and more diverse, and therefore less under the control of the national church.

The fact that the Kirk report failed to gain any credibility outside of traditional anti-Catholic circles is testimony to a growing reconciliation with the Catholic community. It could have been the start of a broader popular campaign to remove 'the Irish'. The various attempts to highlight the 'alien' aspects of Irish Catholicism had conversely awoken concern as to the still unclear status of Roman Catholics in Scottish and British society. An interesting example of this was the resumption of religious parades by Catholics in Central Scotland. Shortly after the end of the First World War, a few Glasgow Parishes started to revive the festival of Corpus Christi. The festival, which occurs in the early summer, was the ceremonial procession of the host 'body of Christ' from the church and through a Parish, returning to the church for its consecration in the mass. The festival is a common-place event throughout Catholic Europe and a day of great celebration. The festival, which could have been a flash point for disturbances, was met with little or no trouble.

However, the growing importance of the Shrine at Carfin in Lanarkshire did provoke a response when, in 1922, the procession was stopped on the instruction of the Chief Constable for the area. It seems that the festival was illegal under the 1829 Catholic Relief Acts, which prevented the parading in public of Catholic clergy in vestments. Each year, the Shrine had attracted between 20–40,000 people on average and had become the highpoint in the calendar of local Catholics. The banning of the parade opened up the debate on the place of Catholicism in early twentieth century Britain. By 1926 the situation was resolved by the passage of a new Catholic Relief Act by parliament, that removed many of the prohibitions on the public display and worship of the Catholic Church.

In an atmosphere of economic and social crisis, the true job of the Church was to help its own worshippers deal with the upheavals of the business cycle. The bitterness and resentment of the Kirk's report did drive a wedge between the churches and seemed to confirm the suspicions of many Catholics that they were unwanted guests in a hostile climate. Further to this problem were the activities of the Scottish Protestant League (SPL). Again it is easy to concentrate on the more colourful elements of the SPL, but they were never more than a minor inconvenience to the Catholic community. The Scottish Protestant League had been founded by a vicious anti-Catholic, Alexander Ratcliffe, a man who was a sympathiser of Adolf Hitler and Mussolini. His main tirades were directed at the institution of Catholic schools: the so-called 'Rome on the Rates.'

The 1918 Scottish Education Act was as much a difficult issue for the Catholic population as it was for the majority Protestants in Scotland. Catholics had been wary of the relinquishing of direct control over their schools despite the economic pressure of paying twice for education, once through rates and direct payment from the pulpit. It was to be the best part of a decade before the Catholic Archdiocese of Glasgow was to fully transfer the ownership of its schools to the School Boards in Glasgow and its environs. By this time, there had been a major change in the structure of Scottish Education with the 1929 Local Government (Scotland) Act. The Act had abolished the locally elected School Boards with the work being transferred to the local authority. In Glasgow this meant that the Corporation of Glasgow now emerged as the main player in education policy. The 1929 Act which came into force in 1930 also abolished the elected Poor Law Authority which became part of the remit of the Public Assistance Board of the Corporation.

With the control of education moved away from the specialised School Boards, the Catholic Union lost its raison d'etre. The idea of

defence of Catholic interests which had involved the CUAG standing candidates in elections for bodies such as the School Boards was
gone. The CUAG had not stood for election for the Local Authorities
for two reasons. First, there was no serious Catholic interest at stake
in the work of the Authority, the main issues were education and
poor relief, both of which had been served up to 1929 by separate
bodies. Second, the electoral system was changed to first past the
post rather than proportional representation. The Catholic vote was
spread unevenly but the larger electoral constituencies used in proportional representation elections had served Catholics by allowing
the CUAG to use the pooled strength of the community in enlarged
constituencies. The CUAG had mobilised the vote and carefully
organised elections to ensure that there was co-operation on the
second and third preferences to get as many Catholic Union candidates elected as possible. In FPTP the fragmentation of the Catholic
population would result in the loss of influence and voting power.
Although there was the possibility of a couple of Catholics being
elected in seats with a large Catholic electorate it would not be
anywhere nearly as large as in the PR system operated before 1930.

Besides the electoral mechanics of the new system there was
another good reason for the CUAG to step back from electoral
engagement. By 1922, the Labour Party was established as the main
preference of working class Catholics. Although the Catholic Union
had stood against and soundly defeated Labour candidates in School
Board elections in many areas, the local authority arena was very
different. The Catholic population had voted Labour for around ten
years in national elections and attempts to change its partisan preference for Labour would have been a major task and not one which
would be guaranteed success. It would also have called for Catholics
to choose between religion and class interests. Prior to 1930, the
division between aspects of identity had been satisfied by the operation of education and general interests in different arenas. The loss
of control was soothed by the realisation that the 1918 and 1929 Acts
had enshrined Catholic Schools through an act of Parliament, and
any amendment could only come through this avenue. Therefore,
any failure to maintain Catholic Schools would bring the full force
of the state on any local authority.

The new local authority education departments organised committees which invited vested interests onto the main policymaking
structures of the council. Catholic representatives went directly to
the heart of the system and were probably able to contribute more

effectively to policy outcomes at the beginning of the policy process than previously in an elected council. To ease concern at the loss of influence, the Catholic Union operated a policy of vetting candidates to see where they stood on important Catholic questions. This may or may not have been a satisfactory way of conducting business, but the CUAG and the Archdiocesan hierarchy seemed relatively happy with the compromise. It was not always such a harmonious arrangement as the enthusiasm of local parishes brought them to scrutinise the opinions of a candidate in a manner which would have put the Jesuits to shame. However, the Catholic Church was shaken by the SPL and its success at elections in the early 1930s in Glasgow. The laissez faire attitude of the CUAG and the hierarchy towards local authorities and party politics was severely tested by SPL councillors. The Scottish Protestant League and its supporters were a danger as they brought with them the threat of sectarian violence to the streets.

An indication of the potential for conflict with the SPL came when Protestant activists broke up a rally by the Catholic Enquiry Service (CES) in early 1931. The issue inflamed Catholic leaders especially when the Chief Constable of Glasgow, Percy Sillitoe, seemed to pass the blame for the incident onto the CES. The incident gives an idea of how the street actions of this period were ripe for exploitation, the environment was one where the extremes of economic decline and a seemingly polarised political situation gave off the signals of increasing militancy. Many organisations were to copy the models of the Communists and the Fascists in organising street rallies to tub thump for the cause; the SPL did likewise. However, it was not the SPL threat that was to bring the CES, an offshoot of the CUAG, to street action but the Communists and Independent Labour Party.

The street action of the CUAG and its satellites was a strange mirroring of the forms of action sponsored by the Communist Party and the Independent Labour Party. Street meetings were a common sight in many cities as various propagandists sought to gain notice. Such meetings could be a focus for violence between left and right as they were in London between the British Union of Fascists and various anti-fascist organisations. In addition to street meetings, the CUAG asked Glasgow Trades Council for the right to march on May Day at the official march of the council. The CES was to march in 1932 and in 1933 but the second march was on a separate route for Catholics. Joining in on the May Day March was not unusual in Europe where many Catholic trades unions existed. Also, the idea of the May holiday could be justified as a celebration of creation (it

was the tradition festival to mark the end of planting crops after all).
But, it seems to be unique in the United Kingdom for a specifically
religious organisation, never mind that it was a Catholic group, to
join the workers' celebration.

The May Day rally may have been a slightly eccentric aspect of
the work of the Catholic Union but it was a manifestation of the
increasingly visible work of Catholics in the social and political
spheres. Much of the inspiration for the work of the CUAG came
from John Joseph Campbell. As Honorary Secretary (latterly as
General Secretary) from the mid-1920s until the middle of the Second
World War, Campbell was to preside over an important period in
recent Catholic history and to help reconstruct the Catholic Union
as an important part of the Catholic community. John J. Campbell
was a Glasgow lawyer and his meticulous approach to the job
brought a new professionalism and energy to Catholic Action in the
West of Scotland. He was a strange hybrid of old British Tory
Catholicism and modern radical European Catholic ideas. He was
totally devoted to the Catholic Union and its place as the senior lay
organisation in the Archdiocese of Glasgow. His contacts were many
and varied, stretching from the House of Lords where he liaised with
senior Tory Peers to the Central Catholic Verein in St. Louis U.S.A.,
a Catholic action body that united the diocese of the Midwest in
America. Campbell pushed the Catholic Union towards becoming a
more active body in line with Vatican thinking on social and pastoral
care as an auxiliary of the clergy rather than being concerned with
elections. Under Campbell's leadership the CUAG arguably became
the most active Catholic society in the United Kingdom.

The Catholic Union represented the very wide and varied types
of activity that the broad theme of Catholic Action could encom-
pass. The Encyclical of Pius XI, Quadregessimo Anno of 1931, set
up the ecclesiastical context of Catholic Action, its aims and objectives. Responses in terms of actual activity were left to the individual preferences and prejudices of the local episcopate. In many
countries a new body was founded to incorporate the ideas of
modern Catholic Action. In the Archdiocese of Glasgow this was
also considered with the Catholic Union effectively recast as the
Catholic Federation of the Archdiocese of Glasgow to act as the
senior umbrella organisation to co-ordinate the range of bodies that
operated in Glasgow.

The Catholic Union Advisory Bureau

The body which came to represent the effort of the Catholic Union more than anything else was the Advisory Bureau of the Catholic Union, known as the CUAB. It brought the Catholic laity into closer contact with the clergy and also closer to the wider community in which Catholics were so long seen as outsiders. It was to have a double consequence in helping the Catholic Church to retain relevance in difficult times but also to forge a very distinctive form of Catholic citizenship. The Church was brought closer to the people by addressing concerns that were the direct consequence of economic depression. The CUAB was also at pains to demonstrate that Catholic social action was not just to the benefit of the Catholic Community but to the wider community. It was also to fulfil a broader objective of the Church, in that it also sought to arrest the influence of the Communist Party and, as we shall see, anti-communism became more and more the object of the actions of senior Catholics. In fact without the Communist Party the CUAB would not have got off the ground in the first place.

For Catholics, the battle for the souls of the people was the pre-eminent concern of all action. The Vatican was in no doubt of the main theatre of war in Europe: between the forces of God and of secular bolshevism. Anti-Communism was an issue with which Catholics and the forces of oppression could find some common cause or at least leave many Catholics ambivalent as to the consequences of the rise of the far right. Dictators such as Salazar in Portugal, Franco in Spain and Dolfus in Austria all used Catholic support or the Catholic Church to present some degree of legitimacy to their authoritarian regimes. In Germany in 1933, the ascension of Adolf Hitler to the chancellorship was aided by the intrigues of the former Chancellor Brunning. Succour or support for the extreme right to gain influence was a price that the Catholic Church was prepared to envisage for the broader objective of rolling back the perceived tide of Communism. Like many others, the Church could not have foreseen the repercussions of this action, though the Catholic Church in Germany was to immediately find out that dealing with the Nazis was a double edged sword. On the one hand the Lautern treaty of 1934 reassured the position of Catholics in the Third Reich but also throughout the 1930s Catholic clerics were to come under the same degree of harassment as Lutherans. Part of the great movement for reconstruction of the Catholic Church in the two decades after 1945, which was to culminate in the Second Vatican Council in 1965, was inspired by the experience of ordinary Catholics in the 1930s who, like many others, were to find that Nazism was not an acceptable bulwark against communism.

In the West of Scotland where the Communist 'threat' was more illusion than reality, the presence of the Communists and the I.L.P served as a means to pull the Catholic community together and assert the superiority of ecclesiastical authority. Where the threat was real was where ideas promoted by the Communists and fellow travellers made an impact on the social and political agenda. Pre-eminent amongst these was the issue of so-called 'Sex' or 'Race' bolshevism. The issue of birth control and its association with eugenics was a serious concern for Catholics because it impacted upon the race and racial characteristics of the 'Irish'.

Anti-Communism provided an unusual insight into the thinking of the Catholic Union and, in particular, its Honorary Secretary, J. Campbell, who went on the offensive against the Communists on a number of occasions by attacking them for stealing ideas, treachery and promoting genocide. The most interesting aspect of the growing hostility of the Catholic Union towards the Communists was the way in which the CUAG both condemned and paid compliments to them. In a speech delivered to the National Catholic Union in 1944, Campbell was heavily critical of a Communist Party

> which has seized on the whole structure and dogma of the Catholic Church and translated the contention for good as one for evil and all under the action by the Communist Party is one of the most amazing feats of the world today.[14]

On the other hand he also praised the Communists for their idea of mutual assistance: 'If that party suffers other members rush to its aid and this is achieved by united action.'[15] The structure of democratic centralism was not a million miles away from the way in which the Catholic Church operated. The idea of instinctive mutual support from a network of cadres had managed to carry the Communists, even the small Scottish Party, into positions of relatively strong influence: especially in the Trades Union movement in the West of Scotland, such as the miners and engineers unions. The Catholic Union emphasised its anti-Communist credentials through support for a London based organisation called the Anti-Communist Union/Anti-Socialist Union (ACU\ASU). The organisation mainly concerned itself with the dissemination of

Anti-Communist propaganda. One book which Campbell took an interest in was called 'Out of the Night' by Jan Valtin. He circulated this book widely throughout the Archdiocesan hierarchy giving it to both the Vicar General and the Archbishop of Glasgow. The book was also sent to the Lord Provost of Glasgow; Patrick Dollan (a close friend of John Wheatley, who had been the minister of health in the first Labour Government in 1924).[16] The hostility of the Catholic Union secretary was to reach its peak in the first two years of the Second World War. The fanaticism of the CUAG secretary could be justified at this time as the Communists in the United Kingdom were supporting the Cominterm's line of opposing war with Germany. The line was maintained until the end of June 1941 when the Wehrmacht attacked Russia. After that the CPGB threw its support behind the effort of the Allies against the Axis forces.

The sinister edge of the anti-Communist activities of the CUAG brought problems, which could hurt the Union financially as well as undermine its credibility. They found themselves in deep water when they tried, in April 1940, to force out an official from the City corporation workforce who had been 'exposed' by the *Catholic Herald* and the Catholic Union as a communist. The man involved threatened to sue the newspaper and the Catholic Union if it persisted in attacking him. The CUAG realised the potential damage, the lack of any form of evidence as well as the fact that being a Communist was not at any time a criminal offence, and they quickly dropped the witch-hunt. The search for Communists went on, nevertheless, with covert operations organised through the Catholic Union. They were primarily based on surveillance of Communist Party meetings, particularly those involving the senior figure of the Scottish Communists, William Gallagher. Verbatim records were kept of the speeches made by Gallagher although only a few survive in the records of the Catholic Union. It is also impossible to determine how deep the infiltration of the Communist Party was by the CUAG or whether this action carried the blessing of any senior figure in the Clergy in Glasgow.

By keeping a close eye on the Communist Party, the Catholic Union was able to pilfer ideas, which might just be of benefit to the Catholic community. One idea was to be the founding and operation of the Advisory Bureaus, which was to prove a spectacular success. On the 30th of October 1931, Campbell received a letter from the secretary of the Catholic Union Mission in Renton, Dumbartonshire.[17] It was a report of the activities of an organisation called the National Unemployed Workers Movement (NUWM). It had set up an office to 'advise, assist, and plead any member's case who had a genuine grievance, either through the Public Assistance Committee or Labour Bureaux or education authority.'[18] The offices were called Advisory Bureaus and anyone could join the bureau for a modest fee of 4d initially and a 3d per month subscription. The idea was simple and effective as it gave the option of legal representation free for an individual as well as advice in a whole manner of other areas relating to work and social security. For the Catholic Union such an organisation was dangerous as it left its people drifting 'like a ship without a rudder' towards the 'propaganda of the left.'[19] Mr. McMonagle proposed that the local Catholic Union mission should form a rival advisory bureau based on the Chapel in the Parish. The response of the Catholic Union was to look further at the idea of the advisory bureau and to communicate with the then Archbishop of Glasgow Donald Macintosh. The response from the Archbishop was very encouraging and also very illuminating. He described McMonagle's idea as 'in every way an excellent one' but that no Catholic was under any 'obligation to seek help from the proposed bureaux.'[20] Macintosh in a further caveat said that the new bureaus should be open to both Catholics and non-Catholics. This condition is an interesting issue as it seems to demonstrate just how sensitive the hierarchy was to the perception that the Catholic Community was insular and only seeking to promote its own interests.

The idea of advisory bureaus was to flower to become one of the most significant forms of mass Catholic social action in the whole of the United Kingdom. The new bureaus were initially to operate within the existing structure of the Catholic Union in Glasgow, and alongside other charitable and social work societies such as St. Vincent de Paul, though there was a fear that there would be duplication and clashes of interest between the different organisations:

> Opinion was widely expressed at the beginning that the work would clash with the activities of other societies, but shortly after the whole scheme was in operation it was found that the work really required the attention of a separate organisation.[21]

The CUAB came to fill a niche in the operation of social security and charity. It was not the job of the bureau to pay out money for those in a desperate situation, though there is evidence that some clerics did indeed dip into Parish funds to help some people. But, rather to provide advice and assistance in claims for compensation, legal claims of wrongful treatment especially in cases of disputes with landlords and employers as well as a host of other areas of civil and legal dispute.

Each of the Parishes was asked to form a bureau as an offshoot of the CUAG mission committee. From each committee an extra levy of £5 per year to support the central structure of the CUAB was demanded, which the majority gave without protest. There was a separate Constitution of the Advisory Bureaus, which set down the precise relationship between the CUAB and the CUAG. The constitution stated that the bureau 'shall not encroach on the general work of the Catholic union.'[22] The main work of the union was, in theory, the collection and maintenance of the electoral rolls for Corporation and Council elections. But, as the CUAB grew and the electoral impact of the CUAG was in complete retreat, it was the advisory bureau which was to become the central focus of Catholic Action in the Archdiocese of Glasgow. Like the CUAG, the advisory bureau was a partnership between the laity and the clergy. The division of labour within the bureau involved the local parish priest providing the main support for the organisation and the senior members of the Mission committee taking the main responsibility for finding out about the nuts and bolts of citizens' advice.

As pointed out earlier, there was no shortage of potential work for the Catholic Union advisory bureau. In just three years it has been estimated that the bureau of the CUAB dealt with no less than 30,000 cases ranging across the whole range of civil, social, employment and legal problems.[23] In addition to his own work load as a lawyer, the honorary secretary himself dealt with and represented free of charge many of the cases sent to him. He wrote over 600 letters on behalf of the CUAB and sent nearly 700 circulars to the CUAB local committees on various aspects of the law. Campbell himself set out the best summary of the achievements of the CUAB:

(a) Counteracted the impact of the Communist Party.
(b) Established political contacts.
(c) Brought awareness of Civil power and interests.
(d) Brought out hidden talents amongst members of the Catholic Union.
(e) Helped thousands of People.
(f) It was an example of United Catholic Action.
(g) Brought recognition of local officialdom.[24]

Taking each in turn, we can determine the magnitude of the effort and the potential influence that the CUAB brought and how it helped to move the Catholic population from the periphery into the mainstream of public life in the Archdiocese of Glasgow.

In March 1935, in the Journal the *Christian Democrat* a prominent Jesuit, Rev. Lewis Watt, concluded that the work of the CUAB was 'an antidote to communist activity amongst our Catholic Poor.'[25] This aspect of the CUAB was headlined as the main achievement of the organisation and as recorded in multiple entries in minutes, letters and messages as the success in eliminating the influence of the Communists. For example, 'one excellent result of the work – apart altogether from the practical assistance given to applicants for relief, etc., – has been that many of our people have severed their connection with the NUWM and similar organisations.'[26] Similar reports came in from around the Archdiocese: 'In Dumbartonshire, Communism had been combatted and generally, the work of the Bureaux had been so successful as to stir up opposition from other political agencies.'[27] Just what sort of opposition is not reported to any great extent and it could be concluded that it was more bravado than actual reality. The Communist threat – whether real or illusory – was a powerful motivation for the Church and provided a strong means to unify the clergy and the laity. It is impossible to determine how effective the CUAB would have been without the spectre of Communism. It would have no doubt pleased some Communists to think of how all-pervasive their influence was thought to be. In this area the CUAB was totally in tune with the broad theme of European Catholicism. Seeing itself as the spiritual and physical bulwark against Communism.

The loss of direct influence in public bodies was a blow to the prestige of the Catholic Union. At a stroke the 1929 Local Government (Scotland) Act had removed the main area of activity of the CUAG. The Union had been primed to mobilise the Catholic vote for elections to the School Boards and the Poor Law authority with a Political Action committee which co-ordinated the maintenance of the electoral register. Each year Catholic Union members would visit door to door all of the Catholic electors within a mission to see that all of the potential electors were on the voting rolls. Though this work was to continue after 1930 it had not the force or the direction which had previously been the case, and although the Catholic community was urged to vote and use their potential influence to ensure the maintenance of Catholic influence in the Council chambers. The Catholic

Church did not exercise nearly the amount of influence on the local burghs and councils as they would like to have thought or their opponents believed. In the corporation of Glasgow only a handful of the councillors were Roman Catholics.

The loss of influence forced by the 1929 Act resulted in the CUAG looking for other ways to influence the work of the council and the Members of Parliament in the Archdiocese. An important way to do this was to arm the local Catholic activists with information on the workings and understanding of the law and procedures in relation to such things as Public Assistance and housing. In doing so they were better able to bring influence to bear on local representatives as well as to join forces with secular organisations to campaign for greater recognition of the shortcomings of legislation relating to issues of importance. A further arena of influence open to the Catholic Union was the House of Lords. As part of the National Organisation of the Catholic Union, Glasgow had an open door to the senior Catholic Peers in London. This had two results, firstly the Peers could help to amend legislation that passed through the upper house, and secondly, Peers could open doors to senior ministers in Government. The Secretary of the Catholic Union throughout the lifetime of the advisory bureau regularly visited London to meet Peers at the Pall Mall Club to discuss a number of issues relating to the work of the CUAB.

Two parliamentary bills particularly represent the fusion of social concern and specifically Catholic concerns: the Employment Act 1934 and the Housing Bill 1935. The Employment Act introduced a new system of training for young people in Juvenile Training Centres. The Catholic Union objected to the lack of religious instruction and the potential for infiltration of Communists. In a letter to Sir Henry Betterton the Minister for Labour, John Campbell promoted the idea of greater Catholic involvement to 'avert moral deterioration', adding that 'Responsible Catholics feel that, so far as this object is concerned, success could be more readily achieved if the atmosphere of discipline and training prevailing into Schools could be maintained to some extent in the training centres.'[28] Campbell asked for the creation of three separate Catholic training centres with Catholic teachers. Mixing concern for work and spiritual welfare he further pointed out that 'it has. . . . to be borne in mind that many of the most active of the communist workers were originally decent boys, who if they had been employed would doubtless have taken more creditable forms of actions.'[29] The message was clear: training for work was a solution to the growth of Communism and as an extra form of spiritual insurance the Catholic Church was also needed. The Housing Act of 1935 proposed to further limit the number of people permissible in a dwelling based on a square footage calculation. The Catholic Union felt that this had the potential to split up Catholic families which were, on average, larger than Protestant families. Throughout 1934 and 1935 the Catholic Union heavily lobbied Glasgow MPs to push for an amendment to the Act to ensure that the equation used in relation to housing would err on the side of the larger Catholic families.[30]

Until the advent of the modern Welfare State with the Beveridge Report in 1941 and a single contributory system introduced in the late 1940s, all of the various agencies relating to unemployment benefit, social security, pensions, disability and the Poor Law were administered by separate organisations. The 'Safety Net' which became a feature of modern welfare provision did not exist and an individual who needed help in gaining financial assistance was required to go through a series of different application forms and in some cases tribunals. By far and away the majority of the work of the Catholic Union was in helping such individuals to fill in applications for poor relief, rent rebates, pensions, and unemployment assistance. Table 1 shows where the work of CUAB was centred. To be able to work effectively members of the Catholic Union had to have knowledge of the structures of the local assistance agencies and the workings of the law. The extensive range of

Table 1.   Returns of the St. Paul's CUAB Whiteinch Glasgow, 1934/1935.[31]

UAB Referee	403
Employment Assistance	124
Employment Compensation	5
Employment Exchange	53
Hire purchase	5
Hospitals	18
Misc.	27
National health Insurance	23
Widows and OAP Pensions	21
Public Assistance	87
Rent and Housing	38
Rent Courts	22
Small Debts	13
Supplementary Grants	58

professions that this predominantly middle class body was able to call upon helped the Catholic Union deal effectively with the workload this initiative inspired. It brought to prominence a number of individuals who were to emerge as senior members of the legal and medical professions, including the future Lord Advocate Lord Wheatley, who as plain John Wheatley LLB represented Catholic Union clients in the highest courts in Scotland for free.

The Catholic community also benefited from its involvement in the Advisory bureaus through gaining closer contact and liaison with the decentralised local welfare agencies. The operation of the National Insurance Acts, Widows and Old Age Pensions Act and the Unemployed Assistance Board presented an opportunity for direct participation in the system. Catholic Insurance and Friendly Societies already had official status as agents for the National Insurance Board, providing both a means to save for hard times and as an adjudicator in times when claims were made. The Widows and Old Age Pensions legislation was administered through a series of local agents who were sanctioned by the government to authorise payment and to be the main judge when dealing with cases. A major bonus for the Catholic Union Advisory Bureau came when one of the senior activists in the Archdiocese, Neil Ramsey of St. Paul's CUAB in Rutherglen, became an agent for the Government department under the Widows, Orphans and Old Age Contributory Pensions Act, 1937.

Under the 1934 Unemployment Act a new system for paying out welfare to the long-term unemployed was introduced, with a new means test for the unemployed administered by the Unemployment Assistance Board. Those who failed to gain relief under the Act had the option of an 'appeal to the Umpire': a classic piece of Cricketspeak so beloved by many at Westminster. The Umpire had power to decide disputed cases and met in a form of tribunal, with an applicant allowed a representative to speak on his or her behalf. The Catholic Union tried for four years to gain the right of representation. The matter at stake was whether or not the CUAB had the right as an association to speak in authority for an individual. Trades Unions could do so when appealing on behalf of a member. Similarly, the NUWM gained recognition to speak at tribunals and also, claimed the CUAB, the Orange Order.[32] The rules of the UAB tribunals prohibited representation by political parties and the UAB chief, Mr Bickerdyke, argued that the CUAB was to a great extent a political party and further to this did not have direct authority to represent an individual as it had no membership. However, the CUAB was eventually to gain the right to 'sit-in' on hearings and advise clients but not to speak for them.[33]

With rights of agency and the right to advise clients, Catholics slowly found a way to become part of the infrastructure of state organisations. This helped to identify members with specific skills in dealing with bureaucracy and built a strong link between the professional life of many Catholics and obligations of religious life. You cannot find a more coherent example of Catholic Action in practice. The possibility could have been that many professional Catholics might have drifted away from the Church and the locality as professional ambition took over from community and religious identity. However, the maintenance of a link between professional life and religion retained a strong bond between the bulk of the Catholic population, which was still for the most part composed of the poorest in society, and a growing professional elite. The issue of Catholic civics in Scotland is still a neglected issue and no doubt there is more than one reason for the maintenance of a strong identity across the classes in the Catholic Community. Family, religious and professional self interest mix in a way in which it is virtually impossible to decipher the true motivation behind such activity.

A final issue which the study of the CUAB incorporates is the issue of citizenship and in particular the relationship between Catholicism and civic identity. The very great mass of activity – 30,000 cases in the first three years, an average of 10,000 people per year in the Archdiocese of Glasgow – indicated that Catholics were becoming more aware of, and involved in, civic and social issues. Added to this were the numbers who were actively volunteering to give their time and services – free of charge – many from the senior professions in the legal and public services such as advocates, lawyers, civil servants, trades union officials, councillors and Members of Parliament. This is strong evidence of the emergence of Catholics as citizens committed to the welfare of the Catholic community but also to asserting the right of recognition for the 'Irish Catholics' as part of Glasgow, Scotland and Britain. An indication of this dual trend of self defence and demand for greater recognition as part of the broader community came in a speech by Baillie John Heenan in early 1935. A report from the speech stated:

> the necessity of the advisory bureaux exercising their influence to maintain our equal rights to make ourselves active in every sphere of civic life and show that we are doing our duty as citizens as well as, if not better than other sections of the community.[34]

This may have emerged as an accidental consequence of the founding and working of the Catholic Union Advisory Bureau but in
dealing with the mass of social, legal and welfare agencies, the
senior laity of the Scottish Catholic Church was forced into dealing
with local and State bodies which they regarded at various times
as either anti-Catholic, anti-God or anti-Irish. We can conclude that,
as the CUAB was initially a tactical manoeuvre to circumvent the
influence of the Communists and their 'fellow travellers', that the
realisation of civic responsibility, by Catholics as an objective, was
an evolutionary process. The deeper the CUAB got into the system
the greater the opportunities were to forge an identity as citizens
just as many Catholics on the continent were to find that campaigning to defend Catholic interests could only be successful through
greater identity with the broader problems of identity and nationality. This issue was not resolved in Europe until the conclusion of
the Second World War and the rise of cross-denominational
Christian Democratic parties.

Conclusion

By 1939, the Catholics of the Archdiocese of Glasgow had reached
a point where they were significant players in the local authority
and that they were more aware than before of the nature of Scottish
society. But as in all countries, the achievement of full status as
citizens and as people in Scotland would require not just political
change and a slight but significant recognition of common interest
with their Presbyterian brethren, but also much broader social
change. Economic change, educational changes with greater opportunity for advancement regardless of income and religion, and a
change in the intellectual atmosphere pushed the Catholic community out of the ghetto. At the start of the Second World War
Catholics had travelled a long way from being strangers in a
strange land. There was an expanding professional class and a
substantial number of Catholics breaking through in the political
parties into positions of influence, though they were still the
minority. The Catholic Union Advisory Bureau brought together
many of these groups in the pursuit of direct Catholic interests
but also demonstrated their commitment to the land that they now
called home.

NOTES

1. The term 'mission' refers to a Church in a national area which does not have its own senior episcopate or autonomy over its internal affairs, but is subject to the authority of the Office of Propaganda in Rome.
2. Ultramontane was a term used by anti-clerical groups in France to describe the growing centralistion of the Catholic Church in Rome. The term literally means 'beyond the mountains', meaning across the Alps to Italy.
3. Pius IX: Giovanni Maria Mastai, 1792–1878.
4. Syllabus of Errors, in L. Snyder (ed), *Fifty Major Documents of the Nineteenth Century* (New York, 1955), p. 120.
5. Rerum Novarum, pp. 177–180.
6. *Ibid.*, p. 179.
7. *Ibid.*
8. *Ibid.*
9. The post-1789 revolutionary government in France proposed to sell Church land, whilst the Papal states around Rome were a constant source of conflict for the new Italian state formed in 1860–1.
10. Rerum Novarum, *op. cit.*, p. 180.
11. *Glasgow Observer*, 24 May 1930.
12. Constitution of the Catholic Union of the Archdiocese of Glasgow, 1930. Glasgow Archdiocesan archive, Box CU1.
13. W. Bishop, *The Menace of the Irish Race to our Scottish Nationality* (Edinburgh, 1923), quoted in T. Gallagher, *Glasgow: The Uneasy Peace* (Manchester, 1987), p. 136.
14. John J. Campbell, draft of speech to the Catholic Union of Great Britain, July 1944, section A, p.8: Glasgow Archdiocesan archives, CU3.
15. *Ibid.*
16. The Catholic Union of the Archdiocese of Glasgow, Glasgow Archdiocesan archive, CU3.
17. John McMonagle to J. Campbell, 30 October 1931, Glasgow Archdiocesan archive, CU3.
18. *Ibid.*
19. *Ibid.*
20. Archbishop D. Macintosh to J. Campbell, 25 November 1931, Glasgow Archdiocesan archive, CU3.
21. First annual report of the advisory bureau of the Catholic Union of the Archdiocesse of Glasgow 1931–2, p. 11. Glasgow Archdiocesan archive.
22. Constitution of the advisory bureau of the Catholic Union, clause 4, 1931. Glasgow Archdiocesan archive.
23. This figure was provided by the secretary of the CUAB, J. Campbell, in a letter to Revd. Laydon, 8 December 1934: Glasgow Archdiocesan archive, CU11.
24. *Ibid.*
25. L. Watt S. J., Christian Democrat, March 1935. Recorded in the minutes of the CUAB, May 1935, Glasgow Archdiocesan archive, CU2.

26. Annual Report of the Catholic Union Advisory Bureau, 1932–3, p. 31: Glasgow Archdiocesan archive, CU2.
27. Dumbarton CUAB report, 1935–6, 28 October 1936, p. 3: Glasgow Archdiocesan archive.
28. J. Campbell to Sir Henry Betterton, Minister of Labour, 23 July, 1934: Glasgow Archdiocesan archive.
29. *Ibid*.
30. The correspondence dealing with the Housing Act (Scotland) 1935, is contained in the Catholic Union Files in the Glasgow Archdiocesan archive, CU3, but are incomplete.
31. Report of the St Paul's CUAB, 1934–5: Glasgow Archdiocesan archive.
32. The correspondence on this issue is spread widely throughout the CUAB box files in the Glasgow Archdiocesan archive. A full assessment is difficult however, because many of the replies from the CUAB have been lost and Campbell only kept carbon copies of his own letters.
33. Bickerdyke to Campbell, February 1939: Glasgow Archdiocesan archive, CU3.
34. Cllr J. Heenan to CUAB committee, CUAB minutes, 7 March 1935: Glasgow Archdiocesan archive, CU2/44.

3

CATHOLICS, THE CATHOLIC CHURCH AND POLITICAL ACTION IN SCOTLAND

Peter Lynch

This chapter offers an analysis of the role of the Catholic Church in contemporary Scottish politics, through examination of the Church's political interests and ability to play a role in the policy process through representation on central and local government bodies. It also identifies the Church's main areas of pressure group activity in Scotland and contrasts its relative success in the area of education with the failure to make progress over the abortion question. Finally, the chapter attempts to focus on the wider role and impact of the Church in Scotland, through its domestic and international efforts in support of social justice and third world development.

> My role is not to tell people for whom they should vote. Instead I have the duty to counsel people as to how they should use their vote.
>
> Cardinal Thomas Winning, *The Herald*, 20 March 1997.

Introduction

Religion and politics are often viewed as an undesirable mix in modern liberal democracies in which religion is presumed to be a private matter and church and state are largely separate. However, in spite of assumptions about the decline of religion and the secular-isation of politics, religion and religious institutions still have a role and some influence in public life.[1] This is certainly the case in Scotland where the churches – both separately and in unison – play prominent roles in public debate on a variety of issues. The Church of Scotland offers a good example of the role of religious institutions in public policy in Scotland. Whether through the annual General Assembly, the Church and Nation Committee or through its role as a service-provider in social services, the Church of Scotland has developed a political role in such diverse areas as housing, nuclear deterrence, the distribution of wealth, Scottish devolution and South Africa.[2] The Catholic Church in Scotland has increasingly played a similar, though less remarked upon, role in political life in Scotland, with an interest in a wide variety of policy issues which has made it an active participant in public life in Scotland. The political role of the Church in Scotland has not merely involved the obvious issues of abortion and Catholic schools, but a broad range of social and political concerns.

The role of the Catholic Church in Scottish political life is an under-researched area. Whilst there has been some analysis of the role of the Church of Scotland, and an annual focus on its activities through the media coverage of the General Assembly, Catholic Church activities are something of a mystery outwith the Church itself. This chapter will focus on the role of the Catholic Church and community in a variety of different political activities, focusing more clearly on the role of the Church and its associated organisations in public policy in three areas: education, abortion and the third world. The Catholic Church and members of the Catholic community are prominently involved in these policy areas, through both religious and secular organisations: a reflection of Catholic social teaching as well as the particular interests of the Church and its adherents.

Understanding Catholics in Politics

The role of religious communities and institutions in modern political life is a complex one. Whilst secularisation has undoubtedly had an impact upon Western societies and undermined the impact of religion on public life, religious institutions retain a significant role in politics. The key to understanding this role is to take account of the Church as an agenda-setting pressure group which has a number of institutional and representational roles within Scotland, rather than as an organisation capable of directing its members to vote in one way or another in the style of Catholic priests urging support for the Christian Democrats in Italy.[3] Church leaders tend to raise issues rather than intervene in partisan debates, though they will sometimes wish these issues to have a partisan impact. Indeed, though the Church often states that it does not wish to tell people how they should vote,[4] this is a rather disingenuous point. In fact, the Church would be extremely happy if its efforts led voters to support candidates or parties who opposed abortion: as was the case with the Pro-Life Alliance at the 1997 general election discussed below.

However, more generally, the Catholic Church can be understood as a type of pressure group within Scottish politics with an important role in some areas of public policy. This role can be understood through consideration of four main factors. Firstly, the Catholic Church has a wide range of social/political views which cannot be easily categorised as an ideology in conventional left/right terms. As an 'active' Church, the Catholic Church frequently expresses these views in a variety of different ways as well as trying to act on these views through political involvement, lobbying and agenda setting. Thus, though the Church seldom has a direct impact on politics in the same way as political parties, it frequently has a role in shaping and reflecting public opinion on certain issues,[5] in addition to shaping societal values in conjunction with other religious institutions.[6] For example, both the Catholic Church and the Church of Scotland frequently express concern for the unemployed, socially disadvantaged and the third world: which feed through into the values and concerns of wider Scottish society. Secondly, as will be outlined below, the Church is actively involved in policymaking and service delivery in a number of areas within Scotland. Church representatives and members of the Catholic community (particularly in education) are involved in government bodies and are frequently consulted on aspects of policy in a range of areas. In addition, the Church itself actually functions as an arm of the welfare state, often in partnership with local authorities in providing a variety of health and welfare services which provide it with an active role in public policy.

Thirdly, the Church has to be understood as an institutional network in a similar vein to a political party. It has a tightly organised hierarchy, which guides activities and opinion within the Church in a top-down fashion,[7] but it also has a grassroots element which is very important to the Church. The grassroots provides it with both a congregation and a membership which can be mobilised in pursuit of certain goals and act as a support network for the Church through providing personnel and resources. For example, in Scotland there is an extensive Catholic organisation which stretches from the Bishops' Conference and its various committees and commissions, to the

dioceses, parishes, schools and various Catholic organisations organised by or associated with the Church such as the St Vincent de
Paul Society, Catholic men's societies and local Justice and Peace
groups, as well as groups organised by individual churches and
parishes themselves. However, though there are a variety of Catholic
organisations in existence, very little is known about the Church's
capacity to mobilise its grassroots in support of its position on
abortion, education or the third world. Finally, it has to be remembered that the Catholic Church is very much an international church.
Its membership spans the globe and includes large sections of the
third world where the Catholic Church is actively involved in a
variety of educational and healthcare activities. This international
aspect is very much reflected in the Church in Scotland, through its
own activities and the functioning of the Scottish Catholic International Aid Fund established by the Church in 1965. Regular readers
of Catholic newspapers such as the *Scottish Catholic Observer* or
Flourish and regular mass attenders will recognise the global aspect
to the Church's activities and concerns through the amount of coverage that third world issues receive within the Church on a weekly
basis, which reflect Catholic social teaching and also demonstrate
the reality of an 'active' Church in Scotland and internationally.

The Catholic Church in Politics and Public Policy

Though the Catholic Church seldom intervenes in party politics
(with the clear exception of abortion discussed below), the Church
and its representatives have a more substantial involvement in the
policy process at different levels of Scottish society. In addition, the
Church is capable of using its position to adopt and publicise certain
policy stances on a wide range of issues, though Catholic political
action often goes unreported beyond the Catholic press in Scotland.
The Catholic Church has a number of roles in politics and public
policy which are attributable to the wide scope of the church's
interests and functions. As far as the public are concerned, the main
role of the Catholic Church in politics probably revolves around the
issues of abortion and Catholic schools. However, this is only part
of the Church's role in political life. Essentially, the church's role can
be understood from three aspects: the 'active' Church as a lobbyist
and agenda setter in a wide range of policy areas, the Church as an
organisation involved in service delivery in health, welfare and
education, and the Church as an institution which is consulted on

many areas of public policy and has institutional representation on some governmental bodies.

Lobbying and Agenda setting

The Church has a social and moral vision of society which has led it to take a wide range of positions on most socio-economic and political questions in contemporary Scottish society. Often, positions are expressed through the forum of the Catholic Bishops' Conference of Scotland and communicated through the media and parish congregations via pastoral letters and statements on issues as different as unemployment and disarmament.[8] In its 1997 election statement, the Catholic Bishops' Conference highlighted issues such as education, health, poverty and unemployment, homelessness, youth affairs, the causes of crime, family life, overseas aid, peace and disarmament and the right to life.[9] Often the Church will seek to act as an agenda setter and lobbyist in these areas, promoting specific problems and issues on its own or in conjunction with other institutions. Significantly, these other institutions often include the other Scottish churches. Writing in the 1980s, Bishop Mario Conti remarked that:

> The degree of consensus or convergence in the Scottish churches on major social and international issues has been significant. On questions of peace, nuclear arms, world development and Scotland's own economic and social issues, the churches have spoken generally with a single voice, and those active in specific areas of social concern have been able to work very closely together in producing common programmes.[10]

Examples of the Church's lobbying and agenda setting roles are numerous. The Church's Justice and Peace Commission took a strong line of opposition to the former Conservative Government's policy on refugees and asylum-seekers coming to the UK, calling on the churches to establish safe havens and sanctuaries for asylum-seekers denied welfare benefits.[11] It campaigned for the government to free 200 asylum-seekers who had been imprisoned in Rochester prison pending their return to their own countries.[12] The Scottish Bishops' conference also sent a petition to the government to change its asylum and deportation procedures following the Joy Gardner Case.[13] Similarly, in 1995, the Church's Justice and Peace Commission, and its local groups, were involved in a campaign against the proposed deportation of a Nigerian-born woman who had been

resident in Scotland since 1982.[14] The Church has increasingly campaigned on socio-economic issues such as the problems of drug
abuse amongst the young,[15] often coupled with the issue of unemployment and Cardinal Winning also became involved in Shelter's
campaign against homelessness in Scotland alongside the Church of
Scotland.[16]

Service Delivery

The Church has a public policy function through its role as a service
provider in education, health and welfare. Though the Church has
a highly restricted role in health and welfare, which has declined as
a consequence of the expansion of a liberal secular state concerned
with individual and not family rights,[17] it does have a clear stake in
the welfare state in some areas, often in partnership with the public
sector. Examples include the Jericho House alcohol recovery centre
in Dundee; the Loretto Housing Association which provides accom-
modation for homeless people in Glasgow,[18] a care centre for the
mentally handicapped in Johnstone and a centre for single mothers
in Hamilton; Hill House home for single expectant mothers in Kil-
marnock; the charity functions of the St Vincent de Paul Society
which runs soup kitchens for the homeless, furniture projects and
home and hospital visits for the sick; the St Margaret's Adoption
Society; Scottish Marriage Care, with 90 Catholic marriage guidance
counsellors; Unity Enterprise, an employment project for disabled
people in Glasgow run in conjunction with other churches; and the
Talbot Association which runs a homeless centre in Glasgow. Such
activities require the Church to keep apace of policy developments
in health and social welfare and in frequent contact with public
services over service delivery: such as the local authorities, Scottish
Homes, local health trusts and social services. The fact that the
Church has an active – rather than merely a rhetorical or moral – role
in aspects of social welfare, also involves it in consultation processes
over policy developments in a wide range of areas.

Consultation and Representation

The Church and its representatives also participate in the policy
process of central and local government in a variety of ways. For
example, the Church is often consulted for its response to policy
proposals and legislation and it also has representatives on a number

of government institutions. The Church made written submissions to the Cullen Inquiry following the Dunblane killings,[19] an official submission to the government's White Paper, *Broadcasting in the 1990s*,[20] and was consulted over the BBC's 'Extending Choice' proposals in 1993.[21] Catholic representatives also play a role on a number of public institutions in Scotland. Catholic educationalists are often represented on Scottish Office Education Department committees and inquiries, either as individual educationalists or as nominees of the Catholic Education Commission. For example, in 1996, the 20 members of the Scottish Consultative Council on the Curriculum (SCCC) included the Principal of St Andrew's College (the Catholic teacher training college), Bart McGettrick, who served as the SCCC's Vice-chair; the Rector of St Aidan's High School in Wishaw; and the headteacher of Our Holy Redeemer's Primary in Glasgow.[22] The Principal of St Andrew's College of Education also served as chair of the Scottish Office's Higher Still staff development committee. There were also Catholic representatives on the Munn and Dunning committees in the 1980s, with Tom O'Mally of St. David's in Dalkeith serving on the Munn Committee and John Oates of St Modan's in Stirling serving on Dunning. More recently, James McVitie of St. Ninian's in Eastwood was a member of the Howie Committee on post-16 education. Similarly, as will be explained below, Catholic Church representatives serve on local education committees and are nominated by the local Bishop under arrangements which have survived since the Education Act (Scotland) 1918. In addition, there are examples of Catholic representation outside education. Bishop Mario Conti was appointed to the NHS advisory committee on appointments to health trusts and boards in 1994,[23] and Father Danny McLaughlin, press officer to Bishop Mone of Paisley, was appointed to the Independent Television Commission's viewer consultative council in 1996,[24] giving the Church some involvement in broadcasting standards policy.

Catholics and Scottish Education

The existence of a separate Roman Catholic school system within the state sector is probably the most public example of the existence of a distinctive Catholic community in Scotland. It also has the effect of maintaining the Catholic community's religious distinctiveness in Scotland to a considerable degree. The reason for the existence of separate Catholic schools can be understood on two levels. First, the

1918 Education Act (Scotland) was an example of an agreement between church and state that education should be a public institution subject to democratic control. The first steps in this direction had taken place in 1872 when the Education Act (Scotland) brought church schools from the Church of Scotland and Episcopalian Church into the public sector. The 1918 act merely added the Catholic schools to the state sector and completed the legislation that had been initiated in the 1870s. Second, the 1918 Education Act (Scotland) can be understood as a form of 'compact' between the state and the Catholic Church, with the state formally recognising the distinctiveness of the Catholic community and providing the Church with a special role within the newly public Catholic schooling system. Such recognition was politically important because it was the state's seal of approval for Catholicism in Scotland, but also functionally important because it provided the Catholic Church with an important role in educational policymaking, with the 1918 Education Act giving the Church a role in approving teaching appointments to Catholic schools, approving the religious and moral aspects of the curriculum and able to nominate Catholic representatives to local authority education committees following reorganisation of local government in 1929.

The strength of the church-state compact over Catholic schooling was probably not all that evident at the time of the 1918 Education Act. However, since 1918 the compact has survived intact despite large-scale social and political change in Scotland. There remains all-party support for the existence of Catholic schools and there have been few real challenges to the continuation of the system. Though much has been written of the development of popular anti-Catholicism in the 1920s and 1930s, with the growth of Protestant Action,[25] the Scottish Unionist Party's varied efforts to play the Orange card,[26] and the Church of Scotland's declaration to reverse Irish immigration to Scotland,[27] these political activities had little impact on actual public policy in Scotland. The Catholic schooling system and the church-state compact which had sustained Catholic education within the public sector has remained in existence, with some changes, since 1918. Indeed, the principal challenge to the continuation of a separate Catholic schooling system in Scotland has not come from opposition to separate schools, even though there appears to be public support for schools' integration,[28] but from two different sources: the popularity of Catholic schools amongst non-Catholics, which has led to

Catholic schools becoming more inter-denominational in composition, and also to the public spending and demographic pressures which have affected primary and secondary education in Scotland across all denominations, leading to school closures.[29]

The continued existence of a separate Catholic schools system into the 1990s was an unpredictable outcome of the 1918 Education Act. It owes its existence not merely to a long-standing cross-party consensus on the issue and the willingness of local authorities to make separate educational provision for Catholic communities,[30] but to the progress made by a largely immigrant Catholic community in Scotland which has generated a community of educational professionals at primary and secondary levels, which itself led to the creation of a Catholic middle class. Whereas Catholic education may previously have been the preserve of religious orders such as the Jesuits, Franciscans and Notre Dame sisters,[31] the combined impact of Catholic schools, the expansion of higher education and the social mobility of Catholics has been to replace the religious orders with ordinary lay Catholics. The fact that there are a substantial number of Catholic primary and secondary schools (and teachers) has given the Catholic schools sector a significant role in the wider educational community. Catholic schools make up a considerable part of the schooling system and Catholic educationalists are involved in numerous aspects of educational policymaking in Scotland.

The principal organisation responsible for education within the Church is the Catholic Education Commission (CEC). The CEC was established by the Catholic Bishops' Conference in 1971 to improve staffing levels in Catholic schools and act as a forum for promoting Catholic education. It is indicative of a more active approach by the Church to educational issues since the 1960s.[32] Before then, educational issues appear to have been dealt with more informally within the Church hierarchy itself. The Catholic Education Commission (CEC) comprises around 30 members and employs a field officer to keep track of policy issues. The CEC is structured with delegates from individual Church dioceses, in addition to representatives from the Catholic headteachers' associations and St Andrew's College. The CEC is the main consultative link between the Scottish Office and the Catholic educational community, though formal consultations between the CEC and Scottish Office are dependent on the pace and scope of government legislation each year. The CEC meets more regularly with the Schools Inspectorate on a formal and informal basis. Whilst the CEC is the official arm of the Church in education, it operates as part of a much broader institutional framework which includes the Catholic Headteachers' Association, the National Association of Catholic Primary Headteachers, Church representatives on local authority education committees,[33] individual schools, school boards of Catholic schools and St Andrew's College of Education. Significantly, the Church itself through the Bishops' Conference, is often involved in the CEC's work. The Bishops' Conference discusses the main educational issues on a regular basis and will act to support the CEC's work in the policy process,[34] often with the active involvement of Cardinal Winning, the CEC President.

The last major consultation between the CEC and central government occurred over the local government reorganisation bill. The Conservative government's proposals for local government reform involved the replacement of the two tiers of Regional and District councils with a single tier of local authorities. The proposals were only peripherally concerned with education, though the impact of local reorganisation on Catholic education in particular was significant. The CEC was sent a copy of the government White Paper on local reorganisation,[35] and was critical of the potential impact of the reorganisation on Catholic schooling. The CEC met with the Scottish Office education department in September 1993 to discuss the reforms. The CEC's concerns fell into two main areas. First, changes in local authority boundaries would have a substantial impact on the Catholic schools system. The new boundaries would cut across the catchment areas of Catholic schools and separate secondary schools from feeder primary schools in some areas. The situation in the former Central Regional Council, which now comprises three separate councils responsible for education (Clackmannan, Falkirk and Stirling), offers a good example of the problems created by the reorganisation. The main Catholic secondary school in Stirling, St. Modan's, was served by Catholic primaries in Clackmannan and Falkirk as well as Stirling itself. Pupils therefore needed to be allowed to attend a school outwith their local authority boundary, with implications for the provision of school transport outwith council boundaries. Unless catchment areas were allowed to run across the new local authority boundaries and councils were required to finance school transport to neighbouring authorities, then there were would be a drop in the school roll at St. Modan's (with implications for its viability), and problems for parents in Clackmannan and parts of Falkirk who would need to find another Catholic secondary school for their children.[36]

Second, the government's proposals abandoned the statutory requirement for local authorities to appoint Directors of Education and establish Education committees. Whereas the system under the Regional Councils involved the provision of professional bureaucracies, clear lines of authority, accountability and consultation, there were fears that the structured approach to education would be lost under local government reorganisation. Professional input would be lost without the Director of Education structure, and education would lose status and importance within local authorities without its own directorate. Also, the absence of an Education committee would damage participation in policymaking, especially if it meant that there was no structure for Catholic representatives to become involved in similar to the pre-1995 situation in which Catholic representatives sat on local authority education committees. In addition, it was questionable whether some local authorities would be able to operate education services effectively given their small size, leading to closures and rationalisations with consequences for separate Catholic schools. The background to this concern was the issue of schools' self-government and the opting-out of local authority control. The abandoning of requirements for local authorities to provide effective internal structures for education were interpreted as reforms intended to undermine education as a function of local authorities and 'encourage' schools to opt out of local authority control, thereby undermining the educational settlement established in 1918. The Catholic Church was opposed to such opting-out, despite its potential use as a weapon to prevent school closures.

When the Local Government (Scotland) bill was published, only two of its 169 clauses dealt with education and it ignored the detailed concerns of the CEC in relation to Catholic schooling and reorganisation. This situation was a reflection of the fact that education had a very low priority within the reorganisation proposals. The Catholic Education Commission published a critical response to the bill and drafted an amendment to the bill to enable school catchment areas to exist across local authority boundaries and co-ordinated a campaign in support of its amendment. Essentially, the CEC was attempting to ensure that the status quo under the Regional Councils was retained under the vague provisions for educational provision in the new unitary authorities. The CEC mobilised the Catholic community through parishes and schools, circulating a petition to the government to protect the integrity of the Catholic education system through amending its proposals. Catholics were encouraged to contact their MPs and the government, and Cardinal Winning used Education Sunday on 6th February 1994 to deliver a pastoral letter to church attenders dealing with the implications of local government reorganisation. Such efforts culminated in a lobby of the House of Commons led by Cardinal Winning in March 1994.[37] At the end of the day, the government accepted the CEC's arguments and amended the bill to ensure that catchment areas and school transport arrangements were not disrupted by reorganisation. Thus the Church and CEC were able to deploy their lobbying skills to pressurise the government, whilst using the Catholic organisational network to mobilise support for amendments to the reorganisation bill to facilitate continued Catholic educational provision. However, such a success did not mask considerable scepticism about the impact of local government reorganisation upon education in terms of special educational services and school closures,[38] and while it was significant that Catholic demands had been accommodated by the government, this success could be explained by the limited nature of the Catholic agenda over local government reorganisation.

Besides such prominent lobbying activities outlined above in which the CEC appears as an outsider in the policy process, there are other occasions when the organisation seems to enjoy insider status within the public policy arena. Curriculum design is one area in which the CEC has enjoyed some influence, especially in relation to religious education. When it came to discussing the content of religious education in Catholic schools under the 5–14 programme, the Catholic Church expressed the view that the Scottish Office proposals, 'Religious and Moral Education' were not suitable for Catholic schools. The result of consultation was a joint Scottish Office-CEC version of the 5–14 programme, 'Catholic Religious Education 5–14', for use in Catholic schools.[39] The CEC role in this area has also been a continuing one, rather than a one-off event, with CEC representatives involved in designing different aspects of the religious education curriculum.[40] Over the longer term, the CEC has also played a role in designing its own religious education units for use in Catholic schools.[41]

The Church and CEC also had to deal with a range of Conservative educational initiatives in the 1980s which altered the characteristics of Catholic schools. The Parents' Charter, which was a component of the Education Act (Scotland) 1988, allowed parents to choose which school they wished their children to attend. This decision created a situation in which non-Catholic parents could choose to enrol their children in Catholic schools: a situation which could undermine the Catholic nature of these schools and remove the rationale for their existence in the first place. For example, in 1995, St Margaret's Academy in Livingston received 230 applications for 180 first year places, many from non-Catholics who could exercise their right under parental choice to have their children enrolled in the school regardless of religion.[42] The local authority resolved this issue to the satisfaction of the Catholic Church and community, but it is indicative of the type of problem which has arisen in recent years. However, in some ways parental choice has been helpful. It has created a new set of supporters of Catholic schools, those non-Catholic parents who favour the moral flavour of Catholic schools in addition to their educational attainment levels, whilst also plugging a gap in the falling school rolls of some Catholic schools which might face potential closure. The Conservative's school boards initiative under the Self-governing Schools (Scotland) Act 1989 has also been something of a double-edged sword for the Catholic Church. On the one hand it has meant that parents became more involved in their schools and could act as an additional pressure group on local authorities and the government, as described above over the government's plans for local government reorganisation. However, on the other hand, the school board system has established a structure in which it is parents not Catholic teachers or priests, who gain more power over the school, with the potential to diminish Church authority.[43] In some situations, therefore, the parents and the Church can come into conflict. For example, the school board of St Bonaventure's in Glasgow responded to proposals to close the school by examining the potential for opting out of local authority control,[44] despite the fact that opting out was opposed by the Church.

Overall, in the sphere of education, the Catholic Church faces a difficult situation associated not with opposition to the continuation of separate schools but with a range of financial and demographic changes which impact upon the school system in general. The Church has become a defender of the status quo within education and appears primarily concerned with maintaining the educational settlement attained since 1918. The range of educational changes and developments over the last decade often makes this approach a difficult balancing act carried out in a rather defensive fashion. Thus, the Church will campaign to preserve such policies as the Secretary of State's veto over Catholic school closures – a right of appeal which non-denominational schools do not enjoy – which limit local author-ity autonomy,[45] whilst also opposing the undermining of local authorities through opting out and reorganisation. How these issues and problems are played out in the context of a devolved Scottish parliament remains an open question. Certainly, in the area of edu-cation, both the Church and the Catholic Education Commission will find they are operating in a much more open and potentially fluid environment, in which Church-Scottish Office contact is merely one of a range of interactions which influence educational policymaking.

Catholics and the Right To Life

With the exception of the issue of Catholic schools, abortion is arguably the most prominent issue that the Catholic Church has been publicly involved in. However, increasingly the abortion issue does not stand on its own as a political / moral question for the Church but has been combined with other issues related to human reproduction such as IVF, embryology and a right to life which incorporates opposition to euthanasia. In recent years, the Church under Cardinal Winning has taken a more pro-active stance on the issue of abortion. Besides acting as a supporter and institutional network for organi-sations such as the Society for the Protection of the Unborn Child (SPUC), the Church itself has taken several initiatives to promote its opposition to abortion. However, it seems to be the case that the Church's position on abortion and its conservative moral voice over lifestyle issues does not have great resonance amongst its member-ship, which may be sympathetic to Church teaching on such issues but does not see them as fundamental issues: reflected in the limited success of the Church in mobilising its grassroots on abortion and other issues.

In advance of the 1997 general election, the Church embarked upon two separate strategies to promote the right to life. First, Cardinal Winning became involved in a renewed dispute with the Labour Party over its support for abortion. The Church had pre-viously sought to make abortion an issue in 1992, when it was critical of Labour for including a pro-abortion commitment in its Scottish and British general election manifestos, rather than leaving the issue to the consciences of individual MPs. Subsequently, there was a dispute between the Scottish Labour Party and the Labour Right to Life group over the group's involvement at the Scottish Labour conference in 1994. The fact that the Right to Life group were initially refused a stall at the party conference brought about a row with the Catholic Church and the intervention of Cardinal Winning. Tetchy relations between Labour and the Catholic Church became more aggravated by Cardinal Winning's widely reported criticism of the Labour leader, Tony Blair in 1996. In a religious programme for the BBC, Winning criticised Blair because 'He says he doesn't agree with abortion but . . . he doesn't condemn it or have a policy on it'.[46] The tone of Winning's remarks about Labour, which included calling them 'Fascists' for initially blocking the presence of right to life activists at their conference, generated considerable media coverage and can be understood as part of the Church's strategy to raise the right to life issue – especially in relation to Labour – on as many occasions as possible before the 1997 general election.

Second, the Church sought to give the right to life a high priority amongst Catholic voters in Scotland. The Church's message to voters ahead of the election stressed the primacy of the right to life as a political issue. Despite marking out education, poverty, health and unemployment as key policy concerns of the Catholic Church at the general election, the Bishop's Conference stated that

> the first priority for Christians in the forthcoming election is to uphold the right to life.[47]

The Church's intention to make abortion a key election issue was aided by two developments. First, evidence of weakening ties between Labour and the Catholic community at the 1992 general election produced a situation in which the Church could seek to challenge Labour to support the right to life and back a position held by its many Catholic supporters, or possibly lose support amongst Catholic voters.[48] Second, the presence of distinct anti-abortion candidates in a number of constituencies at the general election as part of the Pro-Life Alliance, provided a considerable impetus to the Church's efforts to prioritise the abortion issue. It provided a direct electoral challenge to the main political parties, an ability to generate publicity (often controversial publicity over the content of its party election broadcast for example) and assisted the Church in raising the abortion issue in a much broader way at the general election. The Alliance itself was keen to field candidates in Scotland, with one of its UK organisers commenting that 'there is a strong Catholic vote in Scotland and traditionally that is a pro-life vote.'[49] However, in electoral terms, the Pro-Life Alliance was clearly a failure. The organisation had only 9 candidates in Scotland and had withdrawn candidates from seats such as Stirling, Hamilton North and Glasgow Kelvin because sitting MPs were seen to be pro-life. The performance of the remaining candidates on 1st May 1997 was not impressive. The organisation gained a total of 5172 votes in the 9 seats it contested – an average of 1.54 per cent per seat – with its highest share of the vote in East Kilbride at 2.4 per cent.[50] Whether the Pro-Life Alliance continues to contest elections is questionable. Though a pressure group approach to opposing abortion through SPUC seems to have little success in upholding the right to life, an electoral approach has not been any more successful beyond gaining publicity for pro-life campaigners: though publicity and agenda setting may have been the main intention of pro-life campaigners.

The Church has also embarked upon its own anti-abortion initiatives in recent years. Shortly before the 1997 general election, Cardinal Winning gained widespread publicity for his plan to establish a special fund to support women seeking an abortion because of financial pressures, despite financial constraints on the Church itself. The Church established a fund in March 1997 which had received contributions of around £150,000 within four weeks of its launch.[51] This initiative was certainly controversial, but constituted one of the Church's better attempts at agenda setting in the media. Here was a high profile initiative announced by the leader of the Catholic Church in Scotland which appeared on newsdesks on a quiet Sunday when there was not much going on news-wise. The issue provided considerable coverage for the Church and the right to life issue for a number of weeks. The initiative also allowed the Catholic Church to claim that it was taking a practical approach to the relationship between poverty and abortion and seeking to play an active role rather than adopting a purely rhetorical stance.

However, overall, it is difficult to escape the fact that the Church's varied efforts to promote the right to life and prioritise the issue amongst Scottish Catholics have largely failed. The Church has dealt with the right to life question in a high profile manner and created controversy with its attacks on the Labour leader and right to life fund. But the amount of news print dealing with the abortion issue does not seem to have made the issue a priority amongst voters. The political parties have not changed their position on the abortion issue and there has been no evident shift in opinion in support of the right to life amongst the public. Though opinion polling in advance of the general election seemed to indicate that abortion was an issue that some voters would use as a guide for casting their vote, very few

Table 1.   How will a candidate's attitude to abortion affect your vote?

| | % Support | | | |
	Big Effect	Small Effect	No Effect	Don't Know
Male	10	18	70	2
Female	17	18	63	2
All	13	18	66	2

Source: *The Scotsman*, 20 March 1997.

seem to have done so (see Table 1). At the end of the day, the Church's controversial approaches to the right to life question may have succeeded in gaining media coverage and made it something of an issue in the public eye, but these developments have not led to any change in government or party policies towards abortion, and have generally fallen on deaf ears within Scotland.

Aside from abortion, the Church is also involved in a range of human fertility and embryology issues, which have been growing areas of interest given advances in science and technology and the need for government intervention in regulating sensitive areas. The Church has been critical of some of the unintended consequences of human fertilisation treatment, with the freezing and then subsequent destruction of unwanted human embryos,[52] and it is likely that this type of issue will gain the increasing attention of the Church as the right to life issue becomes concerned with a much wider range of questions than purely abortion. For example, pro-life campaigners within the Church have been critical of government policy on the reproductive rights of handicapped people, in response to proposals dealing with the abortion, sterilisation and contraception for incapable adults.[53] The Church has also been concerned about the growing debate on euthanasia which has surrounded controversial cases involving coma patients in Scotland and England and the introduction of a Private Members Bill in the House of Commons to alter the legal framework for euthanasia.[54] One pro-life campaigner, Fr James Morrow, became involved in the case of Janet Johnstone, a patient at Law Hospital in Carluke who had been in a persistent vegetative state following a suicide attempt. Relatives proposed the withdrawal of artificial feeding for Mrs Johnstone, with Fr Morrow seeking to have the Court of Session appoint a new legal guardian for Mrs Johnstone who would not support such euthanasia.[55]

A Third World Church

One of the keys to understanding the Catholic Church and community in Scotland is through an analysis of its commitment to the third world. This commitment chimes clearly with Catholic social teaching and support for a range of missionary works in the third world, but it also reflects its genuine role as a third world church and a global religion. It has been argued that transnational institutions such as the European Union have developed both 'presence' and 'actorness' in international relations.[56] A similar argument can be made about both the Vatican and the Catholic Church in Scotland.

The Church has 'presence' in international relations through its diplomatic activities and network of churches across the globe, with national and regional Bishops' conferences established since Vatican II. The Church's 'presence' is evident through the role of national churches in political life in states such as El Salvador and Poland; Papal visits and interventions, particularly by John Paul II (the modern 'political' Pope *par excellence*); efforts by the Church to develop a role as a global mediator between East and West since the 1960s; and the Church's ability to mobilise its members in support of various initiatives such as the peace movement in Western Europe in the 1980s.[57] The Church's 'presence' comes not merely from its hierarchy through Papal leadership and Bishops' statements, but through its network of churches, congregations and ancillary organisations. Indeed, it can be viewed as a mass membership organisation which enjoys its own communications network and media, similar to political parties. The Church also exhibits a significant level of 'actorness' in international relations and this is most clearly demonstrated in the case of the third world, particularly in Scotland. The Church is an actor in international politics in the third world through its missions and its involvement in the Scottish Catholic International Aid Fund, which has an extensive and long-standing role in development work in Africa, Asia and South America.

The Scottish Catholic International Aid Fund (SCIAF) was founded by the Catholic Church in Scotland in 1965 to finance and co-ordinate development work in the third world. Since its foundation, the scale of SCIAF's activities has grown, through finance provided by Catholic congregations across Scotland. Indeed, the Church's membership across Scotland is one of the primary sources of SCIAF funding and activities and, similar to the case of the Church in general, forms an important part of the SCIAF network through parishes and schools. Donations, parish collections, covenants and legacies form the bulk of SCIAF's annual income which rose from £926,094 in 1985 to £2,435,694 by 1995. Besides contributions and donations from individuals and churches within Scotland, SCIAF has also been successful at gaining financial support from a variety of sources. For example, in 1989 SCIAF received £681,820 from the European Union's special fund for the victims of apartheid for its work in South Africa,[58] and a number of SCIAF projects have been co-financed by the Overseas Development Administration, which were worth £224,912 in 1995–6.[59]

SCIAF has been involved in a number of long-term development projects in the third world, working with other aid organisations and with local communities. The bulk of these programmes would seem to have some political and socio-economic dimension to them. SCIAF's statement of purpose in 1995 stated that its vision of development is 'to empower the poor and oppressed to become agents of change for the benefit of themselves, their communities and the world as a whole. SCIAF supports integral human development programmes which are sustainable and arise out of local initiatives.'[60] Thus its work is concerned with economic and social development, rather than with work usually associated with missionaries in relation to proselytising and conversions. The type of programme SCIAF tends to finance is quite broad. In 1988–9, SCIAF funded a livestock development programme in Kenya, primary healthcare and AIDS counselling schemes in Tanzania and literacy programmes in Namibia and South Africa.[61] In 1994–5, amongst a wide range of projects, SCIAF was involved in supporting skills training and community development projects in India, women's health care initiatives in the Philippines, the work of the Mines Advisory Group in Laos and youth programmes in Columbia. Emergency relief is also an important part of SCIAF's work, in terms of both raising and deploying financial support in specific situations. For example, SCIAF provided £50,000 for victims of the Armenian earthquake in 1987–8, a special appeal to help alleviate the Ethiopian famine raised £586,221 in 1989–90 and raised approximately £800,000 for Rwanda in 1994. Such activities should certainly bury any outdated view of Church responses to third world poverty involving the distribution of bibles.

Educational work is also an important part of SCIAF's activities. SCIAF seeks to undertake development education work in both schools and parishes, so that the Church's organisational network is again utilised to promote specific Catholic themes and concerns (which have the effect of transmitting certain values to a section of Scottish society). SCIAF staff regularly visit schools and parishes to publicise development work and local parishes are often involved in the SCIAF 'partnership scheme', through sponsoring specific communities/projects in the third world. SCIAF has become a funder of development education in Scotland through providing assistance to the Scottish Development Education Centre, the Catholic Institute for International Relations and Scottish Education and Action for Development and produced a SCIAF newsletter for Schools – 'Youth and Schools News'.[62] In 1995, SCIAF organised a 'Solidarity Week with the South' in Catholic schools to educate pupils about development issues and also produced its own CD-ROM dealing with development for use in schools.[63] Overall, SCIAF spent £214,375 on development education in 1995,[64] which feeds its way through schools and parishes to promote the organisation's activities but also provides an important contribution to the Church's teachings on the third world.

Catholic involvement in the third world and international issues is not restricted to SCIAF; there is also significant involvement in these issues at the grassroots levels in schools and parishes. Indeed, without the grassroots level, SCIAF would be ineffective. Third world issues are a frequent topic within the Catholic press, with each weekly issue of the *Scottish Catholic Observer* featuring developments in the third world in a variety of different ways. Coverage has included El Salvador, Rwanda, South Africa, Uganda and a host of other countries where the Church and SCIAF are involved in aid and development projects or wish to express concern about the political situation. In addition, clerical and lay members of the church are often involved in visits to the third world in a variety of capacities which feed into the schools and parishes. For example, one lay member of the Dunkeld diocese was involved in the Scottish Churches World Exchange as a volunteer worker in Hyderabad in India.[65] Such involvement, in addition to SCIAF's activities, provides regular contact and awareness of third world and development issues within the Catholic community.

Conclusion

This chapter has sought to provide an analysis of the role of the Catholic Church in contemporary Scottish politics. By focusing on three key issues – education, the right to life and the third world – it is possible to determine the nature and scope of Catholic political action. However, as indicated above, the Church has policy concerns and interests in a wide range of issues which would require more systematic attention than could be afforded here, particularly in relation to local parish activities and the involvement of ordinary Catholics in Church-sponsored political action. Similarly, whilst it has been possible to outline a number of examples of political activism by the Catholic Church and its associated organisations, it is difficult to gauge the impact of such actions. Participation in the public policy process has clearly given the Church a role in policy-making but it is much more difficult to determine whether the Church actually influences policy outcomes. The case of Catholic schooling and local government reorganisation outlined above offers an example of the Church influencing policy and legislation – though such changes were not in conflict with government policy – but other examples of Catholic political action influencing government are more difficult to discern.

Tracing Catholic influence over particular policy decisions may be problematic, but tracing its impact upon public opinion is easier. Church attitudes towards social justice or the third world for example find reflection in the Catholic community and wider Scottish society, through concern for the homeless, unemployed and socially disadvantaged and support for third world charities. In addition, the fact that the Church has taken a more active role in politics in recent years indicates that it has become more confident of its role in Scottish society, more prepared to speak out on a range of issues and less willing to keep its head down and merely minister to its flock. However, the reason for this change is not merely a result of change in Scottish society and within the Church, but also a result of the growth of secularisation and ecumenicalism. On the one hand, the Church has become an accepted participant in public life because religious institutions are not seen to have much influence in a secular state: merely as one pressure group amongst many, and one that has a clear minority status. On the other hand, the growth of ecumenicalism and convergence of opinion between different religious traditions has provided the Catholic Church with a voice in Scottish politics and an opportunity to escape the isolation of the past in partnership with other churches.

NOTES

1. For contemporary analysis of the impact of religion on broad aspects of public policy see Francis Castles, 'On religion and public policy: Does Catholicism make a difference?', *European Journal of Political Research*, Vol. 25, No. 1, 1994, pp. 19–40.
2. D. Forrester, 'The Church of Scotland and Public Policy', *Scottish Affairs*, No. 4, Summer 1993, pp. 67–82.
3. Douglas Wertman, 'The Catholic Church and Italian Politics', in S. Berger (ed), *Religion in West European Politics* (London, 1982).
4. The Bishops' Conference stated that 'our aim is to provide positive guidance on the issues which should determine how we vote – not to tell electors for whom they should vote', The Bishops' Conference of Scotland, 'Throw Open the doors to Christ . . .', general election statement April 1997.
5. Bruce Millan, 'The Church and Politics', in Alison Elliot and Duncan Forrester (eds), *The Scottish Churches and the Political Process Today* (Edinburgh, 1986), p. 13.
6. Yves Meny, *Government and Politics in Western Europe* (Oxford, 1993), p. 35.
7. It could be argued that the Catholic Church operates through an 'iron law of theocracy', reminiscent of Roberto Michels' iron law of oligarchy, particularly when contrasted with the more democratic Church of Scotland. Roberto Michels, *Political Parties* (London, 1915).
8. Catholic Bishops' Conference of Scotland, *Work and Unemployment* (Glasgow, 1985) and *Disarmament and Peace* (Glasgow, 1987).
9. The Bishops' Conference of Scotland, 'Throw Open the doors to Christ . . .', general election statement April 1997.
10. Bishop Mario Conti, 'Not Strangers but Pilgrims – the inter-church process in Scotland', *Bulletin* No. 3, Catholic Bishops' Conference of Scotland, December 1986.
11. *Scottish Catholic Observer*, 9 February 1996, p. 14.
12. *Scottish Catholic Observer*, 31 January 1997, p. 1.
13. *Scottish Catholic Observer*, 8 January 1994, p. 5.
14. *Scottish Catholic Observer*, 19 May 1995, p. 1.
15. Speeches by Cardinal Winning reported in *Scottish Catholic Observer*, 1 December 1995, p. 3 and 19 January 1996, p. 16.
16. *Scottish Catholic Observer*, 17 March 1997, p. 5.
17. P. Connor, *Catholics and the Welfare State* (London, 1977), p.30.
18. Most notably, it was responsible for taking over the running of the East End Hotel in Glasgow, a centre for the homeless which had run into serious decline. The association renovated the hostel as a short-term measure before relocating its residents in apartments which it ran in Glasgow. See Jennifer Cunningham, 'Great Eastern Sunset', *The Herald*, 17 November 1997.
19. *Scottish Catholic Observer*, 5 July 1996, p. 11.

20. *Bulletin*, No.7, Catholic Bishops' Conference of Scotland, March 1989.
21. *Bulletin*, No. 12, Catholic Bishops' Conference of Scotland, 1993.
22. Members of the Scottish Consultative Council on the Curriculum as at June 1996.
23. *Scottish Catholic Observer*, 2 September 1994, p. 8.
24. *Scottish Catholic Observer*, 2 February 1996, p. 7.
25. S. Bruce, *No Pope of Rome* (Edinburgh, 1985) and T. Gallagher, *Edinburgh Divided: John Cormack and No Popery in the 1930s* (Edinburgh, 1987).
26. J. Mitchell, *Conservatives and the Union* (Edinburgh, 1990).
27. S. Brown, ' "Outside the Covenant": The Scottish Presbyterian Churches and Irish Immigration 1922–38', *The Innes Review*, No. 1, Spring 1991, pp. 19–45.
28. An opinion poll for *Scotland on Sunday*, discovered that 80 per cent of Scots thought that Catholic and Protestant children should go to the same schools. *Scotland on Sunday*, 23 October 1994.
29. Contemporary examples of this phenomenon include the proposals by the City of Glasgow to close St. Augustine's Secondary, St. Leonard's Secondary and St. Gerard's Secondary due to the surplus of school places. *The Herald*, 28 January 1998.
30. Without the state and local authorities, it would have been extremely difficult for the Church to meet the needs of the Catholic community through Church schools. See T. Fitzpatrick, *Catholic Secondary Education in South-West Scotland Before 1972* (Aberdeen, 1986).
31. Frank O'Hagan, *Change, Challenge and Achievement* (St Andrew's College of Education, 1996).
32. The Church in the 1990s would appear to be much more active in educational policy than previously. For example, back in the 1960s the Church appears to have played no role in the *Royal Commission on Local Government in Scotland* (HMSO, 1968) – in contrast to the Church of Scotland and Free Church – despite the fact that it had significant implications for education and Catholic schooling.
33. Each local authority in Scotland has a representative of the Catholic Church sitting on its education committee. Before local government reorganisation in 1995, this situation was relatively simple as education was the responsibility of 9 regional councils (requiring only 9 Catholic representatives). Now, with 32 local authorities, some of which are too small to establish education committees, there is a need for a much greater number of Catholic representatives.
34. The Bishops' Conference discussed the issue of school boards and opting-out in 1989, the implications of the Howie Report on post-16 education in 1991 and the impact of local government reorganisation on Catholic schools in 1993.
35. The Scottish Office, *Shaping the future – the New councils* (Edinburgh, 1993).
36. This problem seems such a basic difficulty for the Catholic education sector that it is surprising that the Scottish Office, and more importantly the education department, did not identify it when it drew up the proposals for local government reorganisation.
37. *Scottish Catholic Observer*, 4 March 1994.

38. Brian Bonnar, Chair of Catholic Education Commission, *Scottish Catholic Observer*, 3 January 1994, p. 8.
39. *Scottish Catholic Observer*, 28 October 1994.
40. The CEC nominated one of its members to work with the Scottish Office to develop new levels for the 5–14 programme for religious education. *CEC News*, June 1997, issue 4, p. 4.
41. *The Bulletin*, No.9, Catholic Bishops' Conference of Scotland, April 1991.
42. *Scottish Catholic Observer*, 4 August 1995.
43. Teresa Gourlay, 'Catholic Schooling in Scotland Since 1918', *The Innes Review*, No. 1, Spring 1989, p. 130.
44. *Scottish Catholic Observer*, 24 May 1996.
45. *The Scotsman*, 26 April 1996.
46. *The Herald*, 26 October 1996, p. 1.
47. The Bishops' Conference of Scotland, 'Throw Open the doors to Christ . . .', general election statement April 1997.
48. For analysis of slippage in Labour support and increased support for the SNP amongst the Catholic electorate see J. Brand, J. Mitchell and P. Surridge, 'Will Scotland Come to the Aid of the Party?', in A. Heath, R. Jowell and J. Curtice (eds), *Labour's Last Chance* (London, 1994) and J. Brand, J. Mitchell and P. Surridge, 'Social Constituency and Ideological Profile: Scottish Nationalism in the 1990s', *Political Studies*, Vol. 42, No. 4, 1994, pp. 616–29.
49. Josephine Quintavalle quoted in *The Herald*, 6 January 1997.
50. *Scottish Catholic Observer*, 9 May 1997, p. 7.
51. *The Herald*, 7 April 1997.
52. Cardinal Winning appealed to the Human Fertilisation and Embryology Authority to alter its rules to prevent the destruction of frozen embryos in 1996. *Scottish Catholic Observer*, 2 August 1996.
53. *Scottish Catholic Observer*, 30 May 1997.
54. The Church was a prominent opponent of the Mental Incapacity Bill and of a ten-minute-rule bill introduced in December 1997 to facilitate some forms of euthanasia. *The Scotsman*, 9 December 1997.
55. *Scottish Catholic Observer*, 24 May 1996.
56. C. Hill and H. Wallace, 'Introduction: actors and actions', in C. Hill (ed), *The Actors in Europe's Foreign Policy* (London, 1996).
57. E. Hanson, *The Catholic Church in World Politics* (Princeton, 1987), p. 9.
58. Scottish Catholic International Aid Fund, *Annual Report 1990* (Glasgow, 1991).
59. Scottish Catholic International Aid Fund, *Annual Report 1995* (Glasgow, 1996), p. 4.
60. Scottish Catholic International Aid Fund, *Statement of Purpose*, 1995.
61. Scottish Catholic International Aid Fund, *Annual Report 1989* (Glasgow, 1990).
62. Scottish Catholic International Aid Fund, *Annual Report 1994* (Glasgow, 1995).
63. Scottish Catholic International Aid Fund, *Annual Report 1995* (Glasgow, 1996), p. 3.

64. *Ibid.*, p. 19.
65. In 1996, one of the issues of the quarterly journal of the diocese of Dunkeld, *Dunkeld News: Diocesan News and Views*, was given over to the volunteer worker's experience in India.

4

LEFT AND LIBERAL: CATHOLICS IN MODERN SCOTLAND

David McCrone and Michael Rosie

Drawing heavily on material gathered in the 1992 Scottish Election Survey, McCrone and Rosie argue that the picture that emerges of Catholics is of a small but significant group in Scottish society. They challenge the usefulness of the ghetto in explaining the contemporary outlook and contribution of Catholics in Scotland. Instead they suggest that Catholics, particularly those of Irish origin, have not been left behind by recent political developments in Scotland and, that while retaining a strong sense of collective identity, have integrated into the mainstream of Scottish political and cultural life.

Introduction

Modern Scottish Catholicism was, to a large extent, created out of the tragedy of another country, out of famine and grinding poverty in Ireland. The Diaspora spread Irish families across the globe: many came to Scotland and settled. However, this is not the only story to be told about Scottish Catholicism. As well as the contribution of Irish immigrants there have been arrivals from Italy, Poland, Lithuania and Ukraine, as well as Catholics from England. Small pockets of Catholicism survived the Reformation in the Gaidhealtachd and North East. All of these groups, to a large extent, have been marginalised in the historiography of Catholicism in Scotland. It will be recognised, then, that the following discussion is selective, and represents only broad patterns.

Catholic Irish immigrants to 19th century Scotland entered a society widely resentful of their presence. Echoing the current discourse on the 'underclass', the Catholic Irish were regarded by many Victorian Scots as indolent, feckless, licentious and dishonest. The arrival of the Irish exacerbated pressure amongst a developing urban proletariat already facing the social dislocations of rapid modernisation, and Catholic Irish labour was, on occasion, used by employers to depress local wage levels. The Catholic Irish were often seen as more than simply economic rivals: many viewed them as a root cause of many social evils. Integration would have been difficult enough, given the differences in speech, custom and religion which divided them from their new neighbours. Crucially, however, a sizeable minority of Irish arrivals were Ulster Protestants who brought their virulent anti-Catholicism with them. Anti-Catholic agitation was common in urban Scotland throughout the 19th century, and this – along with the Catholic Church's fear that assimilation into a largely Protestant society would undermine the faith – led to a ghettoisation of the Catholic community, often in conditions of appalling squalor. The walls of the ghetto were fortified with suspicion and mistrust on both sides.

Social concerns over Scotland's ghettoised Catholics fuelled a pseudo-scientific discourse, in which many Scots argued that the distasteful 'Irish' – who by 1918 were mostly Scots-born – were racially inferior. Such ideas were common throughout inter-war Europe; in all cases the scapegoats tended to be disadvantaged minorities. The eugenicist debate reached its zenith when a 1923 Church and Nation Report was accepted by the Church of Scotland's General Assembly. The Report concluded that the Catholic 'Irish' could never be assimilated into Scottish society due to the 'alien' and 'inferior' character of their race and their religion. However distasteful the Report may sound today (and it must be remembered that 'race' was common currency before Auschwitz) it should be noted that it probably reflected only a minority of opinion within the Kirk, although it had its influential supporters.

The report, however, represented a popular mood amongst many urban Protestants which ended only after the spectacular rise and collapse of militant Protestant parties in Glasgow and Edinburgh. At its height, Protestant Action commanded about one third of the municipal vote in Edinburgh, and could assemble 10,000 to protest – riotously – against a Catholic Congress in the city. Both Protestant Action in Edinburgh and the Scottish Protestant League in Glasgow mirrored fascistic movements throughout inter-war Europe in their populist mixture of demagoguery, simplistic economics, and appeals to a sensationalist – and occasionally esoteric

– anti-Catholicism. Both parties lacked organisational skills, however, and unsupported by the major churches and the Orange Order they could not break out of their municipal boundaries.

The new-found economic and social solidarity during total war undermined the attraction of groups pursuing a militantly anti-Catholic policy, and militant Protestantism disappeared as a meaningful political force in Scottish politics. In the post-war era few sectarian events have had any significant impact. Post-war reconstruction, the economic boom and urban slum clearance all worked to weaken the structural divisions between the two communities. The re-igniting of ethnic hatreds in Ulster did not result in any significant increase in religious tension in Scotland, not least because both communities in Northern Ireland were seen to be suffering. General distaste at events in the Province has dampened enthusiasm for sectarian confrontation. Indeed when Sinn Fein leader Gerry Adams – the supreme 'bogey-man' of Ulster Loyalists – visited Govan in 1995, only 300 Scottish Loyalists demonstrated. The previous day 40,000 had proclaimed their Loyalism at Ibrox. The largest Republican gathering in Scotland – Edinburgh's Connolly commemoration – attracts only a few hundred, and participants tend to be outnumbered by police.

That Archbishop Winning could address the General Assembly of the Church of Scotland in 1975, and, as Cardinal, attend the General Assemblies of both Kirk and Free Kirk in 1995 underlines the distance Scotland has travelled since the 1930s. Perhaps the most telling event has been the Papal Visit in 1982, Scottish Catholicism's 'coming of age'. Huge crowds – of all denominations – welcomed the Pontiff. Demonstrations against the visit of the 'anti-Christ' were small and widely ridiculed – they were seen by most Scots as an embarrassment, fighting a war long since dismissed as irrelevant. Ironically, the greatest threat to the Papal Visit came not from Protestants but from internal tensions in world Catholicism prompted by the Falklands War. Intense lobbying ensured the Visit took place – averting what would have constituted a major embarrassment for Catholicism in Britain. The Pope's speech at Bellahouston Park stressed the Scottish Catholic tradition, and was well received throughout Scotland.

Yet there is some debate over how far the religious divide has actually declined. Sectarianism – or a perception of it – is a widely acknowledged feature of Scottish society. The scandal over Monklands District Council in the 1990s, and the bitterly fought by-election in Monklands East again brought 'sectarianism' under the media spotlight. Yet Monklands displayed the approach so often taken by the media on questions of sectarian bias. The journalist who first broke the story has complained that the wider media over-played the sectarian element of the scandal to achieve good copy. Indeed, enquiries undertaken in the wake of the scandal have uncovered little actual evidence of sectarian policies.

A Sectarian Iceberg?

At this point it would be constructive to review the growing body of literature concerned with religious division in modern Scotland, and to draw out the significant themes and arguments of the various approaches. An appropriate – and chronologically correct – writer with whom to begin is Steve Bruce, whose *No Pope of Rome* (1985) was 'the first serious study of sectarianism in Scotland' for almost four decades.[1] Bruce concludes that sectarianism in Scotland is now no more than 'a boy's game', confined to small pockets within deprived urban Scotland.[2] He commented: 'If we adopt the meta-phor of an iceberg, I contend that the relatively rare public displays of sectarian animosity are not the visible tip of a submerged mass of ice but are rather all that is left.'[3]

Bruce presents an overview of the social developments which caused the melting of what, in the period to 1945 at least, had been a considerable expanse of sectarian 'ice'. Firstly, and crucially, Bruce contends that Scotland did not possess the conditions essential for 'sustained ethnic tension'. The Reformation had developed un-evenly, obstructed for several centuries by Scotland's geology: by the time the Highlands had been 'Calvinised' the Lowlands were widely secularised, and what Protestantism remained 'was moderate, rational, and ecumenical.'[4]

Thus, when the Catholic Irish were arriving in Scotland in any great number, only rural, Calvinist, Highland Scotland had the ideological basis with which to legitimate and sustain ethnic divi-sion: but this was an area left untouched by immigration. Lowland Protestants faced a tangible Catholic presence 'but they did not possess the religious beliefs which would have given a sustainable legitimate basis to their conflict.'[5]

More immediately the Protestant Churches were struggling to adjust to population movements in a rapidly urbanising society. Additionally, much Protestant energy after 1843 was spent fighting over the Disruption and, latterly, attempting to rebuild the bridges thus wrecked. The internal focusing of Protestant energies 'produced a de facto pluralism which hastened secularisation.'[6] By the time Lowland Protestantism had readjusted to population shifts and had, by and large, overcome internal divisions, Catholicism in Scotland was well established – institutionally, culturally and economically – within an increasingly pluralistic and secular society. The political development of the Catholic community also ensured that the materials for ethnic conflict were limited. Despite brief flirtations with Irish Nationalism, the bulk of Scotland's Catholics backed first the Liberals, and then – after manhood suffrage in 1918 – the Labour Party. Involvement in Scottish Labour politics increasingly brought Catholics into the mainstream of Scottish political life, albeit slowly and cautiously.

The differences between Scotland and Ulster are clear: Protestantism in Ulster was faced with a considerable external threat in the form of an Irish Catholic majority and of a sizeable and troublesome Catholic minority in Ulster. Catholicism in Scotland, concentrated within a limited territory, never posed such a threat. Whilst the 19th century had been a period of fission for Scottish Protestantism, Ulster Protestantism became more cohesive in face of an increasingly politicised Catholicism (this process was, of course, mutually reinforcing). Further, the Catholic 'menace' possessed a coherent and powerful political programme: Irish Nationalism. In Scotland, Catholic and Protestant workers were active within the same political formations. Scotland simply did not – and does not – possess the same structural and cultural features which has produced the 'Troubles'.

Whilst Graham Walker notes 'the durability of essentially Irish cultural influences in Scotland',[7] he offers the possibility that sectarianism in Scotland represents 'an exercise in nostalgia which led only into itself.'[8] A metaphor for this would surely be the Glasgow football derby, where fans, polarised into the symbolism of Orange and Green, return to the more mundane, and less colourful, realities of life after the final whistle. On Monklands, Walker urges caution: whatever strategies had been used by local activists, the leaders of all the parties made plain that they would have no truck with the religious card of either colour. One crucial point that had been overlooked is that the allegations were founded on the notion that 'Protestant' Airdrie was receiving fewer resources than 'Catholic' Coatbridge. Given that neither town is religiously homogenous, this would seem a rather inefficient method by which to favour co-religionists. The key question, then, is the extent to which the issue of sectarianism was exploited – or, indeed, created – as a justification for political action. As Steve Bruce notes:

> Sectarianism as a rhetoric for distributing blame is an interesting and important social phenomenon but it is not the same interesting and important social phenomenon as actual discrimination. It is quite possible for the former to endure long after the latter has gone.[9]

Tom Gallagher's argument begins with the observation that: 'the enmity and hysteria sometimes on display at Old Firm matches can serve as a timely reminder of just how thin the crust of civilisation is.'[10] This concern with the frailty of 'civilisation' is a major feature in Gallagher's analysis, and he notes that the Old Firm rivalry: 'does not tumble out of a social void' and that it indicates the sectarian poison which remains.[11] A key feature of Gallagher's work is the extent to which he believes that Scotland still retains the potential – given a particular set of circumstances – for religious conflict. He argues that anti-Catholicism in Scotland has been 'pressed into a number of deep but narrow channels which only rarely burst their banks.'[12] Assimilation of Catholics into Scottish society, Gallagher contends, is very well advanced, but he points out that this gives no guarantee of continued stability. Citing Yugoslavia, Gallagher notes the potential for 'unscrupulous politicians' to exploit ethnic differences at a time of social and political dislocation.

The bulk, in other words, of the sectarian 'iceberg' still lurks beneath the water. Catholics, according to Gallagher, have been historically cool towards the 'national movement' in Scotland, and to expressions of popular 'Scottishness' in general, as the traditional symbols of Scottish nationhood have been too bourgeois and too Protestant to be attractive to descendants of the Catholic Irish. The symbols of Britishness have, for similar reasons, been equally unattractive. Gallagher does not, therefore, find it surprising that there is evidence that Catholics have proved more resistant to Scottish Nationalism than any other group in Scotland. Of crucial importance to the current political developments, post-Referendum, is Gallagher's claim that constitutional change represents too much of a 'leap into the unknown' for Scotland's Catholics.

Whilst much research has been based mainly on archival work and interviewing notable players in Scottish religious and political life, some ethnographic studies have also been conducted. Raymond Boyle has investigated the various forms of identity held by supporters of Celtic Football Club. What emerges from Boyle's research is a fairly negative attitude of the SNP 'as being a party with links with Orangeism and Protestantism',[13] and a high-level of commitment towards the Labour Party. Celtic are widely regarded as the sporting 'flagship' of the Scottish Catholic community, and supporters regularly express sentiments of an Irish Republican, and Irish Catholic nature. In 1996, when the Celtic board launched a campaign against sectarianism ('Bhoys Against Bigotry'), the reaction of a large section of the club's support was 'What Bigotry?' – for them, the problem lay elsewhere. Like the events in Monklands, however, the campaign served to attract attention to the existence of religious prejudice in Scottish society.

Joseph Bradley has also used football rivalry as an entry point into wider issues of religious identity, and a central argument of Bradley's work is that:

> One of the key problems with much of present ethno-religious literature is that it operates with a narrow understanding of religious identity using sectarianism as a key concept. As such, many authors ignore the multi-faceted nature of religious identity in Scotland.[14]

This is a valid and useful point, yet Bradley himself undermines it by repeatedly describing Catholics in Scotland as 'the Irish', and by using 'sectarianism' as a 'key concept' in his own analysis. Bradley, it seems, is concerned with attempting to explain why many Catholics lack the ability or desire to 'articulate an Irish background',[15] and finds his explanation in Britain's 'colonial relationship' with Ireland, replayed within a Scottish setting. A crucial part of this legacy is sectarianism.[16] Of course, as has been noted above, many Catholics in Scotland have no familial link with Ireland, whilst for many others (given the growing rates of inter-marriage) their sense of 'ancestral' identity is far more complex than Bradley appears to allow for. A key problem with Bradley's work is that by using that section of the population – football supporters in the West of Scotland – most likely to be involved in Bruce's 'boy's game', he perhaps overplays the extent of perceived sectarian division in Scotland. One can find evidence of anything in society as long as one looks for it in the right place: but finding it in one location does not mean it exists elsewhere.

In a sense nearly all the work done on sectarianism and religious identity suffers from this to some extent. What is missing from much of the literature is a general view of how Scots relate to the central issues of the debate. Few of the researchers have sought to utilise the data resources which are available, and when they have their usage has been limited. Secondary analysis offers a means of contextualising sectarianism in contemporary Scotland (though not in explaining it). Using data already gathered we can make some attempt to judge how far the 'iceberg' has melted.

The remainder of this chapter, therefore, will examine the evidence contained in the Scottish Election Survey of 1992 with regard to several salient issues. Firstly, has historical hostility made Catholics in Scotland feel less 'Scottish' than Protestants and those of no professed religion? Secondly, how deeply does sectarian conflict characterise Scottish society? Is the 'unique atmosphere' of Old Firm confrontations and the Marching Season a fair reflection of urban Scotland as a whole, or is sectarianism a minority pursuit, a 'boy's game'? Examining the general picture suggests that many assumptions about sectarianism and religious identity in Scotland should be re-thought.

Catholics in Modern Scotland

Where does Catholicism stand today? Our focus is on the social and cultural character of Catholics in contemporary Scotland, using the election studies of 1992, and where it is possible, to compare these with 1974. These studies took the form of surveys of voters at election times, and provide valuable indications of how Scotland is changing in the context of Britain as a whole. Respondents were asked a broad set of questions about their political behaviour and attitudes, but included in the surveys were questions on religious affiliation and practices, as well as on social and moral attitudes. Not all questions were replicated over the two election studies, but where they were, we can use them as the basis for making comparisons to see how the views of Catholics in Scotland have changed over nearly 20 years.

The election studies have two other valuable components: they ask about religious affiliation as well as religious practice; and, secondly, we can make comparisons with those who claim no religious affiliation, as well as with the Scottish population as a whole. Further, we can compare Catholics in Scotland with their co-religionists in the rest of Britain, and with the British population as a whole. Hence, we have a number of points of comparison from which to draw our conclusions. We start from the simple premise that Catholics are those who respond in this way when asked 'Do you regard yourself as belonging to any particular religion?'. There are 148

Catholics and 442 Protestants (which here is taken to mean affiliation with the Church of Scotland), the largest denomination, out of a Scottish sample of 957. We can compare Catholic Scots with Protestant Scots, with 'secular' Scots (those with no affiliation), with Scots as a whole, with Catholics elsewhere in Britain, and with the British population as a whole. Not all these will be used in the discussion below; only key points of interest will be mentioned. Data will refer to the 1992 election study, except where 1974 data is to hand.

How 'Religious' is Scotland? – Church Attendance, Affiliation and Upbringing

On the basis of the 1992 Scottish election study, 16% of Scots claim to be Catholic, 46% Protestant (i.e. have a Church of Scotland affiliation) and 25% to have none.

What is immediately apparent from Table 1 is that the non-religious group is the *only* category which shows evidence of any growth (although there is a small increase in unspecified Christians, suggesting a small amount of people retains a belief in God upon adulthood, but no longer identify with any particular Church). It also seems clear that, of all the denominations, the Church of Scotland is losing adherents at the highest rate. Similarly, the likelihood is that a person brought up within a particular religious denomination will retain an affiliation to it in adulthood: 85 per cent of those with Catholic backgrounds in the sample still regard themselves as Catholics; for the Kirk, the figure is around 70 per cent. Movement between Scotland's major religious institutions – Roman Catholicism and the Church of Scotland – is insignificant, with less than 3 per cent of Catholics brought up in Church of Scotland households, and less than 1 per cent of Church of Scotland identifiers claiming a Catholic background.

Table 1 Affiliation and Upbringing

	current affiliation	upbringing
	%	%
CoS	46	60
RC	16	17
Other Christian	9	8
Episcopalian	4	6
None	25	7
(N	957	957)

Table 2   Church Attendance

	weekly	monthly	irregularly*	never	N
CoS	14%	10	30	37	442
RC	51%	7	11	21	155

* yearly or several times a year

With a quarter of Scots claiming no affiliation, Scotland is marginally more religious than Britain as a whole where the figure is 30%. As we might expect, the Church of England is the biggest British denomination (at 33%), with Catholics at 11%.

In Scotland, Catholics are more frequent church attenders than Protestants, with 51% claiming weekly attendance (only 14% of Protestants attend church as regularly). They also appear to be more active than their co-religionists in Britain as a whole where only 36% attend weekly, and 29% never attend (compared with 21% in Scotland).

In terms of attendance, there is a gradient from male Protestants (60% claim virtually no attendance) to female Catholics, 68% of whom are 'regular' attenders (more than monthly). This mirrors the 1974 results when 52% of Catholics as a whole claimed a 'strong affiliation', but only 18% of Protestants did so.

Adherents of the two religious denominations tend to be female, while men predominate in the 'secular' group. Catholics tend to be younger than Protestants (39% are between 18 and 34), with almost twice as many Protestants as Catholics over 60 years of age (41% to 21%).

Table 3   Gender and Attendance

	CoS		RC	
	male	female	male	female
	%	%	%	%
regular	15	31	46	68
irregular	25	21	12	9
rare/never	60	36	42	23
(N	199	67	243	81)
regular:	once a month plus			
irregular:	more than once a year			
rare:	less than once a year			

At this point it would be instructive to examine the characteristics of our three groups.

Table 4 Gender, Age and Region

	All	CoS	RC	none	N
	%	%	%	%	
male	46	45	45	54	445
female	53	55	55	46	512
	%	%	%	%	
18–34	32	21	40	50	301
35–54	35	38	34	31	334
55+	33	41	27	19	308
	%	%	%	%	
ECS	26	27	20	26	248
NES	19	17	8	25	181
WCS	44	45	68	34	423
Other	11	11	4	15	105
(N	957	442	148	235)	

Catholics live mainly in West Central Scotland [WCS] (68%), but they comprise at most 25% of the population of that region. North East Scotland [NES] has only 7% of adults who are Catholics, with East Central Scotland at 12%. In terms of religious affiliation, then, both East and West Central Scotland have around half of their populations who are Protestant (47% and 48% respectively), with North East Scotland being the most 'secular' (32% claiming to have no religious affiliation).

Perceptions of Sectarian Conflict

How serious do Scots think sectarian conflict in Scotland is? On the whole, religious conflict between Catholics and Protestants in Scotland is not deemed to be 'serious' (two-thirds say there is none or very little, and one-third think it very or fairly serious).

Table 5 Regional Distribution

	All	ECS	NES	WCS	Other
	%	%	%	%	
CoS	46	48	39	47	45
RC	15	12	7	24	6
Other	14	15	23	10	16
None	25	25	32	19	33
(N	957	248	181	423	105)

Table 6 *Religious Conflict*

	All	CoS	RC	none
	%	%	%	%
very serious	9	9	13	6
fairly serious	25	26	19	26
not very serious	49	50	50	49
none	14	14	18	14
(N	957	442	148	235)

Some variations do exist across different parts of the country, with perceptions of conflict strongest in West Central Scotland (where most symbolic manifestations of modern Scottish sectarianism are centred), and weakest in North East Scotland (where there is virtually no history of organised sectarian conflict). It is, however, a minority perception even in this supposed sectarian heartland.

Finally, if we combine age, gender and region (though the sample sizes begin to get small), we find an interesting pattern. We are confining our sample to those between the ages of 18 and 34.

In other words, religious conflict is perceived as 'serious' only among a majority of young males in the West of Scotland. This would seem to lend support to Steve Bruce's assessment that:

> 'sectarianism in Scotland is a boys' game, a leisure activity. It is something that a small number of people do in the evenings and at the weekends associated with other leisure activities like drinking in certain clubs and supporting certain football teams.'[17]

We do find, however, that perceptions of religious conflict vary by age, with younger people more likely to think it serious than older people.

Table 7 *Religious Conflict by Region*

	WCS	ECS	NES
	%	%	%
very/fairly serious	34	27	23
none/not serious	64	69	74
(N	423	248	181)

Table 8   Religious Conflict by Age

	18–34	35–54	55+
	%	%	%
very/fairly serious	43	34	24
none/not serious	53	64	73
(N	301	334	308)

Table 9   Perceptions of Religious Conflict Among Young Scots (18–34)

	WCS		ECS+NES	
	male	female	male	female
	%	%	%	%
very/fairly serious	56	48	39	30
none/not serious	43	52	59	65
(N	70	75	64	64)

Attitudes to Separate Schooling

To what extent is the perception of religious conflict related to separate denominational schooling in Scotland? The policy of state-funded Catholic education has in the past been a focus of sectarian conflict as certain groups have railed against what they regarded as 'Rome on the Rates'. This is not to say that opposition to segregated education is necessarily a sectarian issue – indeed it often manifests itself as an *anti*-sectarian issue. Many Scots object to segregated schooling because they believe that such a system inculcates and maintains *division*. There is evidence of a widespread belief across age and gender that Scottish schools should be integrated.

A small majority of Catholics want denominational schools retained (51% to 47%) — proportionally fewer than in 1974, when the figures were 37% and 29% respectively, with the rest 'don't knows'.

Clearly *Catholic* opposition to Catholic education is a very interesting issue, and one that is by definition wholly free of any anti-Catholic sentiment that could be ascribed to non-Catholic opposition. Opposition to existing educational arrangements is fairly evenly spread throughout the Catholic population in Scotland, with little variation over gender and age.

Table 10   Attitude to Denominational Schools

	RC	CoS	none
	%	%	%
retain RC schools	51	15	12
phase out	47	81	85
(N	147	432	234)

Table 11   **Attitude to Denominational Schools (Catholics Only)**

	male	female	18–34	35–54	55+
	%	%	%	%	%
retain RC schools	54	49	48	51	54
phase out	43	49	48	47	46
(N	67	81	58	49	39)

Attitudes to Northern Ireland

The symbolism of sectarianism in Scotland has an almost exclusive obsession with the politics of Northern Ireland. Urban graffiti proclaim '1690' and '1916'. The songs sung at Ibrox and Parkhead, and the tunes drummed out on Marches often relate not to the *Scottish* past, but to the history of the Irish conflict. More than one in three Scottish Catholics believe that British troops should *not* be withdrawn immediately, whilst two in five Scottish Protestants believe that they should. Our non-religious group (whose family background is generally Protestant) similarly displays a reasonably close split in opinion, with a majority favouring withdrawal.

Table 12   **Should British Troops be Withdrawn From Northern Ireland Immediately?**

%	All	RC	CoS	None
'Yes'	46	57	40	54
'No'	48	35	54	41
(N	957	148	442	235)

It should also be noted that the question gives a specific time scale ('immediately') for withdrawal: it would be interesting to know how many of those answering 'no' would have been more amenable to a gradual withdrawal.

As for where the long-term solution to the 'Troubles' is concerned, there is a marked preference for a united Ireland over the retention of the Union, although it should be noted that this question had a high level of respondents whose position was 'Don't Know'.

Table 13   **Long-Term Policy for Northern Ireland Should Be**

%	RC	CoS	None
Remain within UK	18	42	26
Unify with Republic	65	39	54
(N	148	442	235)

It might seem reasonable to assume that if a 'sectarian' approach were taken by the Scots, then Catholics would favour a united Ireland and Protestants the Union (mirroring the situation in Northern Ireland itself). The Catholic sample fits this hypothesis to some extent, but it is much more difficult to see evidence of it amongst the Church of Scotland sample. Our non-religious group – which does not fit easily with our rather crude 'Ulster' hypothesis – displays a tendency towards unification, though not as pronounced as the Catholics.

When we introduce region as a variable, we find difficulty in supporting the hypothesis over urban Scotland as a whole (the two east coast regions have again been amalgamated) (Table 14).

Certainly the Catholic sample in the West is more heavily in favour of a united Ireland, and Protestants in the West are more in favour of the Union (although a sizeable number do *not* support it). There is little to commend the hypothesis in East Central and North East Scotland: Catholic opinion in these areas seems less heavily in favour of unification (although the sample size in these areas is small). A higher level of support for a united Ireland is evident amongst the non-religious group, and even the Protestant sample is slightly more in favour of an end to the Union than to its retention.

On this evidence it would appear that the politics of Northern Ireland have a different resonance in different areas of Scotland. The crude hypothesis with which we began fits most easily with Catholics in West Central Scotland, but sits less easily amongst the other groups. Scots have, by and large, resisted the temptation to choose their views on Northern Ireland in terms of their own religion – indeed many Scots (as evidenced by the high level of 'Don't Know' answers) have no particular position on the future of the Province. Northern Ireland may well be the cornerstone of sectarian symbolism, but most Scots appear very reluctant to view the Province in sectarian terms.

Table 14   Long-Term Policy for Northern Ireland Should Be:

	WC Scotland			EC/NE Scotland		
%	RC	CoS	None	RC	CoS	None
Remain within UK	15	51	31	24	38	22
Unify with Republic	71	32	46	52	43	59
(N	100	201	80	42	194	120)

Catholics and 'Scotland'

Writing of the inter-war period, Stewart Brown argues that for Catholics in Scotland

> there was not much encouragement for them to feel Scottish while at the same time preserving their religion and their pride in their Irish heritage. For [some] Presbyterian clergymen ... religious and cultural pluralism was an evil, and to be Scottish was to be Protestant.[18]

In political terms, this inability to identify with 'Scotland' has, it is claimed, made the Catholic population of Scotland reluctant to support constitutional change or back the Nationalist party. In this final section we intend to examine these claims – that Scots Catholics struggle to identify with 'Scottishness', and that the Nationalist vote is disproportionately *non*-Catholic.

(a)   Catholics and National Identity

The notion of 'national identity' is hugely complex and slippery: individuals can have a changing attitude to their 'nation', and the meaning of 'the nation' may vary greatly between individuals and over time. However, the data suggest that whatever Catholics in Scotland felt in the past, today they seem just as likely to express feelings of Scottishness as any other group. The first question asks respondents for their nationality – a complex question in a multi-national state like the United Kingdom. The majority of the sample, across the denominational groups, answered 'Scottish'

Two things are notable here. Firstly the level of Scottish identity amongst Catholics is very high, and comparable to the national level. Secondly, while there is evidence of *Irish* national identity amongst Catholics, it is relatively small, and may relate to first-generation Irish immigrants.

Table 15   Denomination and Self-Identified Nationality

%	All	RC	CoS	None
British	25	21	25	22
Scottish	72	71	74	76
English	1	–	–	1
Irish	1	5	–	–
Other	1	3	1	–
(N	957	148	442	235)

Table 16 Denomination and National Identity

%	All	RC	CoS	None
Scottish not British	19	26	17	23
More Scottish than British	40	37	41	45
Equally Scottish and British	33	30	37	28
More British than Scottish	3	1	2	2
British not Scottish	3	1	2	2
Other/Not answered	2	5	1	–
(N	957	148	442	235)

Respondents were also asked how they identified themselves in respect of Scottishness and Britishness.

These figures certainly challenge the claim that Catholics in Scotland feel *less* Scottish than their non-Catholic neighbours. The Catholic sample has the highest proportion of those who failed to identify with either 'Scottish' or 'British'. The most striking aspect of the data is that, for the majority of the sample, being Scottish is of more importance than the sense of being British. Indeed the strongest statement of national sentiment (Scottish *not* British) is highest amongst our Catholic sample.

Further evidence to support the argument that Catholics are embracing a sense of Scottishness to the same extent as other groups can be found where respondents are asked to choose between 'national' and 'class' consciousness. (The question asked: 'Do you feel you have more in common with an English person of your own class, or a Scottish person of a different class?'):

Whilst the incidence of a class identity is highest among Catholics, it should be noted that in all the groups, national identification is more common than class identification. Levels of national identification are remarkably similar between Protestants and Catholics.

This, of course, raises the prospect of Catholics and Protestants having different class profiles. However, in terms of social class measured by occupation, Catholics are similar in profile to the

Table 17 Denomination and Class/National Identity

%	All	RC	CoS	None
Class	27	32	25	25
Nationality	45	43	47	49
Neither	28	25	28	26
(N	957	148	442	235)

Table 18 Respondent's Social Class (Registrar-General)

	RC	CoS	All
	%	%	%
I	3	3	2
II	20	19	21
IIIn	15	25	24
IIIm	23	23	21
IV	24	18	19
V	10	10	8
(N	148	442	957)

Scottish population generally, though there are slightly fewer skilled non-manual workers and more semi-skilled manual workers. In broad terms, 57% of Catholics are manual workers compared with 48% of Scots. The social class profile of Catholics has mirrored that of the population as a whole since the 1970s. The shift from manual to non-manual occupations has occurred at the same rate for both main denominations.

We can produce a cruder measure of social class by collapsing categories I and II as 'middle class' and IIIn to V as 'working class', as well as perceived class identity as follows (Table 19).

In terms of occupation we can see that the similarities between groups far outweigh the differences. In terms of class identification, Catholics are far more likely than other denominational groups to define themselves as working class. The largest group overall, however – representing a majority of the sample – do *not* find class a useful concept for self-identification.

Table 19 Class and Denomination: Occupational Class and Self-Identity

%	All	RC	CoS	None
'Middle class' occupation	23	22	22	20
'Working class' occupation	73	72	76	74
Other	4	6	2	6
	100	100	100	100
'Middle class' identity	10	5	11	7
'Working class' identity	37	49	39	35
Neither	52	45	50	59
	100	100	100	100
(N	957	148	442	235)

Table 20   Attitudes to Constitutional Change

	all	RC	CoS	none
	%	%	%	%
Independence	23	28	19	29
Devolved assembly	50	50	50	47
no change	24	18	28	20
(N	957	148	442	235)

(b)   Religion and the Constitutional Question

Some historians of Catholics in Scotland have pointed to certain reasons why Catholics generally have failed to involve themselves in the Scottish 'Home Rule' movement.[19] They argue that fear that a self-governing Scotland would increase the power of Protestantism (as had happened in self-governing Ulster) worked to separate most Scots Catholics from the early Home Rule agitations, and that as a consequence their support for nationalism is relatively weak. Once more, the evidence runs to the contrary.

Catholics are, if anything, more likely to be in favour of Scottish Independence (28%) than Protestants (19%), and fewer are in favour of the status quo (18% to 28%). Support for devolution is consistent across all religious denominations. Similarly, the notion that the manual working class, both Catholic and Protestant, is, for different reasons, in favour of the constitutional status quo has little to support it.

In 1974, both Catholics and Protestants were broadly in favour of a 'Scottish assembly' (64% and 65% respectively). Since then, differences have emerged between Catholics and Protestants: the former are now proportionally much more in favour of constitutional change than the latter. In 1992, while members of both denominations support constitutional change, Catholics are more in favour than Protestants, a finding which runs counter to much conventional wisdom.

Table 21   Constitutional Option by Religion (Manual Workers Only)

	RC	CoS	none
	%	%	%
Independence	26	23	30
Devolution	53	49	45
no change	17	25	21
(N	107	337	174)

(c) Religion and Voting

Much of the literature on Scottish politics which touches on the issue of religion tends to stress the 'Red-Green' alliance between Scotland's Catholics and the Labour Party. Commentators have also claimed there is a degree of Catholic antipathy towards the Nationalists, for similar reasons to those set out in the debate over Scottishness. Writing in the late 1970s, Jack Brand observed:

> If we are to identify support for the SNP we would not expect to find it in strength among Catholics. We would expect Scottish sentiment to exist in the Church of Scotland since this institution bears much of the tradition of Scotland.[20]

The reluctance of Catholics to vote Nationalist has also been ascribed to a virulent strain of anti-Irish/anti-Catholic sentiment in the early history of the National party. Certain leading figures in the early years of the party were of the opinion that the 'Irish' in Scotland were a 'racial' danger to the 'native' Scots:

> Taken along with the similar outbursts emanating from the Scottish Protestant Churches [in the 1920s and 1930s], this amounted in Catholic eyes to the equation of Scottish nationalism with anti-Catholic bigotry.[21]

What does the data show? With regard to the Catholic vote in the General Elections of 1987 and 1992, two aspects are noticeable: firstly the affection between Catholic and Labour – and Catholic antipathy to the Conservatives – is very evident in both elections. This may, in part, be related to the higher levels of working class identification to be found in the Catholic sample. Secondly there does appear to be some evidence that Catholics *are* less likely to vote for the Nationalists (Table 22).

Table 22   Denominational Group and the Vote, 1987 & 1992 [%]

1987	All	RC	CoS	None
SNP	12	9	13	12
Labour	35	59	32	33
Conservative	23	8	30	12
Alliance	8	5	9	6
1992	All	RC	CoS	None
SNP	20	16	21	23
Labour	32	53	28	31
Conservative	22	6	29	15
Lib-Democrat	9	7	9	9
(N	957	148	442	235)

Catholics have a greater propensity to vote Labour, whereas Protestants were more evenly split between Labour and Conservative. When we compare Nationalist support over the two elections (1987 and 1992), however, we find that it grew across *all* denominational groups. The low Catholic Nationalist vote may have more to do with continuing positive identification with Labour, rather than a negative view of the SNP.

One further point that should be noted is the Conservative reliance on the Church of Scotland vote – whilst it can no longer be claimed that Scottish Protestants are Conservative, it is the case that in 1992 Scottish Conservatives were mainly Protestant.

In other words, the increased mood of political Nationalism in the 1990s, unlike that of the 1970s, was one in which Catholics shared as much as non-Catholics.

Table 23 Composition of Party Votes (1992 Election) by Religious Denomination

%	All	Labour	SNP	Cons.
Roman Catholic	16	26	13	4
Church of Scotland	46	40	48	61
No Religion	245	24	29	17
Other	14	10	11	18
(N	957	304	190	213)

Catholic support for the SNP appears to have risen considerably in recent years. By bringing together the results of a number of surveys, we can see that while in the 1970s the SNP had a very limited support base amongst Catholics, by the late 1980s Catholic support for the party was approaching the same levels found in other groups (Table 24).

Table 24 Proportion of Catholic Voters Voting Nationalist (General Elections)[22]

%	RC	All
1970	3.7	11.4
1974 (Feb.)	6.9	21.9
1974 (Oct.)	7.9	30.4
1987	8.8	14.0
1992	20.0	21.5

Table 25 Party Identified With

%	All	RC	CoS	None
SNP	19	17	19	25
Labour	35	61	31	34
Conservative	26	8	34	16
Liberal Democrat	7	5	6	7
None/Other	13	9	10	18
	100	100	100	100
(N	957	148	442	235)

We can also gauge the attitudes of Catholics to political nationalism by looking at political identification, how the SNP are perceived,
and their party of second choice.

The overall differences between measures of party identification
and measures of voting behaviour in 1992 are not marked and the
level of Catholic identification with the SNP is similar to that of our
Church of Scotland sample. Indeed what separates the denominations on this measure – as on voting patterns – is support for the two
major British parties. Catholics remain solidly Labour, whilst Protestants are split, fairly evenly, between Labour and Conservative.
The non-religious, on the other hand, are split Labour-SNP. Of
central importance here is that Catholic support for the SNP cannot
be dismissed as 'tactical voting' against Conservative candidates: a
significant minority of Catholics, in similar proportions to Protestants, regard the SNP as their party of choice. Indeed, on a number
of specific questions regarding how people feel about the SNP,
Catholics were more positive than Protestants.

Table 26 Attitudes Towards the SNP by Denomination:

THE SNP ARE ...				
%	All	RC	CoS	None
Extreme	51	45	53	47
Moderate	35	40	34	35
United	64	64	66	62
Divided	19	22	17	20
Capable of strong government	30	35	29	34
Not capable	55	47	58	50
Caring	66	66	65	69
Uncaring	16	18	17	14
(N	957	148	442	235)

Table 27   Respondent's Second Choice Party

%	All	RC	CoS	None
SNP	22	28	21	25
Liberal Democrat	22	20	26	16
Labour	14	14	12	18
Conservative	9	8	11	6
None/Other	33	31	30	35
	100	100	100	100
(N	957	148	442	235)

We can also put Catholic attitudes to the Nationalists into per-spective by examining the political parties the SES respondents gave as their *second* choice. If Scottish Catholics were antipathetic towards the SNP we would expect few of them to place the Nationalists as their second choice: this is simply not the case.

Table 27 suggests that there is considerable potential – given the right strategy or political fortune – for the Nationalists to gather far more votes from Scottish Catholics than they are doing at the mo-ment (40 per cent of Catholics who named a second choice party named the SNP). In the debate over 'Scottishness', there has been a re-imagination, a re-invention of Scotland since the 1960s, and to a large extent the SNP has benefited from this new mood of national sentiment. We have seen that Scotland's Catholics have not been immune to this new mood, and, beginning from a very low base, the SNP has made considerable progress in swinging Scottish Catholics round to the party. It may be that a spell of Labour Government, beset perhaps with the problems of power, and the establishment of the Scottish Parliament, will lead to further Nationalist success in weaning more of 'the green' away from 'the red'.

Can we conclude from this data that religious affiliation deter-mines vote? This may seem on the face of it a straightforward question to answer. After all, Catholics are more pro-Labour and anti-Conservative. The problem is, however, that how one votes is related to a number of social characteristics of which religion is merely one. Simply showing that Catholics have a greater propensity to vote Labour does not prove that being a Catholic causes people to vote Labour. It is possible that religion may only be spuriously connected to voting. In other words, it may be that being working class rather than being Catholic explains the propensity to vote Labour. To know whether this is the case or not involves trying to build a model of voting in terms of a number of possible factors to see which, in conjunction with the others as well as separately, is causing votes to vary.

Paula Surridge has built two models of voting, the first looking only at Labour and SNP voters in order to explain what brings people to vote for one party or the other.[23] As we might expect, the most important factor in distinguishing Labour from SNP voters in general in 1992 was their preference for constitutional change. In other words, being in favour of Independence decreases the odds of being a Labour voter as opposed to an SNP one. This, after all, is what we might expect. However, the second most influential factor in discriminating between Labour and SNP voting is whether or not one is a Catholic. In other words, there is still a strong association between voting Labour and being a Catholic, despite the fact that the model allows for one's class identity. Being a Catholic (as opposed to not being one) gives significant odds of being a Labour rather than an SNP voter. Religion, then, has an effect on how one votes over and above one's social class. Hence, though Catholics are by and large working class, their class as such does not explain their greater propensity to vote Labour rather than SNP. It is largely independent of it. The third variable which discriminates between Labour and SNP voters is perceived nationality – how one regards oneself in terms of being Scottish/British.

Religion also remains a significant discriminator of vote when it comes to Conservative versus Labour/SNP voting. What is quite striking is that the best predictor of non-Tory voting is being a Catholic, even compared with attitudes to constitutional issues, class identity, and self-ascribed nationality.

All in all, we can conclude from the data that while Catholics in Scotland still have a propensity for Labour-voting, they are increasingly susceptible to the appeal of the SNP. It remains the case, however, that they are much more resistant than either Scottish Protestants or British Catholics as a whole to voting Conservative.

Left ...

In line with voting habits and predilections, Catholics in Scotland are consistently more left-wing in their political attitudes not only in comparison with the Scottish population as a whole, but also their co-religionists in Britain who are much more similar to the British population in this respect.

Table 28 Political Attitudes

	RC Scots	All Scots	RC British	All GB
'too many rely on government handouts'	3.3	2.7	2.7	2.7
'spend money to abolish poverty'	1.3	1.5	1.5	1.7
'encourage private medicine'	4.0	3.7	3.5	3.5
'get rid of private education'	3.2	3.3	3.8	3.7
'put more money into NHS'	1.3	1.4	1.4	1.5
'redistribute income and wealth'	2.2	2.6	2.9	2.9
'more aid to third world'	2.8	3.1	3.0	3.2
'privatisation gone too far'	2.7	2.8	2.8	2.9

If we examine a broad range of attitudes on a scale of 1 to 5 where '1' is strongly agree and '5' is strongly disagree, and take the mean score, we find that Scottish Catholics are consistently on the left rather than the right of the political spectrum, whether we compare them with fellow Scots or fellow Catholics in the rest of Britain. The lower the score, the greater the agreement with the statement in question.

What these data suggest to us is that Scottish Catholics not only vote for parties of the Left, but take a clear leftist stance on an array of political values. Similarly, there is very little difference between practising and non-practising Catholics with regard to political attitudes; these are consistently on the left of the spectrum.

... and Liberal

While we have relatively little difficulty accepting that Catholics in Scotland are left-wing, given their economic and political history (working class and Labour voting), it comes as something of a surprise that they are on the whole consistently more liberal than Scots as a whole as well as their Catholic counterparts elsewhere in Britain. For example, using a 1 to 5 scale once more, we obtain the following means (The score '1' is the most conservative, and '5' is most liberal; hence, the higher the aggregate score, the more liberal the response) (Table 29).

The lower scores for Catholics (in Scotland and in England) indicates greater belief that availability has gone too far. Nevertheless, we might note that a minority (44%) of Scottish Catholics believe this to be the case, with 36% opting for the view that availability is 'about right', with the rest (7%) agreeing with the view that it is too restrictive.

Table 29   Social Attitudes

	RC Scots	All Scots	RC British	All British
'bring back the death penalty'	3.4	3.0	3.3	3.0
'more opportunities for women'	3.9	3.7	3.8	3.7
'more opportunities for black people'	3.5	3.5	3.5	3.4
'right to show nudity/sex in films, etc.'	2.6	2.4	2.5	2.5
'equal opportunities for gay people'	3.4	3.4	3.3	3.3

On each of these scales, Scottish Catholics are at the liberal rather than the conservative end of the spectrum (and consistently more liberal than their Church of Scotland counterparts). There is only one – expected – exception, and that is as regards attitudes to abortion.

| 'availability of abortion on NHS' | 3.2 | 3.6 | 3.2 | 3.7 |

If we compare 'practising' and 'non-practising' Catholic respondents (as measured by church attendance), we find that practising Catholics are more conservative than non-practising Catholics on attitudes to homosexuality, nudity/sex in films, and abortion, but are just as liberal on attitudes to equal opportunities for women and black people.

Conclusion

We have sought to show in this chapter that the prevailing assumptions regarding the legacy of sectarianism in Scotland require considerable revision if we are to talk of Scottish society in the present tense. Scotland has survived the worst period of economic hardship since the 1930s without a return to the heightened ethno-religious tensions of that decade. Scotland has witnessed a close neighbour with whom she has strong familial links turn in upon itself in an orgy of inter-communal bloodshed – and Scotland has remained peaceful. Now that the Irish situation is dominated by a (albeit fragile) peace process it could be fairly expected that the organised sectarian groups in Scotland will become even more marginalised. A return to war in Ulster would increase the distaste with which the majority of Scots view displays of sectarian triumphalism. Organised sectarianism in Scotland thus appears to have reached a dead end. It is difficult to talk in any meaningful sense of a 'Catholic community' or a 'Protestant community' in present-day Scotland: individuals of all faiths and none now work together, drink together and (most importantly) *marry* each other.

The continuing rivalry between Rangers and Celtic in what is, essentially, the national pastime of Scottish urban males has masked the decline of sectarianism elsewhere in Scottish society. Football's sectarians, by and large, are playing a boy's game, but the songs of Glasgow's terraces represent less than the noise would suggest. They are, to a great extent, nostalgic echoes of another time (and another country). The Old Firm clubs are the *only popular* symbols of sectarian division, football elsewhere in Scotland having shed most, or all, of its religious connotations, and the quasi-masonic organisations of both Protestant and Catholic are now placed firmly at the margins of Scottish life. There is considerable evidence that, for the majority of Scots, political sectarianism is an irrelevance which belongs firmly in the past.

There can be little doubt that the consciousness of Scottish Catholics has been affected by the Catholic Irish experience of immigration, ghettoisation and marginalisation. Most Scottish Catholics from an Irish background retain an affection for their ancestral home – and why not? However, Scotland has changed considerably in the last century, and so too has the lot of the Scottish Catholic. There is little evidence to support the idea that Catholics in Scotland feel less 'Scottish' than non-Catholics. The new mood in Scotland – a mood reflected by the strong 'Yes–Yes' vote in the Referendum – has not left Catholics behind; they are fully participating in the new sense of 'Scotland'.

In sum, Catholics in Scotland are a relatively small but politically and socially important group. Although the survey we are using provides only a snapshot picture of who they are and the values they have, there is every reason to believe that they are much more integrated into Scottish society than ever before, that they feel more thoroughly Scottish, and that they provide an important moral and cultural leavening at a crucial point in Scotland's social and political history at the end of the second millennium.

NOTES

1. S. Bruce, 'Review: political and cultural interaction between Scotland and Ulster', *Scottish Affairs*, Number 15, 1996. p. 32; S. Bruce, *No Pope of Rome: Militant Protestantism in Modern Scotland* (Edinburgh, 1985).
2. *Ibid.*, 1985, p. 248.
3. S. Bruce, 'Sectarianism in Scotland: a contemporary assessment and explanation', in D. McCrone and A. Brown (eds), *Scottish Government Yearbook 1988* (Edinburgh, 1988), p. 151.

4. *Ibid.*, p. 159.
5. *Ibid.*, p. 42.
6. *Ibid.*, p. 160.
7. G. Walker, *Intimate Strangers: Political and Cultural Interaction Between Scotland and Ulster in Modern Times* (Edinburgh, 1995), p. v.
8. *Ibid.*, p. 180.
9. Bruce, *op. cit.*, pp. 33–4.
10. T. Gallagher, *Glasgow, The Uneasy Peace* (Manchester, 1987), p. 1.
11. T. Gallagher, 'Soccer, the real opium of the people?', *The Innes Review*, volume 36, 1985, p. 44.
12. Gallagher, *op. cit.*, 1987, p. 33.
13. R. Boyle, *Football and Cultural Identity in Glasgow and Liverpool*, unpublished PhD Thesis, University of Stirling, 1995, p. 90.
14. J. Bradley, 'Religious Cleavage and Aspects of Catholic Identity in Modern Scotland', *Scottish Church History Society*, volume XXV, part 3, 1995, p. 442.
15. *Ibid.*, p. 456.
16. *Ibid.*, pp. 456–464.
17. Steve Bruce on the Radio 5 Live programme 'Two Tales of a City', 24 December 1995.
18. S. Brown, 'Outside the Covenant', *The Innes Review*, volume 4, 1991, p. 42.
19. Gallagher, *op. cit.*, 1987.
20. J. Brand, *The National Movement in Scotland* (London, 1978), p. 130.
21. Walker, *op. cit.*, p. 105.
22. The sources of this information are for 1970–74, J. Brand, *op. cit.*; for 1987, the Scottish Election Survey (1992); and for 1992, J. Curtice, 'Voters who go to the polls religiously', *Scotland on Sunday*, 26 June 1994.
23. See J. Brand, J. Mitchell and P. Surridge, 'Identity and the Vote: Class and nationality in Scotland', in D. Denver et al. (eds), *British Elections and Parties Yearbook* 1993 (Hemel Hempstead, 1994).

REPRESENTING CATHOLICISM IN THE MEDIA AND POPULAR CULTURE

5

IMAGES, PERCEPTIONS AND THE GHETTO: CONFORMITY AND INVISIBLE IDENTITY?

Joseph Bradley

This chapter focuses on Catholics of Irish origin and argues, in contrast with McCrone and Rosie, that for many the history of rejection and hostility which has characterised the experience of previous generations of Irish Catholics in Scotland has left an indelible mark on the current generation. Bradley argues that the 'Irish' aspect of this community's identity has been rendered invisible by the hostility of the host community and until this is acknowledged and addressed, then a distorted representation of this community will remain.

Historical Context

Writing of the small Irish immigrant community in early 19th century Scotland, Handley reported that the Irish were subjected to all sorts of 'verbal abuse and mockery': the newspapers of the districts where there was to be found an Irish presence being among the chief purveyors of this denigration. Handley quotes a number of newspaper articles having such titles as 'gims of the Emerald Isle' and 'bhoys from the land of the bog and the shamrock'. In addition, 'ape-faced' and 'small headed Irishmen', 'a cruel Tipperary visage', 'a malicious-looking Irishman' and 'a blackguard-looking creature with a plastered face' are all specimens from the *North British Daily Mail* during the 19th century.[1] When the comic reporting became exhausted it usually ridiculed the incomers as the 'low Irish'.[2]

For Handley, the hostility which met the Irish in Scotland stemmed from economic, political and religious reasons: these factors constituting the discourse of the time concerning Irish Catholic immigrants.[3] Handley argues that the chief reason for native animosity was the fact that the immigrants were Catholics, the fewer Ulster Scots Protestants of the north of Ireland who also came to Scotland in their thousands apparently freely re-merging with their former kith and kin. Today we might categorise this antagonism as a form of racism. Certainly, if we care to look at the columns of the *North British Daily Mail*, the *Glasgow Courier, The Witness, The Bulletin*, the *Glasgow Chronicle* the *Glasgow Constitutional, The Glasgow Herald*, and the *Scottish Guardian* among others, there is an abundance of evidence of this animosity. Some newspapers like the *The Scotsman* in Edinburgh were occasionally more favourable towards the immigrants, but this was the exception rather than the rule. Indeed, a discourse of superiority, domination and rejection of the Irish in Scotland was evidenced in the census report of 1871, which stated that:

> As yet the great body of these Irish do not seem to have improved by their residence among us; and it is quite certain that the native Scot who has associated with them has most certainly deteriorated. It is painful to contemplate what may be the ultimate effect of this Irish immigration on the morals and habits of the people, and on the future prospects of the country.[4]

Such reporting on the Irish is important to how Catholics in present day Scotland, in the main the offspring of Irish immigrants, are viewed by others, as well as to how they perceive and represent their past and present, as individuals and as a community. Therefore, this context has a bearing on present Irish identity, that is, the Irishness of the progeny of Irish immigrants in Scotland.

The concept of a ghettoised community is repeated by a number of authors on the Irish in Scotland. The idea is characterised as a physical, cultural and ethnic ghetto, whilst it is often charged with negativity resulting in an evasion of a more profitable exploration of aspects of the immigrant experience. The use of ghetto, with its inevitable conceptual limitations, means that the Irish are frequently seen as being in some way broadly responsible for limiting their own life chances and in becoming victims of prejudice. Tom Gallagher's publication on the Irish in Scotland, *Glasgow: The Uneasy Peace* (1987), remains significant as an informative source comparable with Handley's books of several decades earlier. Nonetheless, Gallagher is typical of some writers on the Irish in that he is often too willing to accept that the ghetto to which Irish Catholics often belonged was frequently self-imposed, particularly by sometimes cruel, prejudiced and small minded clergy,[5] and that the Irish were willing dupes to the will of the cassock and a contradictory emotional attachment to their 'homeland' which invariably kept them in a social, religious and political hinterland. Such notions are important in accounts of the Irish in Scotland, but they are often over emphasised at the expense of more penetrating assessments.

In choosing to remain Irish in Scotland, a common view is one of inevitability at the social consequences of a reluctance to change accordingly: a change which might have resulted in more favourable and more rapid advancement throughout Scottish society. In this view, looking 'back' to Ireland is seen as a largely self-imposed ghettoisation where, owing to a predilection for clinging to antiquated ways, retaining inverted beliefs, of being dominated by the Church, of looking to Ireland politically and of having greater affinity for things Irish than for things Scottish or British, is a self-constructed social barrier. The implication is that those who 'assimilate' are best equipped in breaking from the stigmas of the past, in the process disassociating themselves from old beliefs, perceptions and symbols and adopting Scottish and/or British equivalents. Thus, a perception has emerged that diminishing one's personal as well as one's community's Irish identities is an important mark of progress and achievement for the immigrant Irish in Scotland.[6]

Sometimes authors on the Irish in Scotland imply that in the past, those immigrants who married outside of their community were more likely not to be 'extreme' in religion and politics whilst they invariably lacked the parochialism of other members, eventually enabling them and their children to make social and economic progress in the host society. Such assertions can be over simplistic and, amongst other things, underplay the role of anti-Catholicism and anti-Irishness in the narrative of Irish immigration into Scotland: an inference is that only those Irish who were considered ignorant, bigoted and political extremists retained Irish identity. The implication is that such immigrants to Scotland were compelled to assimilate rather than integrate: a necessary pre-requisite to acceptance and ultimately, improvement and advancement. However, there is little which is certain about changing Irish identity in Scotland, especially in respect of the social forces compelling the Irish in Scotland to change. In addition, and as is suggested here, there is evidence intimating that for those retaining or re-discovering Irishness, the Irish experience has frequently been a negative one in Scotland.

One of the most significant aspects of the ghetto has been a psychological one of stereotypes, ideology, dominant identities and of prejudicial actions and beliefs. In Victorian Britain portrayals of the Irish (and thus Catholics) regularly invoked an ape-like stereotype involving simian features. This portrayal lasted in a number of Scottish newspapers until the outbreak of the First World War and was witnessed throughout Britain more sporadically and intermittently until at least the 1950s. For one writer, this imagery stresses the racial gulf between host and newcomer.[7] In the context of such portrayals, it seems an obvious question to ask: who in society wished to be associated with a race of apes? Although much of this kind of reporting on Irish and Catholic matters has become material for history books, the experience of being subjected to this portrayal, in being sub-human in matters religious, social and ethnic, has had a complex and multifarious influence upon how the offspring of the Irish view themselves. It also has modern manifestations which may be related in a broadly ideological sense rather than linked in some other more obvious, indeed, one-dimensional way.

In the contemporary setting, solely Catholic issues upon which the media have focused have been newsworthy and have merited scrutiny and reporting. Many Catholics as well as the Catholic media in Scotland, although embarrassed by certain revelations in recent years, would view such reporting as being quite equitable. However, falling standards amongst some of the clergy, mixing politics and morality and diminishing numbers of Church attenders are aspects of religion not unique to Catholics and such social features say more about modern society than simply about Catholics in Scotland. Much of society's focusing on the sexual misdemeanours of a small minority of Catholic priests says more 'of how hung up on sex we remain' as one journalist stated in relation to priestly celibacy.[8]

Since 1990, interviews with a significant number of Church attending Catholics has revealed that contrary to media interpretations, many have been supportive of several of Pope John Paul's reportedly contentious social, economic and moral statements.[9] The fact that he is working to a different agenda than many in modern society, one that is essentially spiritual and in opposition to a perceived irreligious, materialistic and impersonal world, also means that his often discerned conservatism in such matters will invariably attract criticism. Catholic or otherwise, religion often has to endure antagonism on the part of the modern media. However, such criticism bears little relation to the mode of reporting on Catholic matters common in the print media until the First World War: indeed, it was characteristic of much of Scottish society until at least the Second World War.

Brown believes that the campaign against the Irish Catholic presence in Scotland during the inter-war years was both institutional
and popular, and was an attempt at 'marginalising, and even eliminating an ethnic minority whose presence was regarded as an evil,
polluting the purity of Scottish race and culture'.[10] Such sentiments
found expression in popular literature, for example in the works of
Andrew Dewar Gibb.[11] Political activists, like Alexander Ratcliffe
and John McCormick, gained success at the ballot by declaring
similar anti-Irish and anti-Catholic opinions. Other significant political figures at the time reflected these widespread feelings regarding the Irish in Scotland. Indeed, Conservative member of
Parliament, Lord Scone, believed that:

> culturally the Irish population . . . has not been assimilated into the
> Scottish population. It is not my purpose to discuss now whether the
> Irish culture is good or bad, but merely to state the definite fact that there
> is in the west of Scotland a completely separate race of alien origin
> practically homogeneous whose presence there is bitterly resented by
> tens of thousands of the Scottish working-class.[12]

There are a number deductions which can be drawn from these and
similar attitudes and opinions. One particular line of discourse, that
which relates to the Irish nature of the immigrants and their offspring
(by the time of the inter-war period the majority of the Irish immigrant population were Scottish-born Catholics), is one which holds
the key to questions relating to a perception of a ghettoised Irish
Catholic community: one unwilling to cease being distinctive, where
integration was widespread, but assimilation less tangible.

Catholics and Sport: Integration or Assimilation

Elsewhere I have referred to the importance of football to many
people in Scotland and the fact that Glasgow Rangers and Celtic –
'the Old Firm' – are two of the major social institutions in Scottish
society.[13] As Celtic were founded by, and in the main for, Irish
Catholic immigrants in west central Scotland at the end of the 19th
century, the experience of Celtic Football Club has frequently
aligned itself with the community it has historically represented.
Linking with the portrayal of the physical and intellectual characteristics of the Irish in the noted press reports, a cartoon published
in a Scottish football newspaper early in this century depicted two
Old Firm players in a bar playing pool. The cartoon portrayed the

Celtic player as stereotypically Irish: dumb with grotesque and brutish facial features. The Rangers player was handsome and with intelligent looking eyes. The cartoon was captioned 'Apes and Aryans'.[14]

Antagonism towards the Irishness and Catholic nature of many football clubs in Scotland in both the last century and the present one has meant that Celtic is the only club in Scotland to survive as perceptibly Irish. However, Celtic's Irishness has long been a focus for hostility. It would be erroneous to believe controversies provoked by a popular Scottish media spokesperson in the mid 1990s in relation to Celtic's flying of the Irish tricolour at its home ground, its supporters singing Irish songs, as well the clubs playing of an Irish ballad over their loudspeaker system, is a recent phenomenon.[15] Such hostility falls into an established pattern.

In the 1950s the Scottish football authorities ordered Celtic to remove the Irish flag from its stadium. Club historian, Brian Wilson MP, states that 'an attempt was made to force Celtic out of business if they would not agree to remove the Irish flag from their home ground.'[16] Ideologically, such a campaign is linked to Brown's assessment of the offensive against Catholics in Scotland twenty years earlier, when he believed there was an institutional and popular attempt to marginalise and even eliminate 'an ethnic minority whose presence was regarded as an evil, polluting the purity of Scottish race and culture.'[17] Robert Kelly, the Chairman of Celtic, saw this latest campaign as an attack upon the nature of the club as well as upon the Irishness of Catholics in Scotland. In two speeches to a lay Catholic organisation, Kelly stated:

> It is necessary that Catholics should become more and more organised, because at present in the west of Scotland they are not making their presence sufficiently felt in proportion to their number. We have no need to be ashamed of our fathers, nor have we any cause to be ashamed that those founders [of Celtic] came from that country that has provided protagonists for liberty wherever they have settled.[18]

Celtic were ordered to take down the flag or be suspended from football in Scotland. With the support of the Celtic followers, Kelly did not comply with the order. The crisis in the Scottish game became a saga and most clubs waned in their attack on Celtic, possibly recognising that the income generated by the club was a major factor in Scottish football's vibrancy. The furore eventually died down and Celtic continued to fly the Irish flag.

In 1991 Scotland's most popular Sunday newspaper the *Sunday Mail* reflected a cultural and political orthodoxy in the Scottish media when, focusing on Celtic's Irish image, it reported the popular group *The Pogues* as guests of the club.[19] The Pogues' IRA connection was considered to have been established because they had written a song protesting about the wrongful conviction of the 'Birmingham Six', who had been imprisoned (on evidence which was eventually discounted) for a lethal explosion in that city in the early 1970s. This song was subsequently banned under the Government anti-terror regulations in 1988. Celtic were consequently 'exposed' as having terrorist links on the basis of this connection.

When Rangers fans became notorious in riots at stadia in England and abroad during the 1960s and 1970s, and the discussion of football hooliganism took on a sectarian dimension, the Scottish press frequently balanced discourse of Rangers 'no Catholics' policy with mention of the symbols of Celtic. Comment also extended to criticism of Catholic schools. In the wake of Rangers supporters rioting in Birmingham in 1976, the *Daily Record*, recognising that too strong a criticism may harm their mainly Protestant readership, and despite the fact that events had taken place in England, tempered their editorial criticism of rioting fans by stating that Celtic should be: 'willing to be recognised as a sporting bastion of Catholicism. They must bear a share of the guilt'.[20]

Catholic Distinctiveness and the Retention of Irishness

The issue of Catholic schools also forms an important facet of observing how a characteristic of the offspring of the Irish in Scotland is considered on the part of the media. It is unlikely there would be Catholic schools in Scotland but for Irish immigration: the schools form part of the immigrant legacy in Scottish society. The schools question has been viewed by some observers as symptomatic of the hostility towards Irish Catholics. In 1935, *The Glasgow Herald* reported a Church of Scotland minister as saying:

> The indignant opposition to the provision of Section 18 of the Education (Scotland) Act, 1918, is that public money is being expanded in educating an increasing section of the population, in the main Free Staters or their offspring, in a faith and a loyalty hostile to the tradition and religion accepted by the vast majority of the Scottish nation. . . . Why should we feed, clothe, and educate these people who everywhere plot and plan for the downfall of Great Britain.[21]

Here, national identity is inductively juxtaposed with anti-Irish and anti-Catholic expressions.[22] Gallagher believes that this particular minister: was only relaying 'what a large number of ministers and their congregations elsewhere shared, if in a somewhat modified form'.[23]

The contemporary debate concerning Catholic schooling is similarly heated though there are a number of additional elements to the controversy giving it greater complexity. Although a small constituent within the Catholic community does not support Catholic schooling, usually viewing the issue as anachronistic, most informed research points towards an overwhelming support for the schools amongst Catholics, particularly amongst their Church-going sector.[24] However, there is hostility towards the schools on the part of the larger society. This is particularly evident on the part of much of the Scottish print media. For the tabloids, discourse is dominated by concerns over young innocent children, their sectarian minded parents and other bigoted elements in society influencing or even controlling them. Such reporting in Scotland's most popular selling regular, the *Daily Record*, periodically proclaims 'Barred, Kids Caught in Storm over Catholic Schools', 'We Are United' (a headline repeated on occasion), and 'It's Pupil Power: Walkout Kids in Schools' Protest'. One article stated:

> They swim together . . . they play football together . . . and last night David became old enough to join his pal in the Beavers. But there is an Act of Parliament that says Douglas, six, and five year-old David could be kept apart during the day – because one is a Protestant and the other is a Catholic.[25]

For some Catholics, the media treatment of Catholic schools is similar to arguments used by their antagonists amongst other groups and organisations in society. The Free Church of Scotland is against Catholic schooling, though they also fear secularisation,[26] which has diminished Christian (i.e., Protestant) teaching in schools in general.[27] The Free Presbyterian Church can be seen to take a similar line, whilst the Orange Order in Scotland has opposition to Catholic schools at the top of its social and political agenda. Like other protagonists engaged in the argument, the Orange Institution view Catholic schools as sectarian and divisive, whilst they generally favour 'integrated education'. David Bryce, the Order's former Grand Secretary, believes that, in the wake of such a religious amalgamation, the number of Catholics in Scotland would steadily fall.[28]

In relation to wider issues relating to this 'community' in Scotland, there are of course a number of conceptual problems in considering Irish Catholics emerging from a ghetto. Not all Catholics in Scotland are of Irish origin. Some thousands of Catholics have migrated from Italy as well as Poland and Lithuania during the course of this century. There is also a small number of Scots who remained Catholic after the Reformation. Inter-marriage, secularisation and the growth of mass and popular cultures can obscure roots and origins and invariably influence identity. These affect our capacity to talk rigidly of social, cultural and political categories. Nevertheless, the vast majority of Catholics in Scotland do originate from Ireland and Irishness is a manifest identity in west central Scottish society. Of course there are problems over how to describe a modern immigrant community: most terms are debatable and less than specific, but then so too are the terms Scottish and British. Such terminology has a variety of dimensions and there are a number of definitions and conceptions relating to these identities.[29]

However, apart from any debate relating to these concepts, one might also ask why many academics, writers and journalists, choose to ignore consideration of the Irishness of the Irish in Scotland? Why is this important component of modern Scottish society frequently assessed through sectarian discourse? In his history of Orangeism in Scotland, Marshall attempts to answer some questions on ethno-religious discord by implying that religious identity is a neglected subject, because it apparently mars the image of Scotland which various people wish to project.[30] Since the 1980s, several authors have contributed significantly to the history of the Irish community.[31] However, neither schools, colleges nor most universities give substantial recognition to these works. Generally, most of the formal educational curriculum excludes study of Ireland or the Irish in Scotland. Despite both countries being linked through migration, a history of British-Irish colonial conflict, and despite the presence of the Irish in Scotland, the Irish and Ireland are largely ignored in Scottish and British education.

The question also emerges as to whether negative images in Britain of being Irish and Catholic have had a critical influence on the self-image and self-perception of the Irish? In 1990, a young Irish-born immigrant to Scotland wrote to *The Herald* in the following terms.

In the wake of all the recent publicity with regard to racism in Scotland towards Asians and Afro-Caribbeans, I find it incredible that no mention has been made of the racism that exists towards the Irish in Scotland. . . . since coming to Scotland, I have on several occasions encountered people who believe that merely because I am Irish, I must either belong to or support the IRA and all it stands for. . . . I have always felt pride in being Irish, but now I feel another feeling creeping into me . . . fear of being Irish.[32]

Troubles in Ireland, particularly Northern Ireland over the course of the past thirty years, form an aspect of the narrative of the Irish in Britain and their portrayal in the British media. Nonetheless, a background of troubles has rarely been required to portray disparaging images of things Irish. For example, the cartoon in the *Scottish Referee* of the early 20th century occurred at a time of little obvious militancy in Ireland, and in 1952 when the SFA attempted to have Celtic remove the flag, there was little trouble in the background of Northern Ireland. The media commentator, who has campaigned to have Celtic remove the Irish flag within the confines of the club's stadium, was also active during the period of a significant cease-fire in Northern Ireland, a time also when many things Irish came to the forefront of popular culture.[33]

In the British media, Ireland is frequently recognised within the limits of a recurring genre: one which draws on images and stereotypes of a religiously backward, poverty ridden country with thick and violent Irish people. In 1993 television presenter, Robert Kilroy Silk, referred to Irish people as 'pixies, peasants and priests'.[34] Writing about a Gaelic football match in Glasgow between two of Ireland's best footballing counties, an *Evening Times* journalist spoke of two teams set to 'knock the daylights out of each other'.[35] A more unreserved derogatory commentary on Ireland was made in 1985 by the then editor of the *Daily Express*, Sir John Junor (the latest in a series of such comments). Junor's remark provoked the following comment from an observer of Irish affairs:

John Junor's remark that he would rather go looking for worms in a dunghill than visit Ireland is but one example of a quite unrepentant anti-Irishness of so much of the Tory press.[36]

Reviewing the London Finsbury Park Fleadh (music festival) for a London newspaper in 1990, Stan Gebler Davies wrote that, 'the easiest way to learn Gaelic is to murder someone for the IRA'. The implication being that the subsequent period spent in the Maze/Long Kesh prison would enable a prisoner to learn the Irish language amongst those incarcerated for similar crimes, a well-established pastime for the prison's Republican inmates.[37] A regular *Herald* columnist also participates frequently in what might be referred to as an attitude of superiority or, 'thick Paddy' cultural stereotyping, a refinement illustrated in the contemporary Irish joke. Writing of a bright young colleen looking for some information regarding an enquiry from a Scot working in Dublin, the colleen admitted there were no rules and regulations regarding the enquiry but would the enquirer still like a copy of the 'unwritten laws.' The same journalist also made mention of tickets for an Ireland – Scotland rugby international which cost ten punts and which he sardonically added, 'included admission.'[38] A spelling mistake on the part of an advertisement for Jury's Hotel in Glasgow was highlighted by the same journalist in 1996. This reporter's penchant for degrading Ireland and the Irish became more obvious when he told his readers to, 'bear in mind they are an Irish company.'[39] Celtic Football Club's Irish identity has also been the object of the 'thick Paddy' sub-culture. *The Herald* reported that after going through sound checks on the public address system came the following words from Celtic's stadium supervisor: 'If this announcement cannot be heard in your part of the stadium, please contact control'. A humorous story, and of course, just as well for Celtic's 'continuing links with Irish ways' added *The Herald*.[40]

There exists a meaningful bond between the Catholic faith and the people and country of Ireland, including its diaspora. For some media commentators, this also provides a means to denigrate Ireland, Irish Catholics and the Catholic faith. In 1996, writing of some Catholic clerical misdemeanours in the *Scottish Daily Mail*, a journalist stated:

> I have never understood why Roman Catholic clergy, as distinct from their Protestant brethren, are expected to forsake the company of women. Especially since, as anyone who has eavesdropped in an Irish village pub well knows, so many of them don't.[41]

One significant member of the print media regularly reflects many of the conventions of reporting things Irish and Catholic in Scotland. Writing in *The Herald*, this journalist described Ireland as 'poor and boggy', and with some disapproval, 'by far the most faithful of all daughters of Mother Church.'[42] The same writer frequently stereotypes Ireland and the Irish. Among his writings he describes the British welfare state and its relative prosperity, as having drawn many

Roman Catholic Irish from the rest of Ireland to Ulster for decades: thus repeating many of the media conventions of the nineteenth and early twentieth centuries in relation to the Irish coming to Scotland.[43]

In 1997 a similar article was again included in Scotland's most popular broadsheet, *The Herald*. The Catholic faith was described as ghoulish, as being associated with bloody degradations, tonic wine, pleas from the pulpit for a new paint job for sanctuaries, showbiz spectaculars, sectarian schooling, crazy priests, as the politics of the body, the sanctity of a few human cells and ethno-religious discrimination being a factor of a long gone history rather than as a recent experience for many people.[44] These phrases were part of an article written by a former Catholic of Irish descent to describe the faith and practices of his former co-religionists.

Again stereotypes were in order when *The Observer Scotland* profiled new author and soon to be MP, Helen Liddell, who originates from the same popularly known 'Catholic Irish' town as the journalist latterly mentioned. This particular correspondent wrote: 'Sex in Coatbridge, after all, had been traditionally a very straightforward exercise in human reproduction, the result in days gone by of a healthy intake of Guinness at the Labour Club.'[45] The abuse of Ireland's national drink, a town with possibly the biggest percentage per head of people with Irish antecedents in Britain, the sexual morality of the Catholic Church, and the strong links between the Labour Party and Catholics in west-central Scotland dovetail with an ethno-religious stereotype in this report in a considered quality Sunday newspaper.

In 1996 *The Herald*, ran a weekend story on Europeans in Scotland; Italians, Poles, French, Icelanders, Russians and Germans. All were presented in a positive light amid their diverse identities and origins.[46] A year previously another weekend article was written on the English presence in Scotland. Such journalism begs the questions, if articles are being written on the various groups which now comprise Scottish society, where are the Irish? Have they disappeared or become invisible? Are the Irish in Scotland simply ignored? If so, why? Other more significant questions might be, have the years of denigration, humiliation and prejudice had a detrimental effect on the Irish in Scotland and exhibitions of Irishness? Have the Irish been marginalised beyond recognition?

In 1996, the *Scottish Daily Mail's* Bruce Anderson wrote of Irish European Union Commissioner Padraig Flynn. Anderson described Ireland thus:

As soon as you arrive in Ireland, you leave the modern world. Every mile you travel west of Dublin is also a mile west of the 20th century. . . . This is a pre-20th century economy, based on the pig and potato and presided over by the priest.[47]

In 1987 the same writer wrote of Ireland's Sean McBride, winner of the Nobel Peace Prize (1974), the Lenin Peace Prize (1977) as well as the American Medal for Justice among other prestigious tributes. Anderson wrote that McBride had two guiding principles throughout his career, 'the first was hatred of Great Britain, the second was a worship of violence'. In contrast, Oliver Tambo, former president of the ANC, described McBride as 'a great beacon, guiding and assisting oppressed people to the path of national liberation and self-determination.'[48]

Where does such negative media reporting and images on Ireland and the Irish leave the traditional Irish Catholic community in Scotland? Has the context of this discourse and style of reporting affected the immigrant's Irishness? In Scotland it seems that it has frequently been the case that to be seen to be Irish, and often Catholic, has meant that relevant attributes are assessed in negative terms. Davey highlights similar prejudice in the treatment of black/brown immigrants in English society. He argues that:

their cultures are negatively evaluated and they are under constant pressure to adopt British habits, customs and values which they are assured will make a better way of life for them.[49]

The former Conservative Cabinet minister, Norman Tebbit demonstrated such reasoning in 1989, when he suggested a novel type of cricket test. Asian immigrants' integration could be tested by asking which cricket team they supported: England or Pakistan/India. He went on to suggest:

that those who continue to cheer for India and Pakistan, are wanting in Britishness. . . . that the only satisfactory way to be an Asian in Britain was to cease being Asian.[50]

In 1997 Tebbit returned to this theme at the Conservative Party conference when he argued that Britain was no place for ethnic diversity and all resident there should be 'encouraged' to see themselves as British and British born immigrants should be taught to see British history as their own.[51] Tebbit's cricket test has proved to be similar to other sporting metaphors or ethnic hurdles. In its form as a 'football test', the qualifying review has also been applied regularly by the Scottish/British press in the 1980s and 1990s as it became common for second and third generation Irish to represent and support the Republic of Ireland in international football.[52] Deprecative comment has constantly characterised the success of the Irish football team.

The *Sunday Mail* described Ireland's Scottish-born soccer international Ray Houghton as a Scot, even though he is a member of the Irish diaspora, an Irish passport holder, of strong County Donegal links and a player for the Republic of Ireland's soccer team.[53] The *Daily Record* disparagingly asserted that 90% of the UK's population could play for the Republic of Ireland: a statement which was a superficially disguised criticism of Ireland's policy of playing members of the Irish diaspora in its international team.[54] The *Evening Times* maligned Motherwell player Tommy Coyne's Irishness during the corresponding period of the World Cup in 1994,[55] while the same paper asserted that 'there will be many in our country temporarily swapping nationalities this month as the Irish go in against Italy': a reference to Catholics of Irish origins supporting the Republic of Ireland?[56] Again, a *Herald* journalist spoke of someone not being sufficiently Scottish enough to play rugby for Scotland, stating 'Jack Charlton's old test for Irish nationality – that the football player in question had once passed through Dublin airport – does not apply.'[57] Such articles rarely reflect seriously on what makes a person or a community what they are, or what they think they are, or how they imagine themselves. The media is nonetheless both influential in terms of how people think of the subject matter whilst it also reflects the preoccupations, beliefs and identities of the readers it serves.

In football, few of the referred-to newspapers have considered it important that Scottish international stars of late, Richard Gough, Stuart McCall, Andy Goram, Bruce Rioch amongst others, were not born in Scotland and few originally spoke with a Scottish accent. Likewise, John Beattie of British and Scottish rugby fame in the 1980s and 1990s, was born in Asia and spent twelve years of his childhood in Borneo before returning 'home' to Scotland.[58] Jean Tigana, one of France's finest footballers of the 1980s, was born in Mali while 1996–97 Celtic player Jorge Cadette has played for Portugal but was born in Mozambique. A sociological and psychological approach to the question of identity and an understanding of the circumstances into which people are born allow differing, less superficial and less insular methods for discussing and reporting identity. Indeed, a more broad-based understanding of identity may also encourage greater acceptance of diversity and plurality in society.

In terms of their style of reporting matters ethnic, it did not occur as somewhat ironic to the *Sunday Mail* that in referring to a possible candidate for the American presidential elections of 1996 Steven Forbes, as a Scot, this was purely on the basis of his Scottish-born grandfather. Of course, Forbes' other antecedents may well have originated from Lithuania, Italy or England. No question here of the criteria for being Scottish.[59] The reality is that Forbes is Scottish-minded and strongly values his ethnic origins in Scotland. Although born elsewhere, he could be considered identifiably Scottish.

Such is the nature of Ireland's history that there are more Irish outside of the country than within its borders. Indeed, former Irish president, Mary Robinson made reference to Ireland's diaspora an intrinsic part of her deliberations.[60] Nonetheless, it is evident that much of the Scottish media have difficulty in comprehending or articulating the Irishness of a significant number of the population in Scotland. Indeed, as is evidenced in these few examples, elements of the media do not ignore Ireland or the Irish, but regularly disparage them. In isolation, these examples may be seen as humorous, insignificant and unrelated comment. Nonetheless, historically, they reflect a well-developed, broad, ideological and attitudinal position. The logic which underpins these arguments was partly exposed by a respected British journalist:

> the assertion that we are one people has always been a lie used to justify the unjust dominance of one group (whites, Protestants or Anglo-Saxons, for example) over the society as a whole.[61]

In British-Irish terms, cultural subjugation has been a process of colonising not only Ireland, but also its people and its offspring. This has been a long historical process linked to British colonialism and Irish identity, as is reflected in a quote from Sir William Parsons about the Irish in 1625. For Parsons, only the depreciation and destruction of Ireland's cultural traits and identity could result in the Irish being absorbed into the Crown's realm. He stated:

> We must change their course of government, apparel, manner of holding land, their language and habit of life.[62]

In reviewing how newspapers (as well as other elements of the wider society) have historically reported on the Irish immigrant community in Scotland we can explore aspects of the Irish and Catholic experience and the nature of contemporary Irish identities in Scotland. Antagonism displayed towards the immigrants and their offspring has reflected upon the Irishness of the Catholic immigrant population in Scotland. As a result, the Irish have emerged as a community which frequently deliberates its Irishness.[63] The fluctuating but ultimately indeterminate nature of this Irishness was summed up succinctly by a Catholic interviewee: 'I'm Scottish, though I've an Irish name. I'm more non-English. I am born in Scotland, but the blood that runs through me is Irish. If my background was black, I wouldn't be a half-caste. I'd be black.'[64] Related to this kind of insecurity or deliberation regarding personal and community identity, several Catholic interviewees have also expressed inhibitions in calling their children by Irish/Catholic forenames. In some instances, the Irish part of their identity was too difficult for them to recognise, they were inclined more towards a Scottish name or a name that had little to do with a conscious identity. In other cases, the reason that 'my child would never get a job', or 'I don't want to be bigoted', were forwarded as the rationale for these decisions. Therefore, for some Catholics in Scotland, their Irish identity is a submerged one: it has become a social and political necessity to conceal their Irishness.

Confusion and argument over the ethnic identity of Catholics in Scotland is reflected elsewhere. The Irishness of the immigrant community is frequently denied or disparaged by some of its members. A number of Catholic newspapers periodically criticise Catholics who express Irishness, especially if it is seen as being at the expense of Scottishness. *The Scottish Catholic Observer* has a history of being critical of Catholics in Scotland who look to Ireland for identity. After one perceived criticism upon the Irish,[65] a number of readers answered back:

> Not for a long time have I witnessed the heritage of possibly 90% of Catholics in Scotland being so overtly dismissed and disregarded, if not indeed attacked. . . . Most of my own social experiences here in Scotland are still very much of an Irish kind.[66]

How close one wants to stay to one's roots is of course a personal decision and the ethnic Irish certainly do not need any lectures on 'valuing Irish ancestry above a Scottish birth'. It is hardly the function of a Catholic paper nor indeed of the Church to tell people where their loyalties should lie. Too many people in the Church in Scotland are ashamed of, and want to hide our Irish ancestry, this is why we never hear them decrying those of Italian or Polish descent who are not all that bothered about a Scottish birth either.[67] Arising from these arguments might be a contention that the idea of ghetto, that is, of being an anachronistic and parochial community, partly adds to the way Catholics in general and Irishness in particular, is viewed by much of the media. In this light, the media fulfils a role as a vehicle for assimilation rather than integration. It also means that the construction of Irish ghettos is more complex than simply being viewed as places where the Irish traditionally resided or psychologically lingered for too long.

Conclusion

The debate and discernible insecurity within parts of the Catholic community over ethnic, national, cultural identities and allegiances demonstrate an Irish identity which has been frequently negated and marginalised within the Scottish media, creating and resulting in negative self-perceptions amidst the immigrant community. Being of the Catholic Irish immigrant community and retaining Irish identity is a diversity which is often disparaged within the dominant Scottish, British and Protestant cultures. One academic who has addressed a number of these issues believes that the antagonism the Irish have faced amounts to racism as well as religious and social prejudice.[68] In recent decades antagonism towards the Irishness of the Catholic community has reflected that the content of the previous historical stereotype has been adapted resulting in the emphasis on genetic (i.e. facial and ape-like features) factors changing. This also allows the arguments in its favour to become more evasive and less encumbered by simplistic notions of genetic superiority, though its legacy remains in terms of the 'Irish joke' or 'thick Paddy' culture. Nonetheless, the form and content retain the consequence of identifying the minority as both a 'problem' and the originators of that 'problem'. As Finn says of anti-black prejudice in the USA, its present emphasis is on socio-cultural factors rather than on genetic.[69] In other words, racism, which had at its centre a conception of blacks as racially inferior, remains an aspect of life in the USA, but its form, relevance and force will be subject to conditions and circumstances. As a consequence, racist discourse has also changed.

In a related sense, social and religious issues in Scotland are often viewed as problematic: in turn, this 'problem' is viewed as sectarian, and many of the attributes of Catholic and Irish identity in Scotland

are judged through a discourse of sectarian concepts and language.[70]
In the mid-1990s a controversial television programme, 'Football,
Faith and Flutes', focused on aspects of Scottish Protestant and Irish
Catholic identity, showing parts of the ethnic and religious mosaic
which makes up Scottish society. The programme was manipulative
and discriminating in its use of political and religious symbolism.
Nevertheless, such programmes may have more to offer if, instead
of dominating this discourse, they came as part of an educational
package in Scottish schools and third level tiers of education. Used
as a source to reflect on bigotry, sectarianism and racism, and to
subsequently explore the true nature of these social characteristics,
such documentaries might have an educational value. Used as a
means to generalise and negatively reflect on cultures different from
those which dominate in Scotland, suggests a sub text arguing for
assimilation rather than integration.

    As a result of limited discourse, not only is Celtic Football Club
and its support regularly seen as sectarian but so also are Catholic
schools, Irish symbols in Scotland, cultural and political support for
a united Ireland and occasionally, the historically strong links between Catholics and the Labour Party. Therefore, the origins of
sectarianism in Scotland are frequently located with Irish Catholic
immigrants, in how they have contributed to change in the socio-
political make-up of the country, how they lack affinity for important
elements of Scottish and British nationhood and, how their institutions, beliefs and practices are impediments to Scottish progress.[71]
Throughout the history of the Irish in Scotland, Catholics from an
Irish background have shown their willingness to integrate into
Scottish and British society. In employment, sport, politics, and
regardless of the distinctions and varying emphasis, unequivocally
in education. In terms of the physical and economic ghetto which the
Irish historically experienced in Scotland, they have long left that
behind and fully integrated into Scottish life. However, as much of
the evidence relating to the Scottish media reflects, Irishness on the
part of the immigrant community has long proved problematic to
many people in Scottish society. As suggested, it is often the case that
the characteristics and nuances of this community are infrequently
discussed in Scotland without reference to sectarianism.

    A letter writer to the *Irish Post* believed that in referring to second,
third and fourth generation Irish people in Scotland, solely as Scots,
people are denying the heritage and identity of this community in
Scotland. Drawing a comparison with similar people in Australia and

the USA, he believed that they would usually be referred to as Irish, Irish Americans, Irish Australians and American- or Australian-born Irish.[72] A regular correspondent to *The Herald* believes that the Catholic faith is frequently distorted by 'a remarkably significant number of *Herald* feature writers, whilst contributions by Catholics, 'are relegated to the letters section.'[73] In 1996, a black footballer playing for Partick Thistle was sent off for two bookable offences, the initial incident for crossing himself in a Roman Catholic fashion: an action regarded as common and inoffensive in many other countries.[74] Recent research, contributing to the social history of a Roman Catholic Parish in Lanarkshire, showed that many Catholics are of the belief that the media is prejudiced against some of their cultural attributes and religious beliefs.[75]

In isolation, many of the instances noted are not socially, culturally or politically significant. Reviewing how the media historically and contemporaneously have characterised and portrayed Irish Catholics in Scotland does not mean that Scottish society is seriously divided or that Protestants, Catholics, or any other group retain one-dimensional identities. Like other societies, Scotland has a number of regional, class and racial features which contribute to wider issues of identity. In terms of the cultural, social and political dimensions of Scottish/British Protestantism and Irish Catholicism, people can have one-dimensional affinities, they can inhabit a multi-layered set of identities or they can lie at any point in-between. In addition, no point is fixed and is subject to a number of influences. Catholics, or indeed religion, are not primary issues for today's media. Indeed, via the media, much of the world's population can relate to a meaningful list of common cultural features.

Nevertheless, a review of Scotland's media treatment of the Irish in Scotland reflects a degree of continuity pointing towards a management of that community and manifestations of its distinctive identities. Essential stereotypes often remain whilst for many others, the Irish are treated as invisible. Sectarian labelling is a threat and an anxiety for many Catholics, both from within and from without their community. As Jim Sillars noted in the context of Catholic schooling in Scotland:

> The day Scotland is relaxed enough to recognise separate schools as the absolute right of a community which contributes to the enrichment of our national life and ethics, and is therefore not questioned as to its rights, Scotland will have arrived.[76]

There is little that is inevitable about Catholics of Irish origins in Scotland becoming culturally or self-identifiably Scottish or British, or about members of that community losing or even rejecting their Irishness. If more accurate conclusions are to be drawn on the Irish diaspora in Scotland we must consider background, circumstance and history. Studies focusing on the Irish in Scotland require a renewed research strategy and a more contemporary and enlightened approach: one less inhibited by an inability or unwillingness to attentively reflect on significant immigrant experiences.

NOTES

1. James Handley, *The Irish in Modern Scotland* (Cork, 1947).
2. *Ibid.*, p. 133.
3. *Ibid.*, p. 131.
4. *Ibid.*, p. 321.
5. This is a frequent theme throughout Tom Gallagher's *Glasgow: The Uneasy Peace* (Manchester, 1987).
6. *Ibid.*, p. 30. In addition, this is also an implication which emerges from qualitative material presently being collected for future publication.
7. *Ibid.*, pp. 18–19.
8. M. Vaughan, 'Faith, Hope and Chastity', *The Herald*, 19 September 1996.
9. J. Bradley, 'St. Mary's Parishioners Today: Schools, Moral Issues and Ireland', in T. Devine (ed), St. Mary's Hamilton: *A Social History 1946–1996* (Edinburgh, 1996).
10. S. Brown, 'Outside the Covenant: The Scottish Presbyterian Churches and Irish Immigration 1922–1938', *The Innes Review*, Vol. XLII, No. 1, 1991, pp. 19–45.
11. A. D. Gibb, *Scotland in Eclipse* (London, 1930).
12. Parliamentary Debates, *Hansard* 261, 22 November 1932.
13. See J. Bradley, *Ethnic and Religious Identity in Modern Scotland: Culture, politics and football* (Aldershot, 1995). Rangers' appeal means that their kit replica is the biggest seller in Britain with around 165,000 per year. A new kit jersey in fact sold 72,000 in its first week of release onto the market in May 1992 (*Evening Times* 11 May 1992). A prestigious report of 1996, carried out on the part of a number of large commercial organisations, not only reflects football in Britain as having a deep significance in popular culture but also recognises football as a rich source of income and advertising on the part of some of Britain's biggest businesses. Rising share prices for clubs who have joined the market and massive sales in football-related items also reflects this. Notably, this particular report marked Scotland out as the most soccer-influenced region in Britain. This conclusion largely arose from the ethno-religious content of the game in Scotland which raised play beyond a level of mere sport. Again, not surprisingly, much of this

aspect of the game manifests itself through support for Glasgow Rangers and Celtic: collectively known as the Old Firm. See *The Herald* 20 November 1996, p. 3 and *Daily Mail*, p. 23, 20 November 1996, p.23.

14. *Scottish Referee*, 3 February 1905.
15. See the *Sunday Mail*, article by Gerry McNee, 23 October 1994, p. 71. Also, *Radio Clyde* 13 January 1996.
16. B. Wilson, *Celtic: A Century With Honour* (Glasgow, 1988), p. 94.
17. S. Brown, *op. cit.*, p. 21.
18. Wilson, *op. cit.*, pp. 97–8.
19. *Sunday Mail*, 17 March 1991, p. 5.
20. *Daily Record* editorial, 13 October 1976, p. 2. Such was also the case in the late 1950s when Glasgow's *Evening Citizen* almost crashed financially after the publication of an article critical of the Orange Institution. 'A readership boycott ensued which caused such panic that Donald MacDonald, then a journalist on the paper, recalls that nothing was written about the Order in the Glasgow press for many years to come.' See Gallagher, *op. cit.*, p. 256.
21. *The Glasgow Herald*, 8 March 1935.
22. See also R. Finlay, 'Nationalism, Race, Religion and the Irish Question in Inter-War Scotland', *The Innes Review*, Vol XLII, No. 1, Spring 1991, pp. 46–67 and S. Brown, *op. cit.*, for other elements of this debate.
23. Gallagher, *op. cit.*, pp. 138–9.
24. Bradley, *op. cit.*, pp. 95–121.
25. *Daily Record*, 13 January 1989.
26. The Free Church's General Assembly in 1967 stated that education cannot be utterly secular.
27. *Free Church Monthly Record*, editorial, March 1986.
28. Author's interview with David Bryce.
29. Some of these identities found in Scottish football were reflected in a 1997 Rangers versus Aberdeen football match played at Ibrox stadium. After Rangers' first goal many of their fans began to sing 'Sweet Chariots' a song associated with the support of the English national side. The retort of the Aberdeen fans was to sing 'Flower of Scotland' which in turn elicited the Rangers' support's response of 'Rule Britannia' followed by 'God Save the Queen' (12 January 1997): thus reflecting British and Scottish identities mean different things to many of these supporters. During the following football season a league encounter witnessed Aberdeen fans responding to Celtic fans singing of the Irish national anthem with the unofficial Scottish national anthem, 'Flower of Scotland'. This was followed by the Aberdeen support chanting 'Could you go a chicken supper, Bobby Sands?', a reference to the significant Irish nationalist identity of the overwhelmingly Catholic Celtic support (20 September 1997).
30. W. Marshall, *The Bill Boys: A Concise History of Orangeism in Scotland* (Edinburgh, 1996).
31. In particular, see Gallagher, *op. cit.*, Bradley, *op. cit.*, and T. Devine (ed), *Irish Immigrants and Scottish Society in the Nineteenth and Twentieth Centuries* (Edinburgh, 1991).

32. *The Herald*, March 1990.
33. A number of people interviewed for this and other research spoke of an increasing confidence in displaying their Irishness in the 1990s.
34. *Irish Post*, 10 April 1993.
35. Reported in the *Irish Post*, 27 February 1993.
36. Reported by Donal MacAmhlaigh, *Ireland's Own*, 5 July 1985.
37. *Irish Post*, 25 August 1990.
38. Tom Shields, *The Herald*, 17 January 1996, p. 15.
39. *The Herald*, 9 January 1996, p. 21.
40. *The Herald*, 9 February 1996, p. 21.
41. Keith Waterhouse, *Scottish Daily Mail*, 23 September 1996, p. 12.
42. *The Herald*, 28 November 1995, p. 23.
43. John McLeod, *The Herald*, 20 September 1994, p. 21.
44. *The Herald*, 9 January 1997, p. 19.
45. *The Observer Scotland*, 10 June 1990, p. 8.
46. *The Herald Weekend Extra*, 14 December 1996.
47. *Scottish Daily Mail*, 1 November 1996, p. 8.
48. *Irish Post*, 9 November 1995, p. 8.
49. A. Davey, *Learning to be Prejudiced: Growing Up in Multi-ethnic Britain* (London, 1983).
50. Quoted by Michael Ignatieff, *The Observer*, 16 September 1990.
51. *The Guardian*, 9 October 1997, p. 8.
52. Such comment was particularly evident during the 1988 European Championships and the 1990 and 1994 World Cup Tournaments. For examples see *The Sun*, 27 June 1990, p. 6; *The Evening Times* 10 June 1994, pp. 58–59; *Daily Record* 16 June 1994, p. 35; and *The Irish Post* 12 December 1992, p. 33 and 27 March 1993, p. 35.
53. *Sunday Mail*, 22 May 1994, p. 59.
54. *Daily Record*, 16 June 1994, p. 55.
55. *Evening Times*, 21 June 1994, p. 55.
56. *Evening Times*, 10 June 1994, pp. 58–9.
57. *The Herald*, Sport section, 23 October 1995, p. 10.
58. *The Herald*, The Commentator, 8 September 1997, p. 29.
59. *Sunday Mail*, 4 February 1996, p. 4.
60. *Irish Post*, 9 July 1994, p. 8.
61. Adam Lively, *The Observer*, 16 September 1990.
62. *Irish Post*, 8 December 1990.
63. This in as much as the vast majority of Catholics in Scotland share a common background and often a common perception of features of their identity. Also, in an era of Americanisation, globalisation including the pervasiveness of popular television and sport, they will also share many cultural, social and political features with other immigrant groups, as well as the non-immigrant or more indigenous population. See Bradley, *op. cit.*.
64. Interview with staff member of *The Celtic View*, August 1994.
65. *Scottish Catholic Observer*, 19 October 1990, p. 7.
66. *Ibid.*, 2 November 1990, p. 10.
67. *Ibid.*, 16 November 1990, p. 7.

68. See G. Finn, 'Racism, Religion and Social Prejudice: Irish Catholic Clubs, Soccer and Scottish Society – 1 The Historical Roots of Prejudice', *The International Journal of the History of Sport*, Vol. 8, No. 1, 1991, pp. 72–95 and 'Racism, Religion and Social Prejudice: Irish Catholic Clubs, Soccer and Scottish Society – 11 Social Identities and Conspiracy Theories', *The International Journal of the History of Sport*, Vol. 8, No. 3, 1991, pp. 370–397.

69. *Ibid.*, p. 73.

70. See Bradley, *op. cit.*, pp. 176–197.

71. See W. Marshall. *op. cit.*, and T. Gallagher, *op. cit.* In a sports sense, further examples can be found in articles by *The Herald's* former main sports journalist, James Traynor, in which he argues for a 'united' support for the Scottish team. The appeal is essentially aimed towards Rangers fans' British Ulster-Loyalist culture and to Celtic fans' Irish identity. It is an appeal which exemplifies lack of understanding of religious and ethnic identity in Scotland. Irish identity and anti-Catholicism are construed as opposites and therefore both are condemned in the guise of 'neutrality' and 'unity'. Despite its claim (and elements of popular argument), Traynor fails to recognise cultural and ethnic diversity and in the process marginalises a large proportion of the Irish community by invalidating their identity. In addition, Rangers' fans' Britishness sits comfortably above or alongside that of Scottishness. A similar view was again expressed by the same writer (22 August 1994, Sports Section, p. 9) when he argued that Rangers in Europe in 1994 should be supported by everyone in Scotland. Everyone had to set aside their 'trivial little loyalties' while 'only the most bigoted' would not allow themselves to support Rangers. This view had been previously forwarded by Pat Kane of the pop group *Hue and Cry*. In this article, Kane, a former Catholic of Irish antecedents, viewed Glasgow Rangers, in their role as a potential European football power, as a fitting model of what a Scottish football club should be like. This argument also disparaged the Irishness of Celtic and their support. See *The Scotsman Weekender*, 'Why must Bhoys always be Bhoys?', 14 April 1990.

72. *Irish Post*, 6 March 1993.

73. *The Herald*, 30 November 1995, p. 18.

74. *The Herald*, 5 February 1996, p. 1; and *The Evening Times*, 5 February 1996, p. 36.

75. Bradley, *op. cit.*, pp. 83–121.

76. *Flourish*, May 1991.

6

CRISIS? WHAT CRISIS?: THE CATHOLIC CHURCH AND THE SECULAR PRESS IN SCOTLAND

Raymond Boyle

In an overview of Scottish national newspaper coverage of Catholic issues from 1996 through to early 1998, Boyle suggests that the Catholic Church in Scotland secures a substantial amount of coverage relative to its counterpart in England. While the main focus of the chapter examines the coverage and handling of the Bishop Wright affair in 1996, it places this against the backdrop of the changing Church–Media relationship which has been evolving over a number of years. He suggests that while investment in the development of more pro-active media strategies by the Church may improve aspects of their coverage, the increasingly market-driven press (in particular the tabloid market) treat the Catholic Church as an important Scottish institution but one which will be scrutinised and at times subject to rather dubious journalistic practices just like any other.

SHOCKING CHARGE AGAINST ANOTHER
ROMAN CATHOLIC PRIEST
News of the World, 1854

BISHOP'S NIGHT OF SIN AT THE HOLIDAY INN
The Sun, 16 September 1996

Introduction

From the perspective of the passive spectator, however, religion makes little sense. The media offer scandalous, simplified, conflict-ridden news stories about religion on the endless information carousel.

So wrote Madeleine Bunting, religious affairs correspondent of *The Guardian*, in *The Tablet*, 16 November 1996.

> . . . it seems as if the Church of Rome is lodged in the popular consciousness at the moment. Whether it's Cardinal Winning squaring up to Blair on abortion or priests caught in sex or abuse scandals, or popular comedies like *Father Ted* and *Ballykissangel* topping the TV ratings . . . Catholicism has certainly broken surface recently.

> Pat Kane, *The Herald*, 9 January 1997

While the Scottish Catholic Church's relationship with the media, in particular the tabloid press, plummeted to new depths during the Bishop Wright affair in 1996, in the parallel universe of television comedy drama, priests, bishops and Catholicism enjoyed a profile they had not had for years. South of the border, the English press were busy fussing over a number of high profile conversions (actual and apparently impending) to Catholicism among the 'great and the good'. Attention was focused on the Duchess of Kent, the then Government minister Ann Widdecombe, and on the glamour wing of the Church, the apparent imminent conversion of actress Liz Hurley. As *The Guardian* leader column of the 16 December noted: 'Catholicism in England has bizarrely enjoyed something of a honeymoon in the media in recent years.'

While the continued success of television programmes such as the BBC's *Ballykissangel* and Channel 4's *Father Ted* is partly explained by their location in differing parts of a mythical Ireland, it also serves to highlight the complex and at times contradictory relationships that exist between an institution such as the Catholic Church and a media serving differing audiences, for differing reasons through diverse channels of communication.

This chapter examines the current relationship between the Catholic Church in Scotland and the secular media. Attention is focused on the Scottish print media, both broadsheet and tabloid. Initially, a brief overview of the relationship between the press and the Church allows us to place the current situation in some context. The initial quote at the start of this chapter about the prosecution of a priest for rape in the 1850s alerts us to the need to take a slightly longer perspective on issues and trends often identified as being solely of the contemporary world. Even over a hundred years ago, the *News of the World* was talking about *another* Catholic scandal suggesting a history that predates even this incident.

Church and Media: Changing Institutions

Like other institutions, the changing relationship between the Catholic Church and the secular media reflects the broader political and social climate. It is unsurprising to find that for much of this century, a Church, representing a community subject to a sustained level of hostility, tended to find few friends among the secular press. With the influx of Catholic-Irish immigrants in the nineteenth century much of the hostility took on both an anti-Irish as well as anti-Catholic focus. For many in Protestant Scotland the terms Irish and Catholic became interchangeable (see chapter 5 by Bradley). What many such communities tend to do in such circumstances is produce their own media and speak among themselves. Thus in Scotland you found the development of a specifically Catholic press which flourished for much of this century.

Fr. Tom Connelly, Director of the Catholic Media Office, notes how 'Catholic news just didn't happen in the secular press. That was why at one stage you had in Scotland three Catholic newspapers'[1] Journalist Rennie McOwen argues that it was not really until the changes set in train by the second Vatican Council in the early to mid-1960s that Catholic issues began to get adequately and fairly reported in the Scottish secular press. He argues that news desks, while often still ill-informed, began 'to look upon Roman Catholicism as something less alien'. This in turn helped lead to both a decline and a change in the nature of the dedicated Catholic press, which McOwen suggests had, at a time when Catholics viewed the media with hostility, acted almost as 'propaganda papers in wartime' and 'served a very useful purpose.'[2] The Catholic Church went through a period where, while never subject to the devotional (and at others times scrutinising) coverage given to the affairs of the Church of Scotland (especially by the *Scottish Daily Express*),[3] it was given coverage by most Scottish newspapers, that was both relatively sympathetic and deferential.

This type of relationship was not of course unique to Scotland. Heneghan has commented on the universal deferential treatment given by the Irish media to the Catholic Church in Ireland,[4] a state of affairs which has radically altered since the late 1980s and early 1990s. Others such as Harries have also noted the shifting attitude of the media to religious institutions (be they Catholic or Protestant in Ireland) from one of deference to one of scrutiny and questioning.[5] Although Harries, a Church of Ireland Press Officer does note that: 'The "media" in Ireland, north and south, are mostly not as aggressive or intrusive as the British media, which leads us to enter into good relations with the journalists we deal with regularly.'[6] While in England, Madeleine Bunting argues that the end of defer-ence is one of the key features characterising Church-media rela-tions. She adds; 'There is a deep, pervasive cynicism in the culture towards any institution which projects itself as having, or as having inherited, a position of authority.'[7] In Scotland this change in the relationship between Catholic Church and secular media was noted by Lesley Riddoch, the then deputy editor of *The Scotsman*, during the Bishop Wright affair (discussed below) when she com-mented that: 'After years of fairly sympathetic, even reverential, coverage by the press, the charismatic Cardinal Winning got a terrible shock at the robust questioning that followed the church's ham-fisted handling of the Roddy Wright affair.'[8]

We are now going through a phase of Church-media relations which McOwen calls 'normality'. A recognition by the secular press, the broadsheets in particular, that the Churches in Scotland are important in the contributions that they make to a distinctive Scottish public agenda. Distinctive, in that they speak as institu-tions whose voices differ in their cultural origins from other churches in Britain and come with a specific Scottish inflection to their accent. A position, one could argue, not dissimilar to that in which the Scottish press find themselves. In addition, some jour-nalists, such as *The Scotsman*'s religious affairs correspondent Mi-chael Paterson, have argued that ironically as Church attendances have declined, religious affairs have become more high profile: 'With the Churches going into decline, they're having to address problems rather than simply drifting along.' From a journalistic point of view, Paterson also suggests that both Protestant and Catholic Churches 'have a more prominent place in [Scottish] public life' than exists in England, which is discussed in more detail below.[9] There remains a deeply rooted suspicion among some sections of the Catholic community, however small, that they are not always given fair treatment by the media. A letter to *The Herald* newspaper at the height of the Roddy Wright affair encapsulated such an attitude: '*The Herald* informs us that "for the hierarchy of the Catholic Church and the way it has handled this entire affair we feel less charity". Any reader of its regular columnists who touch on Catholicism may well ask, "What's New?"'[10]

Political Communication and The Catholic Media Office

Brian McNair and Bob Franklin have outlined the growth in the importance of political communication in an increasingly mediated society.[11] Political parties, public institutions and both commercial and voluntary organisations have all adapted to the need to use the media as a means of communicating with their various publics. The emergence of what McNair calls 'performance politics . . . in the process by which issues emerge in the public sphere to be debated, negotiated around and, on occasion, resolved'.[12]

While the development of media management techniques and strategies has been readily adopted by political parties and organisations with a political agenda, the Churches have been slower to embrace or recognise the importance of the media as a forum through which public agendas are increasingly set. Allied with this, the 1980s and 1990s have seen the increasingly commercially driven media readily extend its scrutiny into all areas of public life. Institutions such as the Monarchy and mainstream churches had previously viewed themselves as being immune from the treatment others in public life had been subjected to by an increasingly intrusive media. The Churches suffered from the combination of a loss of authority and deference in society and a period of competition which saw sections of the British press keen to expose scandal and sensationalism at every opportunity.[13] However it would be wrong to suggest that the Catholic Church was unaware of the importance of media.

One important element which emerged from the sea change in Catholic thinking promoted by the Second Vatican Council (1962–65) was the importance to the church of the modern media. As a result, media offices were set up by the Church throughout the world. In Scotland, the Catholic Media Office (CMO) was set up by a Catholic lay journalist, however the current Director of the CMO is a priest with journalistic experience, Fr. Tom Connelly. The main role of the office, based in Glasgow, is to liaise with the professional media, answer queries from them, and promote the Church's thinking on a range of issues, social as well as purely religious. The CMO however is understaffed and suffers from a serious lack of financial resources. The CMO is largely financed through Church collections and as Connelly notes 'that collection is the poorest we get. People know the Church has access to the media free in this country so Catholics and the Church in general don't see the need why they should pay for anything. So we don't have the resources we might have.'[14]

Despite the changes both in society and in the media already discussed, until recently (see below) a substantial investment in the resourcing and restructuring of the CMO has not appeared to be a priority among the Catholic hierarchy. Indeed what clearly emerges is the extent to which many in the hierarchy have viewed the media with suspicion, often ascribing an anti-Catholic bias as the reason for poor coverage rather than an inept understanding of how news and feature desks operate. This has often been the case despite the best efforts of those working within the CMO. In the past it has not been unknown for an Archbishop to refuse to circulate advance copies of an important speech to the media, the reason being that he claimed that he never gave the text of any speech to anyone until he had actually given it! As a result, much of their work involves being reactive to events rather than pro-active, something that Fr. Connelly regrets, and admits 'in developing a Church media strategy, to be pro-active is what really matters.'[15] Part of the problem stems from the Church's historical attitude to the secular media, which, despite the best efforts of certain individuals and Vatican II, has remained one based on a lack of understanding of how media operate in an increasingly competitive marketplace.

However, the coverage received by the Catholic Church during and after the Roddy Wright affair in September 1996, and the Church's handling of the affair itself, have exposed the inadequate nature of present practice and emphasised the need for the Church to rethink its relationship with the secular media in Scotland. The Wright affair came at a time when the Church was under greater scrutiny from the media than ever before, not least for its handling of a number of high profile cases relating to abuse by members of the Church. This situation mirrors the heightened degree of scrutiny the Catholic Church in Ireland now finds itself subject to following similar damaging allegations. No public institution should be afraid of public scrutiny, and indeed should welcome and encourage a dialogue with its various publics through differing media channels. However, this can prove difficult to achieve for an institution whose internal culture is based around hierarchy and deference.

Media–Church Relations: the Wright Affair

While the attention devoted by the media to the Wright affair and the role of the Catholic Church was extensive and displayed an intensity not often experienced by the Church, this does not mean that it is not worthy of close scrutiny. As is often the case, it is at times of extreme crisis that the fault lines and the tensions within and between institutions are exposed to public gaze. An examination of the relationship between the Church and the media during this intense period helps to expose some of the deeper attitudes and practices which operate between these institutions.

In retrospect, the angry reaction of Cardinal Winning to what he perceived as the 'Gestapo'-like tactics of the tabloid press during the Bishop Wright affair, tells us much about Catholic–Media relations. When the Cardinal, incensed by the insatiable appetite of the tabloids for even more salacious revelations regarding members of the clergy, went so far as to withdraw co-operation with the media, *The Scotsman* announced: **'Cardinal excommunicates tabloids'.**[16] In an open letter to all editors, Cardinal Winning stated:

> I wish to put recent events into perspective and to close our participation in the public debate about what is essentially a Church matter. The Church does not speak the same language as the media. . . . it is not the role, or the practice of the Church, to respond to media speculation. Therefore, we will no longer participate in satisfying the speculative demands of the media . . . During the past two weeks the Church has received an understanding press from most of the quality media, who have reported with dignity the difficulties faced by the Church in dealing with an extremely sensitive subject.[17]

Unfortunately for the Cardinal, as anyone who understands the work practices of contemporary tabloid journalists will realise, all that this action does is to intensify both the level of speculation which often passes for fact in some of these papers, as well as ensuring that journalists will dig even deeper in the hope of unearthing the next front page exclusive. This fact was not lost on a number of Catholics with journalistic experience, who suggested that the reaction among news desks to this move ranged from one of laughter to one of irritation. It also presented an image of the Catholic Church as both arrogant, and one which expected to be able to control the media.

Yet, as Professor Gordon Graham writing in *The Scotsman* noted: 'It is a fact that the British public, and hence the British press, traditionally has a great fondness for stories of "naughty" clergymen, and the further up the hierarchy that the offender has risen, the better.'[18] He continued by wondering why such a story, so obviously constituting part of the staple diet of the tabloid press, should also generate such extensive coverage in the broadsheet press. Madeleine Bunting of *The Guardian* noted: 'The coverage of religion in the print media almost invariably involves sex in one way or the other'. She went on to suggest that this trend, 'has been exacerbated in the English print media as the four daily broadsheets have taken on the agenda and style of tabloids, which thrive on sensation, novelty, conflict, scandal, simplicity and human interest. The fight for readers has led all four broadsheets in the same direction.'[19]

This argument is shared by Engel and Franklin who view this process as being accelerated by among other things: intense competition in all sectors of the print media marketplace for readers and the casualisation of journalistic labour.[20] To what extent, then, might one see the Bishop Wright coverage as providing us with another example of the erosion of the traditional division between the tabloid and the broadsheet news agenda? However, as is argued below, a close reading of the newspapers involved does identify flaws in this thesis, and alerts us to the dangers of simply grouping all the newspapers unproblematically together. This fact is acknowledged by the Cardinal himself who stated that the broadsheet press had 'reported with dignity the difficulties faced by the Church.'[21]

Before examining the background to the story which gripped the Scottish press during September 1996, it is worth briefly outlining some of the characteristics of this section of the media. The newspaper market in Scotland has become increasingly competitive over the last five years or so. The broadsheet market is occupied by the Scottish Media Group's Glasgow-based *Herald*, and the Edinburgh-located *Scotsman*. While Scotland's biggest selling daily newspaper remains the tabloid *Daily Record*, it has been subject to intense competition from its closest rival, *The Scottish Sun*.[22] Although from the same stable as its southern namesake, the Scottish version of this paper has, since 1992, attempted to tailor itself to the Scottish market, even to the extent of supporting the Scottish National Party in the 1992 general election, when the London-based *Sun* was still supporting the staunchly pro-unionist Conservative Party. In addition, developments in print technology have allowed most of the middle market papers such as the *Daily Express* and the *Daily Mail* to produce stronger Scottish editions for this market. However *The Herald, The Scotsman, Daily Record* and *The Scottish Sun* remain the most influential newspapers in Scotland, reflecting a political and social agenda which remains distinct from their southern rivals and counterparts.

The Runaway Bishop

The scandal which broke over the Church during early autumn 1996 centred on Roddy Wright, Bishop of Argyll and the Isles. Initially, it emerged that the Bishop had disappeared, fuelling speculation that he was suffering from extreme stress brought on by a family bereavement. However, it soon became clear that the Bishop had run off with Kathleen MacPhee, a divorcee and mother of two. As a result of intense media interest, the Church, fronted by Cardinal Winning, held a press conference at which they announced his resignation. The hierarchy, while aware that Wright had fathered a child by another woman, were unable to release this information owing to the need to protect the child's privacy. This was compounded by the failure of Wright himself to appear at the conference and take questions.

Later that week, in an exclusive interview with *BBC Scotland*, Joanne Whibley came forward to announce that she was the mother of Roddy Wright's 15-year-old son, Kevin. The media then attacked on two fronts. They criticised the Church, for what they viewed as an attempt to cover up past indiscretions, and protect the former Bishop, leading to wild speculation as to the number of women he may have been involved with. By the time the Church withdrew co-operation with the media, Roddy Wright had already been busy telling his story in an exclusive in the *News of the World*. From a media viewpoint, this story, with echoes of the Bishop of Galway scandal of 1992, contained all the ingredients needed for a classic newspaper tale: sex, a Bishop, scandal, intrigue, betrayal and a story which appeared to have the legs to run and run as each new revelation pushed the story forward. What then was the tenor of the coverage given to the affair in the Scottish press and the Church's role in it?

The Bishop, The Cardinal And The Tabloids

As mentioned earlier there is a long and ongoing fascination held by the tabloid press with the indiscretions of members of the clergy which is not confined solely to members of the Catholic Church in Scotland. To illustrate the point, as this chapter is being drafted there has been an ongoing story running on the front pages of the country's largest selling Sunday newspaper, the *Sunday Mail*, and its sister daily paper, the *Daily Record*. This alleges various misdemeanours, of both a criminal and sexual nature, have been carried out by an Episcopal priest. The story has been running from July to December

1997 with various lurid headlines and exposés. To view the Catholic Church as the sole victims of newspaper enquiries is plainly wrong.

The Bishop Wright story moved through various stages of development. Initially, it was about a runaway Bishop (fairly newsworthy for the tabloids), who it then emerged actually was running away with a woman (very newsworthy) and was then exposed as having had a son by a previous relationship (extremely newsworthy). Such was the news management of the story by the Church, that the media, and newspapers in particular, had a field day as each new development let the story unwind over a period tailor-made to satisfy the deadlines of an insatiable media.

The Church was also unfortunate in that it became the latest victim of the ongoing intense newspaper rivalry between the Scottish market leader, the *Daily Record,* and its challenger, the Scottish *Sun.* Both papers are locked in a titanic struggle to eat into each other's circulation figures. Something they believe will be achieved in part, by the production of exclusive stories (and no little carping at the authenticity of each newspaper's right to claim to speak for the Scottish people). While Scotland has had competition in the tabloid market place before, it fails to match the intensity with which this current phase is being waged. This phase was initiated in 1992, when a serious financial investment was made by News Corporation in *The Scottish Sun* (it also came out in support of the Scottish National Party) in an attempt to dislodge the *Record* from its position of prominence within the lucrative Scottish market.

Both papers threw considerable resources at the story. Between the 16 and 23 September when the story was at its height (or the 'mad week' as some journalists called it) the *Daily Record* had at least fourteen journalists working on differing aspects of the story, while *The Sun* deployed at least eleven. The nature of the coverage in both papers followed a very similar pattern of development, suggesting a clear tabloid structure into which such stories are placed. The *Record's* bizarre splash of '**I LOVE YOU FATHER STARSKY**' ran the risk of confusing its younger readers by making reference to a 1970s American police series *Starsky and Hutch,* based on the premise that Bishop Wright looked like one of its stars, Paul Michael Glaser. Inside, the four-page coverage focused on the apparent breaking of his celibacy vows by the Bishop. The Editorial comment was broadly sympathetic however, calling for the Church to move with the times, asking 'should we pillory a good man for a very human flaw?'[23]

This sentiment was echoed in *The Scottish Sun* editorial (*The Scottish Sun Says*) which commented: **Church Living in the Past**. It called on the Church to rethink celibacy rules, claiming that the Bishop had been pilloried 'Because he is a normal man who has fallen into a perfectly natural relationship with a woman.'[24] Interestingly, *The Sun* revealed something of its complex English/ Scottish identity – something on which the *Daily Record* is quick to attack its competitor – by more or less restating this position calling for the end of celibacy again the following day under a *Sun Says* editorial (no sign of Scottish in its editorial masthead) which appeared to be lifted straight from its English edition. Both papers set up phone lines on which readers could contact them if they had spotted the Bishop, with the *Record* running a phone poll asking readers if priests should be allowed to marry (86% Yes, 14% No). The *Record* also brought a national dimension to the story by commenting on an apparent difference of opinion between Cardinal Hume in England, who seemingly suggested that change could be on the way regarding the issue of celibacy, and the hard-line view of Cardinal Winning. The paper concluded: 'For once, Record readers are on the English side – by an overwhelming majority of 86 per cent of our poll.'[25]

Initially, the coverage in both papers centred around attacks on the Church's demand that priests remain celibate, although one could speculate on the extent to which the tabloid press may have a degree of self-interest in maintaining the status quo given the amount of copy such stories generate. However, the Church was also praised for its actions in other areas. The *Record* was generous to the Church on its handling of another issue that has dogged it in recent times, that of allegations of abuse by priests. On Thursday 19 September its editorial stated:

> **The problem of pervert priests in the Catholic Church has recently been eclipsed by sexual lapses of a more understandable nature.** But the Church has shown courage by bringing it into the open. Instances of abuse culminated in a recent damaging case that provoked allegations of a cover-up. Now, by addressing the issue so openly, the Catholic hierarchy shows it is moving with the times. **There will be many who wish it would give such consideration to the question of celibacy.**[26]

When BBC Scotland broke the news that Bishop Wright had a son, the mood of the media, and the tabloids in particular, changed. From

Friday 20th September, the *Daily Record* headlined their coverage with **Sins of the Father**, while *The Sun* used the more tabloid vernacular of **Scandal of the Bonking Bishop**. While much of the coverage focused on 'A Church in crisis' the issue of celibacy disappeared as the tabloids went on the offensive, attacking both the Bishop and the Church hierarchy for what they viewed as a cover-up. When Cardinal Winning had held a press conference earlier in the week, he did not mention the Bishop's previous relationship nor that he had a son although he had knowledge of both. Joan Burnie in the *Record* under the headline: **MATCH MADE IN HELL**, attacked both the hypocrisy of the Bishop and the woman he had run off with, Kathleen MacPhee, but also alleged a Church cover-up adding that 'the higher echelons of the Catholic Church cannot, and must not, absolve themselves. They, too, are guilty of hypocrisy.'[27] While *The Sun* led a more personalised attack on the integrity of Cardinal Winning:

Cardinal must pay for sins:

'Cardinal Winning's face should be as red as his robes this morning . . . the Cardinal in trying to save the Church's already tarnished reputation – deliberately deceived the entire Catholic establishment. *He must now stand up and be counted for his sins . . . the same way Bishop Wright did.'*[28]

Aside from the fact that withholding information may or may not be viewed as 'a sin', and that Bishop Wright did not exactly voluntarily accept his responsibilities, the attack on the Cardinal was made clear – even if how exactly one makes a Cardinal 'pay for his sins' was not.

At this juncture the story took on a dynamic of its own, with both the *Record* and *The Sun* happy to mix fact and speculation regarding how many other women the Bishop had been involved with and how many other priests might be in similar situations. In particular, *The Sun* now displayed all the trademarks of this style of door stepping journalism. Numerous quotes were attributed to 'a friend', 'a close friend', 'a family friend', 'a close family friend', 'a neighbour' 'pals said', 'Catholic sources' and so on and so forth. The sympathetic editorials disappeared as *The Sun's* editorial of 23rd September, **So Selfish** made clear: *'Two words sum up the bonking bishop: Selfish pig.'*[29] At the same time the Church appeared to adopt a siege mentality to its media relations with the *Record* noting: '**Bosses quiet on claims:** The Catholic Church stayed tight lipped last night over the latest revelations regarding Roddy Wright. The highest Churchmen . . . were unavailable for comment.'[30] There is little doubt, that the Cardinal's attempt to end 'the public discussion' by not speaking with the press was counterproductive. The information vacuum was simply filled by ever more speculative material.

Within this storm of accusations and attacks on the Church's handling of the affair, there were also calmer moments of more considered and rational comment from the tabloids. The *Daily Record* allowed a parishioner from Oban to defend the Church in an open space article which interestingly began by stating that: 'Decent people have had enough of the gutter press, so I say to the media; "You are not welcome in our town . . .".'[31] While *The Sun* columnist Jim Sillars under the headline: **A FEW GOOD MEN**: painted a sympathetic picture of a Church let down by one man, but containing many doing good and important work, he suggested that 'Tom Winning is a religious leader, not a politician served by spin doctors. He gave us an honest shambles. . . . Scots Catholics have reason for disappointment in one man, but have a lot to be proud of in their Church of many good people.'[32]

The exclusive confessional interview given by Roddy Wright to the *News of the World* on the 22nd September added the final ingredient to a classic tabloid tale of sex, power, deceit and exposure. While on this occasion it had been public figures in the Catholic Church who had been subjected to trial by tabloid, in many respects they were being treated no differently from others in positions of authority in society. Something, which while perhaps unpalatable for the Church, simply reflected a broader shift in the media's relationship with religious institutions.

The view from the broadsheets

> In just one week the Catholic Hierarchy in Scotland has become entangled in as much carnality as might be found in Graham Greene.
>
> Anne Simpson, *The Herald*, 21 September, 1996

It can appear at times that the journalistic boundaries between the popular and the broadsheet press are no longer as rigid or as clearly defined as they may have once been. However, there is little doubt that a reading of both *The Scotsman* and *The Herald* newspapers' coverage of the Bishop Wright affair show clear differences in the tone and style of their journalism to that which was to be found in the above tabloids. Michael Paterson of *The Scotsman* noted that as a journalist working within the broadsheet market, he was put under no pressure to distort or take sides in the story, a practice often associated which the tabloid sector.[33] Paterson also noted that broadsheets were not under pressure to simplify Church issues for a non-Church readership with all the attendant dangers of 'caricaturing people in the religious community.'[34]

Initially, the story was covered with a degree of sympathy towards Bishop Wright, with uncomplicated reporting of the facts leading to his resignation. In a leader, *The Scotsman* called for: **Compassion for Bishop Wright** and asked that the Church face up to the problems that enforced celibacy appeared to be having for many priests.[35] In the light of what was to unfold, *The Herald's* front page headline was a rather misleading one: **Bishop quits to end Church crisis.**[36] However, as the revelations began, the tone of the coverage changed as more and more coverage was devoted in both papers to the emerging scandal, and the fallout that it would have among the Catholic community in Scotland.

In general, the reporting in the Scottish broadsheets of the affair was either factual or centred around informed comment. Indeed a number of common themes emerged in both papers' coverage. Throughout, there was a continual concern both with the undermining of the Church's authority and the need to address the validity of the continuation of celibacy among priests. Parallels were often drawn with the Bishop Casey of Galway scandal in 1992. Typical were pieces such as: **Questions the Church can't avoid**: 'Just as the Bishop Casey scandal rocked the moral authority of the Catholic Church in Ireland, the revelation that Bishop Roddy Wright had an illegitimate child who he helped to support may well have longer term implications.'[37] Again, in the same edition a piece by the Irish-based John Cooney carried the headline: **Paternity claim mirrors case of Irish bishop**. Both newspapers focused a good deal of their attention on the handling of the crisis by the Catholic Church itself, and gave much attention to Cardinal Winning's role in the affair. After initial sympathy, *The Scotsman* was unhappy both with the Bishop and the Catholic hierarchy: **Tribulations of a turbulent priest:** 'The unpleasant fact is that Father Wright lied to his superiors. The equally unpleasant fact is that the Catholic church in Scotland has handled the matter with at best clumsiness, at worst an apparent succumbing to the deeply entrenched instinct for a cover-up.'[38]

The charge of cover-up centred around the press conference earlier in the week at which the Cardinal had announced that the Bishop had resigned. When it later transpired that at this conference the Cardinal had known of the existence of Roddy Wright's son – something the Bishop had admitted to the Cardinal over the previous weekend – the mood towards the Cardinal became hostile. The Church clearly felt it could not disclose this information without the prior consent of all involved, and while Roddy Wright would claim in the *News of the World* of 22nd September that he gave this at the weekend meeting, this is something that the Church strongly denies.

The attacks on the Cardinal from the tabloids find echoes in *The Herald's* leader, although it is careful not to mention him by name.

> **PRICE OF LIVING A LIE:**
> *Cover-up has damaged Catholic Church:*
> For the hierarchy of the Catholic Church and the way in which it has handled this entire affair we feel less charity. . . . The first instinct of the Church in situations of this sort is to cover them up. This is a most serious misjudgement.[39]

However in an apparently contradictory stance, *The Herald* stated in a report elsewhere in the same edition that ' . . . commentators agree that the Church was not in a position to disclose the confidential information that Bishop Wright had an illegitimate son.' More surprisingly, Ron McKenna conducted a sympathetic interview with the Cardinal in that same paper the next day in which he noted that, while the Cardinal knew of the Bishop's son at the press conference, 'there was no possibility of him making it public.' The article entitled: **Winning faces up to the flak,** also documented some of the pressures the Cardinal had been under from sections of the press, noting how the police were called to move on journalists from his under siege home.[40]

There is little however in the way of the speculation and flyers that characterises much of tabloid reporting once a story starts to snowball. While *The Herald* noted that **Church is Braced for More Scandal,**[41] and *The Scotsman* hinted at more revelations,[42] neither newspaper printed detailed claims. Their coverage also lacked the use of extensive quotes attributed to anonymous sources which so regularly make up the bulk and substance of tabloid stories. Both papers tended to report on-the-record comments from senior

Church figures and commentators both in Scotland and in Rome. There were also a number of pieces in both papers which attempted to place some of the issues within a broader context, and provide more thoughtful and rational comment. Articles by Anne Simpson and James MacKay in *The Herald* and Gordon Graham and Rennie McOwen in *The Scotsman* are some examples of such writing. Over-all, then, what lessons should the Church take from the coverage it received during the Wright affair?

The Church and (the Lack of) Media Strategies

The latest story concerning Bishop Wright is a public relations disaster for the Church . . .

The Herald 20 September, 1996

A number of issues regarding the Church's media relations emerged from the Roddy Wright affair and the attendant media circus. It highlighted to those in the hierarchy of the Church the need to rethink their strategies regarding media relations, and strengthened the hand of those who had been advocating change. The Catholic Media Office now hopes to have a lay journalist in place by 1998, overseen by a Director of the Office who will remain a Priest. This process, of what within the police service media relations is called 'civilianisation',[43] was also strengthened by the appointment of former ‛Scottish television reporter, Ronnie Convery, to advise and to carry out research for the Cardinal on social issues as well as to help liaise with the media. Of course this is not the first time that lay journalists have been involved with the Church. Historically however, it has been difficult for lay media experts to be allowed to have any input into policy decisions within such a hierarchical Church.

Despite the protestations of the Church, Convery's appointment is a clear recognition of the poor handling by the Church, and Cardinal Winning, in particular, of the Wright affair which was allowed to spiral out of control when an initial press conference with the Bishop in attendance would have taken the impetus out of the story, a point which in hindsight is acknowledged by individuals within the Church. In an editorial, *The Scotsman* welcomed the appointment of Convery, but noted how: 'The Catholic Church in Scotland has in recent months become so detached from earthly reality, including the views of its faithful, that it will take much effort and wisdom to restore its credibility.[44]

There is also the extent to which much of the Church's media relations are driven by the charismatic Cardinal Winning. In media relations' terms there are clear advantages in having a single authoritative voice speaking on behalf of an organisation (a point recognised by a number of journalists who come into contact with the Catholic Church). However, in all organisations, religious or secular, it is important that that person takes advice from the media advisors close to him, something which appears not to have happened in the handling of the Roddy Wright affair. While the Cardinal is respected by many journalists, they also note that this does not mean that he is expert in handling the media.

The Church must realise that the media is crucial to communication not simply with the Catholic community, but also with the broader Scottish public. To simply speak to the faithful is no longer an option for such an important Scottish institution at such an historical juncture in the history of Scotland (see chapter 3). Another issue relates to the danger of over-centralisation and the stifling of democratic debate within the Church. Journalists commented on the extent to which much of what is happening at grass-roots level in the Catholic Church goes unreported owing to the hierarchical structure of the Church. All media enquiries are referred to the Catholic Media Office, which has tended to focus issues through the eyes of the Bishops' Conference of which Cardinal Winning is the President. The Church needs to develop structures which facilitate both a flow of information from the grassroots to the hierarchy, but also understand the workings of news and feature desks in the Scottish local and national media which are always on the look out for stories. Despite the temporary collapse of Church–media relations during the Wright affair, what becomes clear on a broader examination of secular press coverage is the relatively wide-scale reporting of Catholic issues which is already taking place.

Reporting the Church

While the Bishop Wright affair and its continuing fallout dominated much coverage relating to the Catholic Church during 1996, it would be wrong to suggest it was the only type of coverage. The affair was crucially important because it marked the end of doubts – if any existed – that the Catholic Church was now subject to the degree of media scrutiny enjoyed (if that is the right word) by most other Scottish institutions. Thus issues relating to the Church – such as cases of abuse – are widely reported, as are the Church's responses in dealing with these problem. The danger of the Wright affair, from a media relations' viewpoint, is that it could mark a return to the siege mentality which has dominated much of the Church's thinking regarding media relations throughout the twentieth century. The futility of any such retreat seems to have permeated, if not all, then considerable elements of the Church's hierarchy. As the commercialisation of the media continues apace, burying your head in the sand and ignoring the media simply is not an option.

Indeed, what emerges from a reading of the Scottish broadsheet press during 1996 and 1997 is both the considerable coverage given to issues relating to the Catholic Church, and the relatively fair shake down the Church enjoys in the rough and tumble world of the media marketplace. *The Scotsman*, in particular, provided broad coverage on a number of fronts relating to Catholic matters. The ongoing rapprochement between the Church of Scotland and the Catholic Church is given considerable coverage by the paper throughout the year through articles by its religious affairs correspondent such as: **Churches unite for millennium**[45]

While not enjoying the profile one might have expected, debates surrounding the future of Catholic education can be found particularly in the broadsheets. Among them is a thoughtful and interesting piece by Tariq Tahir from *The Scotsman* which focused on the increasing interest being shown by non-Catholics in attending Catholic schools:

> Church's Valued Approach
> Which school did you go to? For years, this simple question has served thousands of Scots as a relatively foolproof way to find out a person's religion. If it has a Saint in the name, you can be pretty sure you are not dealing with a Rangers fan. However, the reliability of this universal school test is being slowly diminished as Catholic school headteachers across Scotland say they are receiving an increasing amount of interest from non-Catholic families.[46]

Within the political arena, although the Church may view this as simply speaking out on moral/ethical issues, Cardinal Winning in particular generated extensive coverage with his clashes with the Labour leader Tony Blair over abortion (articles and news stories running through October 1996 – January 1997). With other Church pronouncements on issues such as poverty and homelessness the Cardinal found himself in broad support of the Labour leader (see chapter 3 by Peter Lynch). Overall, the tone and style of the reporting appear fair, and while the comment from columnists such as Jack McLean, Michael Kelly and Pat Kane at *The Herald* may be negative, positive, humorous, intelligent or intelligible it remains exactly that: comment. The aim of such writing is to entertain, annoy and inform readers, while generating both debate and, ideally, a bulging letters bag to the editor.

The tabloid press of course operate to a different news agenda. They tend to focus on stories with a human interest angle, and engage in a degree of hyperbole and speculation that is not found to the same extent in the broadsheet press. In Scotland, this agenda is broadly applicable to all the daily national papers outwith *The Herald* and *The Scotsman*. However, it is also the case that at particular moments the tabloids will give broader coverage to specific Catholic issues. Recent examples of this have been clearly evident around the Church's outspoken condemnation of abortion. In particular, Cardinal Winning's attack in the run-up to the last election of the Labour Party's stance on the issue generated much coverage in the tabloids. The *Daily Record* ran a centre page, double spread, news Focus special: '**Holy War**: The abortion row that threatens to split the Catholic church and Labour'[47] which focused on the attitudes of individual Catholics and Catholic families to the Church's stance. However, this type of longer, more thoughtful feature is not particularly typical of the treatment of Catholic issues, which are more likely not to be covered in any great depth by this section of the press. So while religious issues are not covered in any detail, the tabloid press will carry Church-related stories as long as they are pitched towards their 'softer' news agenda.

Conclusion: The State of Play

For such an old institution the Roman Catholic Church in Scotland has acquired that most modern of afflictions: a crisis of public relations.

Leader comment, *Scotland on Sunday*, 25th January 1998

While the decline in general Church attendance continues both in Scotland and England, proportionally attendance remains higher in Scotland at about 15% compared to 10% south of the border. From a reading of the broadsheet press, both UK national and Scottish, it is also clear that the main Churches in Scotland enjoy a greater degree of exposure and coverage in the Scottish press than their English counterparts do in the UK nationals.[48]

In part this is explained by the size of the country, but according to Michael Paterson, religious affairs correspondent with *The Scotsman*, it also reflects the greater prominence enjoyed in Scottish public life by the Churches, both Protestant and Catholic, than their counterparts south of the border. This position is also echoed from within the Catholic Church, where the Director of the CMO, Fr. Tom Connelly argues: 'There is still a consciousness about religious issues in Scotland which there simply isn't in England. While people may not be practising, they are aware of religious issues.'[49] Indeed, given the specific Scottish agenda within which they operate, the Catholic Church will often liaise more closely with their colleagues in the Church of Scotland than with their English counterparts. However, despite this situation it should also be noted that apart from *The Scotsman* there are few, if any, dedicated religious affairs correspondents within the secular press. The increasing casualisation of journalistic labour requires journalists to wear a multitude of hats, a process that is particularly evident in the tabloid section of the market.

In the 1990s, the Catholic Church is viewed by the Scottish media as an important voice within Scottish public life, as an institution whose voice should be heard in a public forum, but also subject to both scrutiny and questioning in a manner that a hierarchical religious organisation can sometimes be uncomfortable with. This can be particularly difficult for a religious organisation such as the Catholic Church in Scotland given the turbulent history of Catholicism in this country. Within the CMO, there is a view that any poor press received by the Church is motivated and driven, not by an anti-Catholic bias, but rather the increasing competition from market forces in the media marketplace and a broader decline in journalistic standards.

As is increasingly the case in Ireland, the media now view the Catholic Church as simply a public institution, albeit an important one. As Scotland enters a period of substantial constitutional change there is no doubt that the Scottish Catholic Church has an important role to play in defining Scottish public culture and debate. This role will increase with the development of a Scottish parliament committed to reflecting all shades of opinion within Scottish society. Writing in *The Observer*, this point was recognised recently by the former editor of *The Herald,* Arnold Kemp. In the run-up to the publication of the White Paper on a devolved Scottish Parliament, it emerged that Tony Blair had intervened to ensure that policy on abortion should remain in Westminster and not in Edinburgh. According to Kemp, an astute observer of Scottish affairs, the reason for this was that' . . . Blair and the [Labour Party] leadership have been intimidated by Cardinal Winning who has on occasions implicitly linked the abortion issue to the support Labour traditionally enjoys from Catholics, particularly in the west of Scotland. Last October he launched a personal attack on Blair, accusing him of 'washing his hands' of the issue. Later he reaped a rich media harvest when he offered to remunerate mothers who declined an abortion'.[50] This clearly demonstrates that the Church, through a strong focal point such as Cardinal Winning, can use the media to flex its political muscles. However, as Rennie McOwen has argued: 'Of all the problems facing the Catholic church today, the issue of open and frank debate. . . . and how it is reflected in the internal and secular media, is all important. . . . Secular public opinion about the church is an essential input for modern evangelisation.'[51]

As we have noted above, the Catholic Media Office suffers from both underfunding and understaffing, a situation which may now be partly being addressed as a result of the fallout from the Wright affair. More difficult to change may be an autocratic and hierarchical Church culture, suspicious of change, and resistant to dissent and debate. The ongoing revelations, and adverse publicity, about allegations of child abuse in Catholic run children's homes between the 1930s and 1970s continues into 1998. *Scotland on Sunday*, in a leader quoted above, noted how for too long the Church was quite happy to deal with any problems 'in house', when public action was necessary. Any change in that culture must extend beyond any simple adaptation of a more positive public relations strategy.

Having spent much of the last twenty years or so emerging from a media ghetto (both real and imaginary), and taking its place – at times however uncomfortably – within the mainstream Scottish media, there can be no return to the comforts and constraints of ghetto life. On issues such as education, poverty and sectarianism, when the Church speaks publicly, the media are quick to give these thoughts a wider audience. This of course does not mean that any pronouncements are not subject to criticism within that media coverage, but for any institution to expect anything less smacks of naiveté. Of deeper concern for the Church should be the gulf which exists between the hierarchy and many grassroots Scottish Catholics on core areas of dogma. This is a point emphasised by the failure of the Church to convince large sections of Catholic voters that the abortion issue should take precedence over support for the Labour Party at the 1997 general election. Without change and adaptation by the Church, no combination of media strategies and positive press coverage, however welcome and helpful, will necessarily begin to bridge this gap.

Acknowledgements

I would like to thank all the people who spoke with me about the issues discussed above and, in particular, Rennie McOwen, Tom Connelly and Michael Paterson.

NOTES

1. Interview with the author, 27 June 1997.
2. Interview with the author, 2 July 1997.
3. T. Gallagher, 'The Press and Protestant Popular Culture: A Case Study of the Scottish Daily Express', in G. Walker and T. Gallagher (eds), *Sermons and Battle Hymns: Protestant Popular Culture in Modern Scotland* (Edinburgh, 1990).
4. P. Heneghan, 'The Church and the Media: Can They be Friends?', paper presented at *The Churches and the Media in Modern Ireland*, All Hallow's College Summer School, Dublin, 30 June to 4 July 1997.
5. L. Harris, 'The Church and the Media: Servants not Friends', paper presented at *The Churches and the Media in Modern Ireland*, All Hallow's College Summer School, Dublin, 30 June to 4 July 1997.
6. *Ibid*, p. 6.
7. M. Bunting, 'God's Media Image', *The Tablet*, 16 November 1996.
8. *The Scotsman*, 4 October 1996.
9. Interview with the author, 26 June 1997.
10. *The Herald*, 21 September 1996.
11. B. McNair, *An Introduction to Political Communication* (London, 1995) and B. Franklin, *Packaging Politics: Political Communications in Britain's Media Democracy* (London, 1994).
12. B. McNair, *op. cit.*, p. 188.
13. M. Engel, *Tickle the Public: One Hundred Years of the Popular Press* (London, 1996).
14. Interview with the author, 27 June 1997.
15. *Ibid*.
16. *The Scotsman*, 27 September 1996.
17. Open letter from Cardinal Winning, Catholic Media Office, 27 September 1996.
18. *The Scotsman*, 2 October 1996.

19. Bunting, *op. cit.*
20. Engel, *op. cit*, and B. Franklin, *Newszak and the News Media (London, 1997)*.
21. *The Scotsman*, 27 September 1996.
22. Scottish-based newspapers comfortably outsell the London-based nationals in the Scottish market. The broadsheet Scottish market is dominated by the Glasgow-based *The Herald* (cir. 104, 844) and the Edinburgh-based national *The Scotsman* (cir.78, 691). *The Herald* is part of the Scottish Media group which also owns *Scottish Television* which holds the ITV franchise for the Scottish central belt. These figures are trade estimates provided by John Menzies and published in *The Drum*, September, 1997. The *Daily Record* is Scotland's largest selling newspaper with a circulation of almost 690,000 (Jan–Jun, 1997). During this same period its main rival in the popular market, the Scottish edition of *The Sun* had a circulation of 392,000. These figures are trade estimates provided by John Menzies and published in *The Drum*, September, 1997. For an overview of the position of the Daily Record in Scottish life see P. Meech, 'The Daily Record: A Century of Success and Neglect', *Scottish Affairs*, No.13, Autumn, 1995. There is no love lost between the papers, and they quite often openly attack the credibility of the other. For example on the 21 September 1996 *The Sun* announced, '*The Sun* 20p: Why pay 8p more for a load of lies attack', while the *Daily Record* (23 September, 1996) attacks its rival as 'Second rate and a downmarket English-based newspaper.'
23. *Daily Record*, 16 September 1996.
24. *The Sun*, 16 September 1996.
25. *Daily Record*, 18 September 1996.
26. *Daily Record*, 19 September 1996.
27. *Daily Record*, 20 September 1996.
28. *The Sun*, 20 September 1996.
29. *The Sun*, 23 September 1996.
30. *Daily Record*, 23 September 1996.
31. *Daily Record*, 24 September 1996.
32. *The Sun*, 24 September 1996.
33. For an overview of tabloid practices in Britain see P. Chippendale and B. Horrie, *Stick It Up Your Punter* (London, 1990), and Engel, *op. cit.*
34. Interview with the author, 26 June 1997.
35. *The Scotsman*, 17 September 1996.
36. *The Herald*, 17 September 1996.
37. *The Herald*, 20 September 1996.
38. *The Scotsman*, 21 September 1996.
39. *The Herald*, 20 September 1996.
40. *The Herald*, 21 September 1996.
41. *Ibid.*
42. *The Scotsman*, 21 September 1996.
43. P. Schlesinger and H. Tumber, *Reporting Crime: The Media Politics of Criminal Justice* (Oxford, 1995), pp. 130–6.
44. *The Scotsman*, 4 January 1997.

45. *The Scotsman,* 17 January 1997.
46. *The Scotsman,* 12 December 1996.
47. *Daily Record,* 10 June 1997.
48. The UK national broadsheets examined during 1996 were *The Guardian, The Times* and *The Independent.*
49. Interview with the author, 27 June 1997.
50. *The Observer,* 13 July 1997.
51. R. McOwen, 'Media Epiphany of the Faithful', *The Scotsman,* 8 November 1996.

7

YOU ARE THE PEOPLE, WHO ARE WE? – SOME REFLECTIONS ON THE IRISH CATHOLIC CONTRIBUTION TO SCOTTISH SOCIETY

Patrick Reilly

Through analysis of a variety of poets and writers, in addition to Scotland's most famous living comedian, Reilly traces the Catholic and Irish influences in Scottish popular culture. The contrasting perspectives of Thomson and McDiarmid towards the Irish and the Scots; the enduring impact of Catholicism found in the work of (very) lapsed Catholics such as Billy Connolly and Tom Leonard; and the role of roots, community identity and Catholicism in the writing of William McIlvanney, form the core of the chapter through discussion of the legacy of religion in the work of some of the most prominent figures in contemporary Scottish culture. Finally, the chapter seeks to place the emphasis on a changing community and the difficulty in categorising cultural figures from the Catholic and/or 'Irish' community in Scotland when their contributions and attitudes to religion, community and society are so varied: evidence that the Catholic community has become part of the mosaic that is Scottish society.

Introduction

The most important single event for the development of Scottish Catholicism took place in Ireland. The famine of 1845 led to an Irish influx into Scotland and to this day the country bears the imprint of this migration – that distant agricultural disaster continues to mould our character and shape our destiny, leaving its mark on almost every area of our corporate and cultural lives. The newcomers had to be tough to survive: destitute, ill-educated, despised and feared as Romish interlopers, they cultivated a defiant solidarity, a tribal

sense of kinship, as the sole means of preserving cultural and religious identity in an environment that often was, and was always
perceived to be, hostile – 'the black country with the cold heart', as
Patrick MacGill, earliest fictional recorder of the immigrant experience, described Scotland.[1] The native reaction to the intruders was
as understandably predictable; when the scourge of wandering,
famishing Irish began, so, too, did the fear that Glasgow would
become a city of paupers and the plague. The Irish were a triple
threat: to native employment, to the poor rates, to community health.
They were accused of their afflictions and found guilty of being
victims. When the cholera epidemic of 1848 ravaged Glasgow, bad
sanitation and the worst overcrowding in Europe were responsible,
but, the Irish being the principal sufferers, it was easy to identify
them as the agents of the plague – death proved complicity. They
were regarded as improvident, intemperate and unreasonable, the
mammoth task of civilising them intensified to despair by one last
insuperable obstacle – they were not simply savages, but Romanised
savages, and in their advent the Protestant Scots descried a plot to
annex Scotland as a papist colony.

I have written elsewhere about the experience of the post-Famine
immigrants as reflected in the literature produced by and about
them.[2] My present intention is to describe our current situation in
the light of the radical changes now occurring both within Scottish
society and Scottish Catholicism. The so-called Irish Catholic contribution to Scottish culture is, today at least, a much more complex
affair than was previously envisaged, whether by those who deplored the coming of the Irish as a disaster or those who celebrated
it as a deliverance. One way of highlighting this complexity is to set
it against the over-simplistic pronouncements of earlier commentators, and to this end I wish to contrast two totally opposed views of
the newcomers, one violently hostile, the other surprisingly sympathetic, both advanced at a time when Scotland was still trying to
come to terms with their arrival on our shores.

The Irish in Scotland – Annexation Versus Cultural Liberation

Caledonia, or the Future of the Scots, written by George Malcolm Thomson and published in 1927, illuminates certain attitudes towards the
Irish Catholic element in the Scottish population prevalent among
leading Presbyterian thinkers in the first third of the century and still
encounterable today.[3] Two years after the book's publication a report

to the General Assembly of the Church of Scotland recommended the repatriation, by whatever means necessary, of these unassimilable aliens back to the land of their origin as the only way of safeguarding the purity of Presbyterian Scotland. Thomson, while sharing this view, was altogether more pessimistic. The Catholic Irish are here in Scotland, not merely to stay, but eventually to dominate. The future of the Scots is that they have no future. They face displacement and eventual ejection, as the intruders, driven by the priest and the party-boss from their power-base in the West, gradually extend their tentacles over the whole country. Thomson's book can be classified as a dystopia, a nightmare vision of the future, on a par with Huxley's *Brave New World* or Orwell's *Nineteen Eighty-Four*, extrapolating certain malefic tendencies already at work in society, that will, if unchecked, end in catastrophe. The calamity Thomson dreads is a papist annexation of Scotland and he sees no way of preventing it. He imagines the future a hundred years hence when a young man of Scottish, i.e., Presbyterian, ancestry (the terms are synonymous) comes from the Antipodes to see what has become of the land of his forefathers. It is the year 2027 and Scotland is now an Irish Catholic colony looking to Dublin rather than London for leadership. In Edinburgh he sees the gleaming white spire of the newly-built St Patrick's Cathedral towering over Princes Street, and there is much talk of thuribles and incense and processions in honour of Mary and the Sacred Heart choking the streets of the capital. It is significant that the new cathedral (Catholicism is clearly thriving) is named after Patrick of Ireland and not Andrew of Scotland – the Scots are on the run.

In Glasgow he meets in a hotel one of 'the old stock', who, asked if he is English, emphatically retorts that he is a Scot, but it is an evidence of decline that to the young man it sounds like a Yorkshire-man denying that he is English. The term Scot is clearly on the wane, and the root cause is the parasitical Irish, who, since their first coming in 1845, have repaid their hosts by ingesting and destroying them. After first prudently ascertaining his questioner's identity – it is presumably dangerous to speak too openly in this papist colony, especially in its Irish heartland – this Scottish equivalent of the last of the Mohicans opens his heart on the racial, religious and cultural disaster that has befallen his country. He provides 'a rough resumé' of the history of the last fifty years, that is, from 1977 to 2027. A hundred years ago in 1927 Scotland was still largely inhabited by Scots. Today the Irish element in the population is predominant. Not only did the Irish undercut Scottish workers; the immigrants were, in addition, more suited to the demands of mass production than the Scot, who, with his intensely individualist psychology, was unsuited to work in which he became the servant of a machine. Catholics, by contrast, are mindless conformists, as easily dragooned to the requirements of an industrial machine as to the dictates of a mechanical religion.

The problem of Irish and Scot sharing the same country is, for Thomson, the nature of the total and radical incompatibility between them. The English can tolerate and even occasionally be amused by the Irish, but the Scots simply cannot stand them, as anyone who contemplates Ulster will agree. There the descendants of the Scottish Presbyterian planters obligingly and abundantly demonstrate their total detestation of Irish religion and culture. The two races cannot get on and ought not to try. Thomson points to what he calls 'the sociological failure of mixed marriage between the two races' as what must occur when wrong-headed attempts to defy the laws of nature end in miscegenation. Such misalliance produces a half-breed type, combining the worst qualities of both stocks, and breeding, in addition, a strange nullity, an abnormal lack of character and vigour. The only way for the Scots to survive is to have nothing to do with these pestiferous intruders – but, lamentably, as Thomson himself knows, the warning comes too late: Scotland is already well down the road to irremediable racial pollution.

While the Irish pour in, the best Scots move out. Scotland by 2027 is simply an outpost of Greater Ireland, and the former age-old relationship with England is in fatal disrepair. The old Protestant alliance between Scotland and England crumbles as Dublin supplants London, its artists and writers becoming exemplars for their Scottish counterparts. Thomson's vision ends with a Caledonian version of Ragnarok or Götterdämmerung, a last desperate stand of doomed Scottish heroes against their tragic destiny, when in the late 1980s the True Scots League, a nationalist, semi-military society against Irish domination of their country, rises in rebellion only to be suppressed with much bloodshed by English troops. After this it is all downhill: it is 'now possible to calculate almost to the exact decade when the last Scot will leave Scotland'.

It is certainly a melodramatic scenario, and most of us presently living in Scotland, only thirty years away from Thomson's fateful date, whether we are 'true Scots' (native Presbyterians) or 'Irish' (people with Irish names who have lived in Scotland for four

generations) may permit ourselves a smile at the wild sensationalism of Thomson's prophecies. But it would be a mistake to dismiss
all this as no more than the bigoted ravings of one demented
individual. There are still a number of respected commentators
who deplore what they see as the hibernianisation of a Protestant
country (Graham Walker's description) and the slow contamina-
tion of its culture – on a recent radio programme Steve Bruce
questioned the gratuitous and undesirable importation of a term
like 'the crack' into Scottish discourse and wondered why so many
Irish pubs are sprouting up all over Glasgow. Trivial, perhaps, but
a sign, however small, of a new and dangerous instability in our
traditional culture, a sapping of old certainties, as attitudes and
ideas alien to the national spirit take inauspicious hold upon the
young.

Even the errors in Thomson's lugubrious jeremiad, absurd as they
now appear, are revealing and instructive. To begin with, the so-
called 'Irish', as defined by Thomson, are no longer Irish and are
increasingly ceasing to be Catholic. Thomson denies the first and
never envisages the second. The 'Irish', whom his young visitor finds
in pernicious control of Scotland, are the descendants of the post-
Famine refugees. Most of them have been in Scotland for well over
a hundred years (by 2027 it will be something like five generations).
No matter. Once Irish, always Irish. However long they stay, they
will never, for Thomson, qualify as Scottish. Scottish equals Presbyterian, Catholic equals alien. Thomson would still find many supporters of this equation among us today. The equation has, of course,
been modified to accommodate the modern phenomenon of religious decline. One need not be a practising or even a believing
Presbyterian – atheists are acceptable, provided they are Presbyterian atheists. But everyone in the country with an Irish surname is a
candidate for repatriation, regardless of what he may think of Ireland or religion here and now. True, not everyone from Ireland is
unwelcome; those Ulster Protestants who came in such large numbers after 1918 to work in the shipyards of Glasgow are as secure in
Thomson's eyes as though they had been domiciled here since the
days of John Knox. They, too, are of 'the old stock' and there is no
threat to the purity of the race from this kind of Irish. Thomson
knows very well whom he wishes to exclude. Nor does the possibility of lapsation seem to have crossed his mind. Once a Catholic,
always a Catholic. The Scottish Catholic hierarchy might even
manage to smile through their pain at the naiveté of this assumption.

Thomson's dark forebodings seem almost comically irrelevant to our present situation. His 'Irish' are no longer Irish, save in some vague, nostalgic, sing-song sense, though it is true that even today 'The Fields of Athenry' has a strange capacity to anger some of those obliged to hear it. Secondly, many of the most significant contributors to Scottish culture from the people abhorred by Thomson have broken decisively with the religion of their forebears. What would Thomson have made of people like Tom Leonard, William McIlvanney, Billy Connolly, Meg Henderson (the list could be easily extended), indisputably descended from the post-Famine immigrants, but clearly Scottish and just as clearly not Catholic? His thesis, after all, is that nothing good, so far as Scotland is concerned, can come out of Catholic Ireland, that the 'Irish' can only contaminate and defile, that, even when intermarriage occurs, this is miscegenation, racial, moral, and cultural pollution. He assumes, wrongly, that the children of the immigrants will never abandon the faith. But the question is not whether the people he calls 'Irish' are still devout Catholics. It is enough to prove him wrong if it can be shown that those he denounces as poisoners of the well of Scottish culture have in fact richly contributed to the country they were supposed to destroy, regardless of how they stand in relation to Holy Mother Church. Their religious beliefs, or lack of them, are irrelevant, if it can be shown that, despite their descent, they have culturally enriched the country to which their ancestors once came.

It is startling to compare Thomson's nightmare of Irish infiltration with C. M. Grieve's rhapsodic speculations concerning the same event.[4] Where others from Carlyle onward had viewed the Irish as benighted savages – even a Catholic convert like Fionn MacColla could join in this jeremiad of racial adulteration – Grieve astonishingly hailed them as potential cultural liberators. The story of Sleeping Beauty helps to explicate this surprising metamorphosis. Scotland, cursed to cultural sleep by the bad fairy of Calvinism, would awake at the touch of the Hibernian prince. Grieve argued that the return of Catholicism to Scotland would help restore that pre-Reformation atmosphere in which Scottish culture had flourished and that future cultural progress in Scotland depended on the emergence of a new generation of Catholic artists.

For many years Grieve's utopian expectations seemed as extravagant as Thomson's dystopian dread. The newcomers did not immediately rush en masse to release Scotland from the prison-house of Calvinism – most of them could scarcely read or write, and all of them were much more concerned with 'getting on', with escape from the rat-pit (the title of MacGill's novel), than with becoming the avant-garde of Scottish culture. In the children of immigrants the world over, the drive to economic success often consumes every other consideration, and this general tendency was probably intensified by the special historical circumstances of the post-Famine period. These survivors (one thinks of the post-holocaust Jews) were so intensely aware of the fate they had escaped that the very thought of art would have seemed to them frivolous and irresponsible. To make themselves safe was their sole preoccupation. Grieve's dream of a flowering of Catholic artists was not shared by the immigrants; they concentrated instead on becoming teachers, lawyers and doctors. Yet in the long run there can be no doubt that Grieve was a better prophet than Thomson. However belatedly, his prediction that the Irish would become Scotland's cultural saviours, has, allowing for the element of hyperbole, proved truer than Thomson's Cassandra-like warnings of ethnic cleansing and racial extermination. But prophecy is always a hazardous venture. The whole Irish-Catholic-Scottish relationship is a far more convoluted business than any too straightforward account, Grieve's included, allows. Native Scottish writers did not remain imprisoned in an anti-artistic Calvinism; Irish Catholic writers had ceased within a generation or two to be either, though it is, of course, also true that total amnesia seldom occurred. If Thomson was completely wrong, Grieve was only partially, and in a way unforseen by himself, right, as a consideration of figures such as Tom Leonard, Billy Connolly, and William McIlvanney easily demonstrates.

Billy Connolly and the Legacy of St. Gerard's

Consider Billy Connolly, unarguably the outstanding comic talent produced by Scotland in the last twenty years. Ian Pattison, one of our foremost contemporary writers of comedy, employs a BC/AC chronology to call attention to the major significance of his impact: Before and After Connolly. The coming of Connolly is, on this assessment, the decisive watershed, the truly ground-breaking event. Before him there is Andy Stewart and the Kilt Police; after him comedy is indissolubly wedded to real life. Pattison describes him as basically an observation comedian, nourishing himself upon the everyday epiphanies (I shall have more to say about his affinity with Joyce later on), picking up the rough mineral ore of daily experience and polishing it until it gleams to the heavens. His achievement was the Columbus-like one of discovering a world of comedy that had always been there, but that everyone else had missed.

In one sense, it is simply stating the obvious to claim Connolly for the Irish Catholic tradition within Scottish society, yet he is Glaswegian to the core and some of his fiercest opponents are to be found within the ranks of orthodox Catholicism. In examining this paradox, we shall uncover certain crucial facts about the development and present situation of the descendants of the Irish within Scotland today. True, there are moments when his lineage is unambiguously, if farcically, discernible. In his send-up of the sentimental tearjerker, 'Nobody's Child', the absurdly lachrymose narrator tells sadly of always being left abandoned in the orphanage because potential adopters turn away when they hear that he's a 'Tim' – 'they always take the Prodistants and I am left alo-en'. The laughter that unfailingly greets this points to something remarkable in our society: what provokes angry resentment as straight factual statement is gleefully welcomed when comically packaged. Say straight out that there is anti-Catholic prejudice among us, whether in football or business or anywhere else, and you risk being denounced as a paranoiac trouble-maker (see Paolo di Canio). Make a joke out of the masonic or Orange connections of Scottish referees and you will have everyone rolling in the aisles (see Rikki Fulton, Tony Roper, Jonathan Watson, *et al*). 'Nobody's Child' obeys this unwritten law by turning discrimination into farce, but that does not necessarily mean that Connolly really finds it funny.

His own original, anti-army, anti-recruiting song about Northern Ireland is another matter altogether; there is no farce because there is no parody. The young soldier, lured into signing on by the posters depicting the Army as *la dolce vita* – skiing in the mountains, sunbathing on the beaches – has been posted to Ulster where these delights have been conspicuously unforthcoming. Plaintively, accusingly, from his hospital bed, he puts the question to the siren-sergeant who took him in: 'Ah'm askin' ye, sergeant, where's mine?'. There is nothing funny about this song – this is Connolly at his most sombre. But the song goes beyond the disillusionment bred by the gap between promise and reality, between brochure and life. The singer refers to facing a crowd of 'weans' in a Belfast street with his machine-gun trained upon them. It is not simply that the seductive posters didn't show *this*, true though it be. Much more provocatively and tendentiously, Connolly seems to be saying much the same as

Republican apologists when they put forward their version of what is going on in the Six Counties and insist that any meaningful decommissioning of arms must apply to much more than simply the armalites of the IRA. Just as Seamus Heaney has provoked criticism of himself for certain poems he has written on the Troubles, so Connolly, too, leaves himself open to the charge of being a Republican sympathiser. George Malcolm Thomson would have instantly cited this in vindication of his thesis: what else can we expect from someone with such a name, such an education, and such an ancestry?

Yet, in another sense, Connolly can hardly be paraded as a shining product of the Irish Catholic tradition. Some of his most significant work has provoked unqualified condemnation from the leaders and spokesmen of official Catholicism, and Thomson himself might have been baffled when confronted with Connolly's ribald parody of the Crucifixion – it makes such a ruin of Thomson's neatly precise pigeonholing of the Irish Catholic element in Scottish society. The best way to engage this paradox is to consider 'The Crucifixion' as his most famous single piece, as well as the one most fully depicting his complicated relationship to the faith into which he was born and subsequently rejected. Anyone familiar with Joyce is unlikely to find in 'The Crucifixion' a revolutionary new departure. Both Joyce and Connolly exhibit the same tradition of negative Catholicism and inverted religion – each approaches his subject with the expertise of an insider and the sarcasm of a sceptic. In the opening chapter of *Ulysses*, Buck Mulligan mocks the birth of Christ, as Connolly in 'The Crucifixion' ridicules his passion and death.[5] Even as the believer bridles at the blasphemy, he will simultaneously acknowledge how intimate the culprits are with their subject-matter, and, though this may not assuage his wrath, it is, in a perverse way, a tribute to the thoroughness of their religious education. Centuries of theological argument, well known to Joyce as prize student of the Jesuits, lies behind Mulligan's 'Ballad of Joking Jesus':

> I'm the queerest young fellow that you ever heard,
> My mother's a jew, my father's a bird.

However offensively expressed, it nevertheless summarises the key mystery of salvation cherished by all Christians, and, in an especially reverential sense by Catholics: the incarnation of the Son of God through the descent of the Holy Spirit upon the Jewish maiden, Mary. The 'Ballad' goes on to refer to the miracle of the wedding-feast at Cana and ends with Christ's resurrection and ascension into heaven after his death on Calvary. Incarnation, miracle, resurrection, ascension – the *content* of the 'Ballad' could not be more orthodox. What outrages the believer is the jeering tone in which these sacred things are discussed – the speaker is demeaning the tradition from which he comes and the privileged knowledge it has conferred. Yet the person who comes off worst from the episode is not the blasphemer Mulligan, but the patronising Englishman, Haines, 'laughing guardedly' at the performance. He addresses Stephen:

> We oughtn't to laugh, I suppose. He's rather blasphemous. I'm not a believer myself, that is to say.

Two thoughts occur. First, Stephen had not been laughing at all. Second, there can be no blasphemy without belief. What Joyce thinks of Haines is plain from Stephen's curt reply to the foolish question asking him what kind of believer he is. 'There's only one sense of the word, it seems to me'. If you believe, then you believe in creation from nothing, miracles, a personal God. If you cannot accept these, then you are not a believer. Stephen's statement of the situation could not be more Catholic, and his clarity of thought and conciseness of expression are a tribute to his (and Joyce's) Jesuit teachers, even if this education has taken him down a road not at all what they desire. It is the lapsed student of the Jesuits who writes the 'Ballad of Joking Jesus'.

Just as surely is it the lapsed pupil of St Gerard's Secondary, Govan, who writes 'The Crucifixion', however much his erstwhile mentors may deplore the production. Here, however perversely presented, is an insider's view of the whole tragic sequence – and this is precisely what the orthodox Catholic finds hardest to forgive. Connolly knows Christ as no simple pagan, no uninstructed disbeliever, ever could. It is as if a man were to turn his own brother's death from, say, asbestosis, into a jest, as Connolly turns the Crucifixion into a piece of coarse tomfoolery. It is a member of the family – for who else would know the details so intimately? – who drags the drama of suffering down into the dirt. Yet even if Jesus was not the Son of God come to die for us, he was a man who suffered grievously, and it is always wrong to make fun of another human being's agony. Recently, Connolly appeared on television, looking suitably shocked at the tragic death of his friend, the Princess of Wales. One imagines how justifiably angry he would be at any attempt to reduce *that* death to farce, and that he himself would ever dream of doing so is simply inconceivable. There are some things not to be joked about, some things that are no laughing matter. So that Connolly can do to Christ what he would never dream of doing to Diana is explicable on one supposition alone: he has no grudge against Diana as he has against Christ. 'The Crucifixion' is an act of revenge for his own religious upbringing, and, like Joyce, he uses the instruction he has received to affront his instructors. Only an ex-Catholic bent on retaliation could have written the piece.

When his Jesus rebukes the 'eedjits' who demand 'holy tricks' because they don't know the word 'miracle', Connolly is justifiably exempting himself from the condemnation. Religiously speaking, he is very well educated and it is because he knows what he's talking about that he can parody so pitilessly – his comedy is parasitic upon the story it ridicules. The blasphemer cannot operate without a believer to scandalise, even if that believer is his own former self. If no one knew the story of the Crucifixion, if millions did not continue to believe in its salvific message, Connolly would be wasting his time. Just try getting some comic mileage out of the death of Adonis or Baldur. There have to be believers for the belief to be mocked. If Christ were universally regarded today as merely a poor misguided or misreported man who died atrociously two thousand years ago, who would be foolish or heartless enough to turn such torment into farce? Connolly, like Joyce, is still sufficiently Catholic to think it worthwhile to ridicule the religion into which he was born. Someone completely secularised would not even bother to do so.

Certainly, Connolly goes further than Joyce, is coarser and more extreme, if only in selecting for ridicule Christ's death rather than his birth. Whenever Joyce refers to Christ's death (see the end of *The Dead* or Tim Finnegan's triumphal resurrection at the end of his song: 'Thunderin' Jasus, d'ye think I'm dead?') it is in reverential acknowledgement of the mythic hero who overcame the tomb. True, Leopold Bloom comically misinterprets the inscription on top of the cross to mean Iron Nails Run In (Jesus of Nazareth King of the Jews), but the joke here is clearly on the well-meaning, good-natured ignoramus. It is altogether different when Connolly, speaking as himself, tells us that the inscription reads Mad Mental Rules OK, a Glasgow housing-scheme gang graffito. Connolly is as aware of the true meaning as Joyce, but he pretends to be as ignorant as Bloom for the sake of the easy laugh from his audience. One wonders just how many of those who laugh at the joke know what the letters really mean. What they do know is that Christ was not one of the Tongs and the comedy comes from the incongruity of the association. But Connolly, pretending not to know, is simply playing to his Glaswegian gallery: anything for a laugh. In similar vein, he goes into guffaws of uncontrollable laughter at the apparently wild coincidence of 'The Saracen's Head' pub being near the *Cross*, as though he does not know how Glasgow Cross comes to be called as it is.

It is because he knows the story so well that he can so comprehensively parody it – hence the believer's indignation. To quote T. S. Eliot, after such knowledge, what forgiveness? The Last Supper, we are advised, took place in the Gallowgate; only a printer's error mislocated it in Galilee. It is presented as a drunken melee, with each new arrival demanding a glass of wine – and even without the benefit of biblical scholarship, Connolly's audience knows that wine-drinking in Galilee and wine-drinking in Glasgow have nothing in common. Very few working-class Glaswegians drink wine, and most of these tend to be alcoholics and down-and-outs. Connolly's Last Supper is a rabble of Glaswegian derelicts. The same incongruity is exploited when we hear that the wine-guzzling Apostles, waiting in the pub for the Big Yin to turn up, are 'getting tore into the Mother's Pride'. There was bread and wine in Jerusalem, so there must be bread and wine in 'The Saracen's Head' – yet who among us familiar with working-class pubs in Glasgow has ever seen a loaf on the premises? When concern is expressed at the Big Yin's non-appearance, an older Apostle ('Ah've been in this gemme a wee while') reassures the doubters. The Big Yin will keep his promise to come, the more so since he does not need to; he could just as easily sit at home and turn pails of water into wine – Cana is in Connolly's mind as it was in Joyce's. When the Big Yin finally does arrive, he complains of being 'knackered' with miracles, and is especially peeved because the very first question put to him by the dumb boy he cured that day is, 'Is it awright if ama Prodistant?'. When Joyce was asked if he had rejected Catholicism in order to become a Protestant, he acidly replied that he had not abandoned a logical absurdity in order to embrace an illogical one. There spoke the pupil of the Jesuits, just as through Connolly's Christ speaks the pupil of St Gerard's – for this Christ, obviously a Catholic, is irked at having squandered one of his debilitating miracles on someone who kicks with the other foot.

At every point the narrative matches the original. When it is explained what prophecy means, it is, appropriately, Judas who wants to know the winner of tomorrow's three-thirty. In the gospels

Judas is a Thatcherite, value-for-money man; he resents the precious ointment wasted on the Master's feet when it could so easily have been sold for a handsome profit; he finally sells Jesus for thirty pieces of silver. Connolly's Christ predicts with exact accuracy the details of the arrest, passion and crucifixion as given in the gospels: the crown of thorns, the assistance from Simon of Cyrene, the garment gambled for by the guards, the inscription on the Cross, the demand of the bad thief that Christ should miraculously save them both, the final, terrible cry of abandonment, the spear thrust through the side, the placing of the body in the tomb, the resurrection and ascension into heaven. Connolly clearly did not waste his time in the RE class at St Gerard's and his teachers must have been delighted with so attentive a pupil. What will dismay them is the use to which he has put his learning, his debasingly demotic reduction of the great story to the argot of the Glasgow slums. The crown of thorns becomes a jaggy bunnet. Christ is a first offender with every hope, given normal circumstances, of a one-night lie-in and probation to follow. The seamless garment is the good dress stolen and pawned, the tomb of Joseph of Arimathea is an old air-raid shelter, and so on. The most appalling cry of despair ever heard in life or literature – 'My God, why have you forsaken me' – is bathetically reduced to, 'C'mon, Da, geeza brek'. The Ascension ends with the Big Yin 'sittin' in the clouds wi ma Da'.

But the affront is not the description of Christ and his Apostles as a group of raggle-taggle Glaswegians drinking in a working-class pub. The historical Christ was born in a stable, chose his followers from the poorest sections of society, and told us that he was even worse off than the foxes, for they, at least, had a roof over their heads. Nor would it be the first time in the two-thousand-year history of Christianity that Christ was appropriated and adapted to suit the beliefs, traditions, life-styles of those to whom he was being intro-duced. The missionaries who carried him to the ends of the earth often adopted precisely this strategy in order to make him more acceptable to the peoples among whom they came. The newly con-verted Norsemen saw in him a young Viking warrior, defying his enemies to the death, heroically accepting his fierce destiny. How else could they have embraced him without ceasing to be them-selves? In his short sketch 'Today is Friday', Hemingway presents him as yet another of his laconic, disciplined tough guys (boxer, bullfighter, old fisherman), suffering agony without complaint, the classic example of grace under pressure. Pacifists celebrate the gentle, non-violent man, unprotestingly being nailed to the cross, forerunner of Gandhi and passive resistance. Throughout history Christ has been all things to all men; why object when Connolly presents him as a low-class Glaswegian?

Not what Connolly makes him, but the scabrous motive behind it: this is the offence. All the others – Vikings, Hemingway, pacifists, and so on – appropriate him in admiration; they admire him and they wish us to do likewise. But Connolly makes him a Glaswegian, not as a tribute to the city, but as a degradation of the Saviour. The general imbecility of the situation is conveyed in the football-like chants of Christians and Romans alike. The Big Yin finally makes his appearance, steamin' and calling for the best of order. We have all met such people, but only when we could not avoid them. Connolly is determined to make Christ a clown. His chief objection to the crown of thorns is that he had taken such care with his split ends that morning. Simon is able to help with the carrying with the cross because he has 'just run oo 'a pies'. The water that accompanied the blood after the spear-thrust is rendered as Jesus urinating on the soldier because he can neither 'hook' nor kick him. This Christ is an object of derision and contempt, not of admiration; Connolly strives to besmirch the story and all concerned. Do some people sometimes talk and act like this in Glasgow? Regrettably, yes, but that is scarcely justification for making the Son of God one of them.

The final insult is to have John, the beloved disciple and author of the Gospel in which the claims to divine sonship are most strik-ingly advanced, put the drunken blowhard in his place. Having listened to the detailed prophecy without interruption, John at last decisively intervenes. We all like you, he tells Jesus, and we all know that you chipped in mair for the kerryoot than anyone else. But, when you get a few of these cheap wines, 'yur patter's rotten'. Friendship and the Big Yin's largesse notwithstanding, the truth must be told: Jesus is simply a drunken loudmouth and everything he has prophe-sied about his impending death, resurrection, and ascension is sim-ply the result of imbibing too much cheap wine. Every working-class pub in the city has a loudmouth fool of this sort, but it is not something that we care to boast about. But, as always, Connolly, good student of the gospels that he is, knows exactly what he's doing. It is no fluke that he should give the final devastating word to John, since it is John who begins his gospel with the logos, the word incarnate, from which all things began and in which all shall end. But where St John's Word is mystical and salvific, Connolly's is shameless and rowdy. Catholic educators throughout Scotland would be delighted to have pupils who knew the Gospels so well as Connolly, but appalled to see them treat them with such disrespect. It is Connolly's good luck that he is a lapsed Catholic and not a lapsed Moslem – Salman Rushdie is in hiding, under sentence of death, for writing about the Prophet in terms that are almost eulogistic compared to what Connolly has said about the Christ.

McIlvanney and Leonard – The Literature of the Lapsed

The paradoxes of Connolly can be replicated in writers such as William McIlvanney and Tom Leonard. Though not born a Catholic, McIlvanney is descended from Irish Catholics who fled the Famine, and his finest work, *Docherty*, bearing all the stigmata of an intense personal experience, has a direct literary ancestor in the writings of Patrick MacGill.[6] Navvy gives way to miner in this new hagiology, but there is the same rage against social injustice, whether the subject be the General Strike ('Initiation'), the Famine ('The Graveyard at Skibereen') or urban deprivation ('Incident').[7] What redeems all this from the embittered conviction that 'remedy is none' is the second major element of the work: ancestral piety, a loyalty to Burke's 'little platoon', which, radiating outwards from the beloved father, becomes the model for all relationships between the wretched of the earth. Against the impersonal industrial system, McIlvanney marshals the loyalties of the tribe. Docherty is a lapsed-Catholic, first-generation Scot who discards the religion that left his father supine before injustice, 'a galley slave kissing his oar', meekly exchanging starvation in Ireland for exploitation in Scotland. Docherty's rout of the brutally dictatorial priest, as seen by his youngest son, is one of the book's Homeric moments; underlying his refusal to send the boy to the Catholic school is the gulf between institutional religion and the lives of the poor: 'they wanted you to respect authority when authority had no respect for you'. Furious at a child absent from the Catholic register, 'they' easily acquiesce in a system of breeding children and ponies alike for the pits.

The boy's grandfathers – Connemara Catholic, Ayrshire Protestant – incarnate the divided legacy of West of Scotland religion, a tradition of shared exploitation the only unifying factor; and, as always in McIlvanney, what makes him so sure a guide to vital areas of Scottish culture, is the deep sense of *pietas*, love of the roots whence one sprung. Tam Docherty has little sympathy with his father's

Irishness, but when he hears his sons mocking the old man's reminiscences of 1845, he turns on them in one of the book's key moments.
'D'ye ken who ye're talkin' tae? ... He's where you come fae. An'
whaurever ye go, ye'll have to take 'im wi' ye.' Aeneas with Anchises
on his shoulders – it is the cultural emblem of the Scot, his defining
characteristic – and McIlvanney exalts the grateful acknowledgement of the burden as the supreme value. The old man is saved
from the workhouse by his lapsed son and Protestant daughter-in-
law just as his Catholic children are slamming the door on him. To
abandon Anchises, renege upon the past, be it by a snobbish educational clambering upwards or the use of any other superior ability,
is the supreme perfidy.

Docherty is about history and love, cherished tradition, its beauty
a triumph over the most apparently inauspicious material. The
atmosphere of the Ayrshire mining-town with its Irish-origin family
is magnificently evoked, its epic-like hero one of the great creations
of Scottish fiction. Tam dies explicitly as redeemer, and, if his world
is not beautiful, messiahs are born in stables. That his funeral lacks
a priest is a trifle set against the sacrificial death and his epitaph is
reverently intoned on the street corner: 'a lot of hert'. The heart
signifies both courage and compassion, that so prized, so elusive,
combination of qualities. In one son the courage becomes brutality,
in another the longing for justice a rage against the past – only the
youngest inherits the whole man who was his father. Heroism with
insight. *Docherty* teaches us how to find in the past the values that
will preserve us in the future.

Tom Leonard is closer in origin to Billy Connolly, and his poetry,
giving a voice to the voiceless, reproduces with stunning authenticity the idiom of Glasgow.[8] One of its salient characteristics is a
violence forever threatening to explode. It is a volcanic poetry whose
eruptions would be gratuitous and excessive were we to forget the
beleaguered communal mentality from which it derives. It is a poetry
of the deprived, of the underdog, and Leonard is a direct descendant
of Patrick MacGill, eighty years on and enraged at social injustice
rather than religious affront. But here, too, we are still in the armed
camp of the early Irish immigrants, still waging a war; there is still
a siege, still enemies to be encountered and bested. The poetic
imagination is still very much on the defensive, mistrustful, watch-
ful, resentful – it is the same mindset as MacGill and Fionn MacColla,
though with a crucial change of adversary. The target is now unwar-
rantable, self-promoting elitism, a new elect, a modern clerisy,

educational rather than religious: not Presbyterian disdain, but the arrogant privileging of certain accents, speech acts, modes of discourse, is what now provokes resentment.

But if religion has fallen from its centrality of importance, it has not disappeared – the legacy is still detectible, even if in an inverted, ironic, subversively critical form. Consider, for example, a poem such as 'Impressions', an account of a mission preached by a thickly-brogued Irish priest to a class of twelve-year-olds in a Glasgow Catholic school. The inspiration is, of course, literary as well as personal – Joyce's hell-fire sermon in his *Portrait of the Artist as a Young Man* is its openly acknowledged source:

> Authentic? Joyce *authentic*? I'll tell you.

But it is also a significant marker in a process of religious disaffection among the young that is at the root of the current crisis in Scottish Catholicism. 'Feed Ma Lamz' is equally subversive as it daringly translates the God of Mount Sinai to the heartland of Glasgow to deliver the ten commandments anew in a language appropriate to his new chosen people: 'nay fornirz or communists', 'nay laffn ina Sunday'; but, if the accent is new, the vindictiveness is constant:

> Oaky doaky. Stick way it
> – rahl burn thi lotha yiz.

The poem exploits the contradiction, embarrassing for Christianity, between a loving, merciful Christ (speaker of the title) and the xenophobic, killjoy Glaswegian despot-god –

> Doon nyir hungkirz. Wheesht –

as well as the frogmarching of the commandments to suit the needs of modern society: 'thou shalt not kill' becomes 'nay GBH (septina wawr)'.

But the religious allusions are not always hostile, as the playfulness of 'The Miracle of the Burd and the Fishes' makes plain (even if the 'burd' in question is a wee Glasgow lassie who has dumped her disconsolate boyfriend). The reference is to one of the great miracles of collective compassion worked by Christ in the feeding of the five thousand, as well as to the Glasgow coat of arms associated with the legends of St Mungo. The irreverence here is of a sort that betokens an affectionate familiarity, much in the way that one might tease an old friend. I can remember as a boy hearing the Celtic forward line described as The Five Sorrowful Mysteries, and when the Jungle at

Celtic Park was first renovated, it was referred to as the seating of the five thousand. Far from malice or enmity, such remarks reveal a sympathy, an affection; it would be foolish and misguided to resent this as an insult to religion.

Faith and football, however much this is deplored, are intimately interconnected in the working-class areas of the west of Scotland. The old complaint at religious discrimination recurs in the poem 'Crack' (1975), when Kenny Dalglish of Celtic is pulled down in the box and the penalty kick predictably refused: 'wan mair upfir thi ludg'. The bigotry may be trivial, but it is bigotry nevertheless. Which brings me finally to 'The Good Thief' (1975), a poem admirably uniting with classic economy the cardinal Glasgow preoccupations of football and religion. The drunk supporter is, like his gospel forerunner, headed for Paradise (nickname of Celtic's stadium), and, just as the darkness over the earth at the moment of Christ's death is dispelled by the promise of salvation ('this day thou shalt be with me in paradise'), so the threat to the game from the darkness over Glasgow near three o'clock (hour of both Christ's death and the kick-off) is countered by the consoling thought of the floodlights towering over Parkhead: 'good jobe they've gote thi lights'. Christ is still with the good thief and is, of course, still 'wanny us' . 'Ma right insane yirra pape'; naturally, the good thief is right – Christ is a pape, what else could he be? He, too, is headed for Paradise – the good thief can see it in his eyes. Such a poetry is incomprehensible without its religious matrix. Perhaps some will be as scandalised by 'The Good Thief' as many are by Connolly's 'Crucifixion', but this is to miss the world of difference between them. Connolly's purpose is to debase, to make Christ part of a drunken rabble; Leonard's is to elevate, to raise the tipsy supporter to the level of the thief who died assured of salvation. 'The Good Thief' is completely free of the jeering tone that pervades 'The Crucifixion' – no one should mistake it for an anti-religious poem.

Conclusion

If such radical divisions on identity and religion can be discovered between people such as Connolly, Leonard and McIlvanney, who, on the old classification, ought to be inseparably linked then it is surely time to forsake that classification as no longer relevant to our present concerns. Any taxonomy that leaves us helpless as to where to place the likes of Leonard, Connolly, McIlvanney or James

McMillan, is simply not worth retaining – whatever usefulness it
may once have possessed has gone forever. The static simplicities
and fixed certainties of the past, so easily adopted by Thomson and
Grieve, are fast dissipating. What was once obvious and transpar-
ent is now complex and confused. Change is our norm. In a world
seized by a sense of movement, of ever-increasing *accelerando*, old
modes of coming together no longer seem pertinent to the changing
situation, and it would be miraculous indeed if religion were
somehow immune from the processes transforming the rest of
society. 'We shall not be moved' roar the massed supporters in the
confrontational idiom of old, redundant world, but any footballing
Galileo among them might whisper his concealed dissent with an
equal measure of being right: *E pure si muove* (but it moves nevertheless). The glib, age-old equations – Catholic = Irish, Presbyterian
= Scot – will no longer serve, and it is long past time to have done
with such misleading and perniciously anachronistic labels.

In the sixth circle of the Inferno, Dante is challenged by the man
of history, the disdainful aristocrat, Farinata, so touchily obsessed
with yesteryear: *chi fuor li maggior tui?* – who were *your* ancestors? It
is the characterstic, all-sufficient question of the zealous tradition-
ist, living wholly in and for the past; assigning to history the task of
determining friends and foes: tell me your origins and I'll tell you
who *you* are. It is a question based on the assumption that the answer
supplied will determine both recognition and response. For many
years Scotland had its own equivalent of Farinata's question, similarly designated to identify strangers and to relegate them, if need
be, to their proper, subordinate status: *we* are the people – who are
you? To marginalise, to discriminate, to exclude. These were the
underlying purposes of the question and, for more than a century
after the coming of the Irish in 1845, it was fully understandable to
all parties involved and even accepted by those who were its intended targets and victims. Tradition was the single, indispensable,
all-sufficient key to identity. Few of those involved had read the
Inferno, but their business together was transacted on the same stern,
simplistic principles as those employed by Farinata in his dealings
with Dante.

However, this situation is increasingly not the case any more.
Today we are all sharers in any identity crisis, as old mindsets wither
and Farinata's question – once so crucial in the matter of self-
definition – ceases to apply. Today the all-important question is the
anti-traditional, democratic, individualist challenge: never mind

your ancestors, who are *you*? And the response is increasingly couched, not in terms of a body of beliefs providentially bequeathed by the past, but a series of concerns existentially thrown up by the present. Where one came from is no longer so unhesitatingly proposed as the sufficient clue to where one is going. Forget your origins, tell us your destination: who are *you now*? A failure to acknowledge this simply disqualifies one from appreciating what Connolly, Leonard, *et al.* are all about.

Who were *your* ancestors? The curt answer is 'the same as yours', in the sense of being domiciled in this country long enough to be on an equal footing without fear of discrimination or reprisal with any other citizen of our present multi-cultural, multi-faith or no-faith society. As to the long answer, it is for most people standing on the threshold of the twenty-first century, too tedious and troublesome a trek back to a distant, increasingly irrelevant source, to justify the bother to answer. The onus has shifted from those being asked to those asking the question: why do you want to know?

Yet, in some quarters, old attitudes die hard and the redundant, offensive question lingers on to plague and impede Scottish life. In the story, Rip Van Winkle slept through the most important period of American history, dozing off in the reign of King George and awaking, a stranger in his own land with George Washington's portrait over the village inn. Rip remained himself, simply growing older while America was transformed. Yes, it is possible to walk around and still be asleep, to seem awake even when one slumbers and the danger is that Scotland may have become a haven for somnambulists: those who refuse to wake up to our changed reality, the wilful Rip Van Winkles, with eyes wide open and minds stubbornly shut. Yet, the last word is Galileo's: whatever is said and whoever says it, nevertheless it moves. No more than the heavens is Scotland exempt from this all-embracing law.

NOTES

1. Patrick MacGill, *Children of the Dead End: The Autobiography of a Navvy* (London, 1914) and *The Rat Pit* (London, 1915).
2. Patrick Reilly, 'Catholics and Scottish Literature 1878–1978', in David McRoberts (ed), *Modern Scottish Catholicism 1978–1978* (Glasgow, 1979) and 'The Mirror of Literature: The Development of Catholicism in Scotland Since 1845', *Scottish Affairs*, No. 8 (1994).
3. George Malcolm Thomson, *Caledonia, or The Future of the Scots* (London, 1927).

4. C. M. Grieve, *Albyn or Scotland and the Future* (London, 1927).
5. James Joyce, *Ulysses* (Harmondsworth, 1986).
6. William McIlvanney, *Docherty* (London, 1975).
7. William McIlvanney, *The Longships in Harbour* (London, 1970).
8. Tom Leonard, *Three Glasgow Writers* (Glasgow, 1976), *Bunnit Huslin* (Glasgow, 1975) and *Poems* (Dublin, 1973).

'THE LONG NINETEENTH CENTURY': SCOTLAND'S CATHOLIC GAIDHEALTACHD

Ray Burnett

While much of the book has focused on the experience of Catholics of Irish origin, Ray Burnett's research focuses on Catholicism in the Western Isles. He argues that Gaelic Catholicism has been largely ignored by researchers pre-occupied with the west central Scotland Catholic experience which has then become generalised, wrongly, as being representative of the entire Scottish Catholic community. In addition, he persuasively argues that much of what was originally the epicentre of Scottish Catholicism has, over the years, been usurped by the increasing influence and dominance of the lowland Catholic hierarchy, leaving only traces of the original, Western Isles Gaelic Catholic identity. He suggests that while some have claimed that the Irish Catholic identity has been rendered invisible by the host community, it remains ironic that the Irish section of the Catholic population has been in part responsible for submerging an important aspect of a Scottish Gaelic Catholic identity which predates the Irish influence in Scotland.

Introduction

Fidelity, devotion, loyalty, the unquestioning commitment of an unsophisticated but tenacious faith, sustained across the centuries in an unbroken tradition since Columba in the mountain fastness and island outpost of the Gael. Mass stones in the heather, secret seminaries in the glens, a cross above 'Blessed Morar', Madonnas in Eriskay and Barra, roadside shrines in South Uist. All under the benign protection of 'Our Lady of the Isles', the biggest religious

statue in Scotland and the icon of the Catholic Highlands and Islands. An image is as enduring as it is irreducibly romantic. Nor is
it necessary to take the high road or cross the Sea of the Hebrides to
be aware of this ancient and abiding dimension of 'the Faith'. Every
week the memorial columns of the Scottish Catholic press remind
the diaspora of the Gael and the wider Catholic community that
there is more to Scottish Catholicism than Ireland.

> The other glory of Scotland is the living devotion to Mary in the Western
> Isles. Mary entered there into the fabric of everyday life. She guided the
> helmsman over the deep waters of Barra. She guarded the cattle on the
> lands of Uist. She was in the night croons of the Island Mothers. She was
> there and she belonged . . . At other times different parts of Europe have
> paralleled and sometimes even surpassed the devotion of the Isles. But
> whatever these traditions in Europe, none are as unbroken as those of
> the Western Isles. . . . Out in most of the Isles, the robe of Christ was not
> torn, so that when their men sing of Mary the bitterness of history falls
> away. By a kind of magic we touch an unbroken tradition, in that their
> voice when they sing of Mary is still the voice of the one Church, that in
> Columba's time embraced the world, from Iona to Mesopotamia.[1]

Within and without the Catholic Gaidhealtachd there is an implicit,
seldom articulated yet widely felt belief that the Catholicism of the
Gaidhealtachd is distinct and different from that of the rest of
Scotland in its devotional practice, belief system and values, a difference arising from linguistic, ethnic and cultural factors, rooted in
the history of the Gael.[2] It is this unchallenged assumption which this
chapter seeks to question. The proposition advanced is that while
there was once a complex social and cultural Catholic Gaidhealtachd, it has evolved into the present not through an unbroken
continuum but through a series of key pivotal breaks, or moments.
The most recent of these have fostered both the social reality which
survives as Catholicism in the Gaidhealtachd and the cultural creation of an image of the Catholic Gaidhealtachd which is an illusory
denial of reality and a contradiction of history. The Catholic Gaidhealtachd has been emasculated from within and re-created from
without resulting in a steadily decaying husk encasing a sadly
deracinated religiosity and a re-aligned societal matrix for the function and practice of religion, in effect a translocated, surrogate
ghetto, painfully mismatched with a fading, increasingly irrelevant
externalised image of triumphalist fideism, the faltering pulse of its
'long nineteenth century'.[3]

The restoration of the hierarchy in 1878 is the first pivotal break, the key to the social delineation of the modern Catholic Gaidheal-tachd. The cultural moments of the 1890s-1900s and the 1920s-1930s are the second pivotal break, the double-phased creation of the image of the Catholic Highlands and Islands. Both fuse and synchro-nise in the cumulative moment of the 1950s, the ultimate defining moment of the modern Catholic Gaidhealtachd, the high water mark from which the subsequent slow but palpable ebb can be measured. As the formative moments in the creation of the modern era, the context within which the present must ultimately be set, these are the moments with which this essay is concerned.[4]

The Peripheralisation of the Gaidhealtachd

In the parish of Lochaber the priests swarm like locusts, running from house to house, gaining multitudes to their anti-Christian Idolatry.[5]

The failure of Presbyterianism to establish itself, the reconciliatory missions of the seventeenth century, the conversions within leading families and geographical fastness have combined to give an identi-fiable pattern of entirely, predominantly, or significantly Catholic areas which stretch right across the Highlands and Islands. Ben-becula, South Uist and Barra in the Outer Hebrides, Rhum, Eigg and Canna in the Inner Hebrides. From Kintail and Glensheil through to Glen Cannich, Strathglass and Glenmoriston. From Knoydart and Glengarry to Fort Augustus, the Great Glen and Stratherrick. From Moidart, Morar, Glenfinnan into Lochaber and Glencoe, through Brae Lochaber across the watershed to Badenoch and the Spey. And in the east from Upper Deeside and Braemar through to Glengairn and Strathavon, from Tomintoul and Glenlivet to the Cabrach and Strathbogie.[6]

The names of these districts resonate with traumatic moments in Highland history. The failed Jacobite campaigns of 1688–1745, the mass voluntary emigrations of the late eighteenth century, the clear-ance and land expropriations of the nineteenth century, the depopu-lation and decline of the early twentieth, the relentless retreat and eclipse of the Gaelic language and culture. For the communities of the Catholic Gaidhealtachd these successive dislocations had a particu-larly severe impact. The disastrous repercussions of an involvement with defeated Jacobitism was a key moment in the shaping of the modern Catholic Gaidhealtachd as was the wilful encouragement of mass emigration of entire Catholic districts in the late eighteenth century was another. The disregard of the Church authorities for the existence of the Gaidhealtachd as a distinct, organic, cultural and linguistic entity was a third. The restoration of the hierarchy in 1878 took no account of the Gaidhealtachd in the diocesan delineation between Aberdeen and Argyll and the Isles. No account was taken of historical and cultural associations and bonding.[7] Kintail was left adrift on the west, the old Gaelic Catholic communities of east Inverness-shire, Glen Cannich, Strathglass, Glenmoriston were isolated in the east. Strathavon and Glenlivet, Upper Deeside and Glengairn were subsumed into a non-Gaelic setting, their Gaelic identity and past effectively abandoned. At a stroke the Catholic Gaidhealtachd was dramatically reduced to the single diocese of Argyll and the Isles, or rather a peripheral part of that single diocese. The Argyll area of the diocese was essentially outwith the old Catholic Gaidhealtachd.[8] Badenoch and Brae Lochaber remained important surviving Catholic communities but they were already being increasingly drained and eclipsed by a wider Lochaber dominated by the growth of a Fort William vortex. Only the rump mainland west Inverness-shire districts of Glenfinnan, Moidart, Morar and Knoydart along with the outlying small isles, Barra, South Uist and Benbecula, remained as natural, organic, overwhelmingly Gaelic Catholic survival. This was the axis – Brae Lochaber, the western seaboard, the Hebrides – to which the Catholic Gaidhealtachd was effectively reduced.[9]

In the romantic recreation of the Highlands and the Highlanders from without, the association of the Catholic community with Jacobitism was a tie to the 'past', defeat, a lost cause. The mass emigrations encouraged by the Church carried the implicit notion that there was no future for the Catholic community, *per se*, in the Highlands and the core area was greatly weakened. Further debilitating, demoralising devastation came with nineteenth century clearance. Even after 1878, this creation of a subaltern position continued. As there was no significant contribution from Catholic thought to the popular ideology of the land agitation of the 1880s–1900s, Catholic inferiorism was reinforced. The Church authorities preferred the patronage of peers to the promotion of popular politics. The result was the 'grounding' of modern Highland Catholicism in a set of associations with defeat, dislocation, marginalisation, inferiorism. It needed the rebuilding of a popular-cultural bloc. Instead, 1878 brought cleavage, fracture and further fragmentation.

Centralisation through 'hierarchology'

The formation of the diocese of Argyll and the Isles as part of the restoration of the Scottish hierarchy in 1878 provided a focus, albeit reduced and truncated, for Catholic Gaidhealtachd. But the sustenance and development of an ethnic, cultural or even linguistically based Gaelic Catholicism was never the concern of the Church authorities. Having Gaelic-speaking priests for a Gaelic-speaking area was obviously useful but it was never essential. Within an institutionalist ecclesiology which essentially perceived of the Church 'as a machinery of hierarchical mediations' with the power and function of the church devolved into the three central functions of teaching, sanctifying and governing, the creation of Argyll and the Isles brought the Catholic Gaidhealtachd firmly within the context of a 'hierarchology' which had developed from Trent, culminated in Vatican I and which continued to evolve and entrench through a series of subsequent papal encyclicals by Leo XIII, Pius XI and Pius XII.[10] This was the bedrock on which the Church within the modern Catholic Gaidhealtachd was built to a template of ultramontanist orthodoxy, uniform throughout Scotland and Europe, the 'institutionalist ecclesiology' succinctly characterised by De Smedt as clericalism, juridicism and triumphalism.[11] Not just the practice of religion, but the rhythm of communal social life itself, was focused through the key diocesan institution of the parish, built on the authority and power of the parish priest, mediated through the promotion of devotional orthodoxy, cemented with the mortar of Catholic education.[12]

The landscape and cultural legacy of the Gaidhealtachd may have been imbricated with a distinctive, deeply-rooted religiosity, the benefaction of successive generations of early Celtic saints but it received scant acknowledgement within the formal re-establishment of the Church within the islands and western seaboard. As the new diocese embarked on a major programme of church building provision, the architectural style, the furnishings and decor of the new buildings were more reflective of the ultramontanist influences and the predilections of diocesan aristocratic benefactors than of any sense of Celtic continuity.[13] Dedications to the early Celtic saints were the exception to the rule; only the new Oban Cathedral was dedicated to Columba, no parish was dedicated to Bride, and even the pre-eminent dedication to Mary are not in any Gaelic form or variants, but in such 'official' forms of Tridentine Mary or Coronation

Mary as, *Our Lady Star of the Sea, Our Lady of the Assumption*.[14] The account of the opening of the new Morar parish church of *Our Lady of Perpetual Succour and St Cumin* in 1889 reveals the extent to which these influences so totally permeated the formal manifestations of Catholicism in its enduring Gaelic heartland. The late Lord Lovat, who owned the property, had provided the site and the funds, Lady Sausse donated the bell, Lady Mostyn a chalice, and Lady Lovat gave a luncheon for 'the clergy and leading members of the congregation' after the service at Morar Lodge. The architectural style was thoroughly English, the High Mass and liturgy thoroughly Roman. Aspersions and the Litany of the Saints followed by Webb's Mass in G, 'very creditably rendered by the choir of the neighbouring parish of Knoydart', the proceedings ending with the Litany of Loretto, Solemn Benediction and a sung Te Deum. The Bishop gave a Gaelic sermon and a portion of the Rosary was recited in Gaelic but the Mass Celebrant was Dom Hunter-Blair OSB and the principal preacher was Dom Oswald OSB, both from Lord Lovat's other principal foundation in the diocese, the Benedictine community of Fort Augustus Abbey.[15]

Founded in 1879 in the ruins of the old Hanoverian fort, the Abbey community was soon to develop a long and distinguished record of Gaelic and Scottish historiographical scholarship but its initial profile was more reflective of anglocentric orthodoxy and ultramontanist conservatism.[16] At its foundation the monks had evoked the ire of a local minister into complaining bitterly that they had been seen in the winter out skating on the frozen loch on the sabbath. When, with the advent of summer they were to be seen out boating on a sabbath evening, the exasperated divine had implored:

> If this be not attempting to bring French Sundays, French sins, and I may add, French judgements into British territory, I don't know what is.[17]

Or, as the Glasgow, Protestant campaigner, George Hay bluntly put it:

> The 'Fort' was erected to protect the pure and undefiled religion from the corruptions of the Man of Sin: but now, alas! On its battlements waves the red flag, mystic symbol of the papacy. On the banks of the great waterway of Scotland, where once paced the loyal soldiers of our beloved Queen, now swarm the black locusts of Egypt, holding out to passers-by the cup of abominations of the Scarlet Woman, drunk with the blood of the saints.[18]

Certainly papal influence was not far to seek. Throughout Scotland personal and parochial Catholic devotional practices were transformed by papal injunction. Successive popes reinforced a Tridentine Christocentrism through the rigid uniformity of the Latin Mass. A Christology of the Eucharist developed beyond the Mass into a series of secondary devotions whereby the Eucharist developed into a subjective kind of piety, with a passive spectator role for the laity and an all-important custodial role for the clergy. Leo X had introduced the Rosary, devotion to St Joseph, the Holy Family and the Sacred Heart. Pius X re-emphasised the Sacred Heart and introduced the notion of daily communion. Novenas, octaves, benediction, devotion to the Blessed Sacrament and October devotions transformed the practice of religion, in the Catholic Gaidhealtachd no less than elsewhere, as it felt the impact of this far-reaching 'devotional revolution'.

This devotional orthodoxy and spiritual uniformity permeated the Catholic Gaidhealtachd through the training of its priests. Neither at Blairs, Valladolid or elsewhere was there any suggestion of a distinct, far less distinctive, Gaelic training. Seminarians might be given a copy of Fr. MacEachen's Gaelic dictionary or *Leanmhuin Chriost*, the Gaelic translation of *De Imitatione Christi* on which to maintain their Gaelic proficiency in their own spare time.[19] But while the a Kempis eschatology may have awoken a resonance with popular Gaelic religiosity, the meagre remainder of available Gaelic spiritual texts reflected an orthodoxy *in* and *through* the medium of Gaelic rather than any subaltern popular Gaelic religious culture, with *An Cath Spioradail*, a translation of Lorenzo Scupoli's *Il Combattimento Spirituale* and *Cràbhadh do'n Tighearna Iosa*, a translation of a short English collection of devotions before the Blessed Sacrament augmented by the Gaelic prayer books, *Iùl a' Chriosdaidh* and *Làchran an Anma*, both in essence collections of translations of the Rosary, litanies, the Stations of the Cross and other 'official' prayers.[20] The results were quite noticeable by the time Anthony Ross first went to stay in Catholic Morar in the 1930s:

> The house had the usual Catholic emblems, but nothing which appeared distinctively Gaelic. French and Italian repository art and style of devotion had taken over in Morar very effectively by 1937.[21]

The Feast of Corpus Christi, the Feast of the Assumption were important dates for every parish and all parishioners. The Feast of Bride and Columba passed by unnoticed. This adherence to the focal moments of ultramontanist orthodoxy could be dressed up as no more than a continuation of popular religiosity, clothed in the common legend-history of Catholic Scotland and given a grounding in the 'simple Faith' of a dutiful people as in a 1957 official survey of parish life:

> Our people loved the October devotions. For centuries they had lived on the Rosary, often on it alone. It was the prayer of the hearth 'smoored' for fear of the visiting elders of the kirk. It was the prayer of the men who had to take to the heather or shelter in the cave. It was the prayer of the men, Scottish and Irish alike, who crowned the long line of victories by the battle of Kilsyth on the feast of the Assumption 1645. It was the prayer of those who were driven down to sea by dogs to be transported beyond the seas after Culloden. Surely then it was fitting that through it should come the wonderful gift of Benediction of the Blessed Sacrament.[22]

In reality, in the Catholic Highlands, as in Glasgow and elsewhere, the concentration on the Eucharist and Penance merely followed the revivalist techniques of consolidating the role, the power and the authority of the parish priest.[23] Where the Catholic Gaidhealtachd differs from the rest of Catholic Scotland, however, is that the Gaelic core of the diocese is numerically very small and in essence geographically confined to the two contiguous districts of the islands and a small part of the adjacent seaboard. It is also a very close-knit community, a very small reservoir from which to draw a regular supply of priests. Since 1878, six of the eight bishops of Argyll and the Isles have come from this Gaelic core of the diocese: from 1919 to 1959 three cousins succeeded each other as bishop,[24] virtually all the priests come from the same community they return to, often with close relations not just in one but in several of the parishes they subsequently serve.[25] Initially the diocese suffered from a shortage of priests, then it was hampered by early deaths.[26] But as the Catholic Gaidhealtachd entered the modern era, a pattern of stability emerged in which several of the key figures who contributed to the formation of the modern Catholic Gaidhealtachd entered pastoral duties in the area.[27]

What this meant in practice was that over the two decades of 1940s and 1950s, the critical years for the formation of the Gaelic Catholic community of the post-war era, only fourteen priests served all of the island parishes of Benbecula, South Uist, Eriskay and Barra in rotation. One other priest had charge of Moidart for the 1940s and two others held Morar and Arisaig respectively for all of the 1940s and 1950s.[28] Some of this core fourteen had been there in the pre-war years, others were to continue their parochial careers into the 1960s and 1970s. They rotated amongst the five island parishes with occasional sojourns on Eigg. Like their predecessors before them, they all came from the area they served, seven from South Uist, three from Barra and four from Morar[29] (see Table).

The result was an extraordinary degree of familiarity both amongst the clergy and between priests and parishioners, a genial intimacy which, as the bishops in Oban were also drawn from this same small group, extended to include the latter in the passing on of parochial news and gossip, as in Fr. Duncan MacLean's request to Bishop Campbell in February 1940:

> Yesterday also we buried old John MacKellaig – the last of the Land Leaguers. He had been failing for some time. [*Màiri Nìl Bhain had been asking if he had any news of her daughter who was in Oban.*] People tell me she does not go to Mass or duties, & is quite up to date in her habits. I presume she smokes a cigarette without a holder! Could you get one of the young ones to interest himself in her mode of living? The mother says, 'Cha'n eil aice ach Beurla shasunnach . . .'[30]

Parish Priests in the Isles 1936–80			
Benbecula	1940–51	Joseph Campbell	(Barra)
	1951–56	John MacCormick	(Barra)
	1956–66	Colin MacPherson	(South Uist)
Ardkenneth, South Uist	1941–46	Angus MacSween	(Morar-Arisaig)
	1946–62	John Morrison	(South Uist)
Bornish, South Uist	1940–48	Neil MacKellaig	(Morar)
	1948–52	Alex MacKellaig	(Morar)
	1952–59	John MacLean	(Barra)
Daliburgh, South Uist	1941–48	Patrick MacDonald	(South Uist)
	1948–80	Neil MacKellaig	
Eriskay	1940–46	Malcolm Morrison	(South Uist)
	1946–51	Colin MacPherson	
	1956–59	Donald MacDougall	(South Uist)
Castlebay, Barra	1941–56	Ewen MacInnes	(South Uist)
	1956–66	John MacCormick	
Northbay, Barra	1936–46	Dominic MacKellaig	(Morar)
	1946–59	Malcolm Morrison	

The late Fr. Anthony Ross OP, an astute observer of the Scottish Catholic community to which he was initially drawn as a convert and which he subsequently served as a historian, has characterised the situation in the late 1930s as one in which many priests were tinged with fideism and were markedly anti-intellectual, working to the general belief that 'all will be well' if the people 'kept the Faith', a commitment most easily measured by regular attendance to Mass and duties and the reproduction of approved views.[31] In the Gaidheal-tachd there is more than a suggestion that this general, uncritical contentment was tinged with an added edge of clerical paternalism. As Fr. MacLean observed to the bishop when told he was to be moved from South Uist in the core Gaidhealtachd to Dunoon, in Argyll:

> 'the life of the Isles is ever attractive for it is carefree generally and has much to commend it . . . [while in Dunoon] life shall lack much of the consolation derived from ministering to an unsophisticated people. But the work remains the same.[32]

Any attempt to profile the nature of the modern Catholic Gaidheal-tachd must seek to assess the role, influence, and enduring legacy of this small number of men who served as parish priests in these formative years and balance the sometimes conflicting, often contra-dictory, evidence of surviving record and personal recollection. The high regard in which the clergy is held within the Catholic commu-nity has meant that, as a rule, uncritical filial reverential memory prevails. Thus according to the historian of 'Blessed Morar':

> Morar has always been blessed with a succession of saintly men, who devoted their lives to the spiritual and temporal welfare of the people entrusted to their care.[33]

The several priests who came from Morar itself to serve elsewhere, mainly in the Catholic islands, are also profiled in similar vein. Evidence, oral and otherwise, from within the communities some of them served, however, can give a very different picture. In a rare departure from the convention of filial pietism, a recent and unusu-ally candid account from Eriskay contrasts the assistance given by a relieving priest in helping islanders to write letters, to the attitude to his parishioners shown by the incumbent parish priest in the pre-war years:

> The resident priest at the time, Father Gillies, would not write for anyone and between him and his two sisters, apart from a few cronies, would

scarcely even speak to anyone, one day telling somebody who went to complain that if the window was nearer to him than the door to jump through it. . . . Mainland folks had a tendency to look down on island folks, and that trio had a good share of it the day they were moved to go somewhere else, with the sisters hoping a few bombs would fall on the island. The people were glad to see the last of them.[34]

If the reality within the Catholic communities was not always what it seemed, in broad terms, to the objective observer of both Protestant and Catholic areas of the West Highlands and Islands, there was a marked difference between the leadership role exercised by the clergy within the two communities. In the late 1940s, the *West Highland Survey* examined the social life of every crofting township in the islands and on the western seaboard and considered the influence of religion on the social life of the crofting townships in both areas. It concluded that whereas in the Protestant community, 'the tyranny of religion has driven many questioning young folk away from the townships' and 'too many ministers seem unable or disinclined to enter into any other side of life than the religious', in the Catholic areas, despite the community being even less well served than Presbyterian areas with social organisations, the attitude of the church to social and cultural activity was markedly different:

> The different attitude to sabbath observance enables the Catholic con-
> gregation gathered for Mass to go afterwards into the hall or the school-
> house and have a secular meeting. The Catholic priest is commonly busy
> about the townships seven days a week and exercises a very real lead-
> ership and pastoral influence. Our observations lead us to the opinion
> that a very small and remote community would have greater chance of
> survival if it were Catholic than if it followed one of the stricter sects.
>
> —Catholic priest.[35]

With the core of the Catholic Gaidhealtachd lying entirely within Inverness-shire, this 'very real leadership and pastoral influence' led many priests into an active role as District and County Councillors, a combination of parochial and political power which gave them a singular position of authority within small, close-knit island and isolated communities. For forty years, from 1940 to 1980, for example, Fr. Neil MacKellaig was a parish priest in South Uist, and for most of this period he was also the County Councillor. He is remembered as a 'strong priest', a man who enjoyed the authority of his position. This authority was not infrequently exercised behind the scenes to try to ensure that the priests, not the people, stayed in firm control, as in 1941 when the nomination of an incoming non-Catholic for the vacancy in the Benbecula ward was privately promoted, 'in the interests of the church', against the people's own choice of a local Catholic layman. An innate sense of mainland superiority is also attributed to Fr. MacKellaig and cited by many as the reason why no local island Catholic was ever appointed headteacher of Daliburgh secondary school.

At the inception of the diocese, the lack of provision for Catholic education, the lack of Catholic teachers and control teaching appointments had been the central issue on which the Church authorities had focused their energy. The situation was particularly acute in the Hebridean properties of Lady Gordon Cathcart where estate policy was resolutely resistant to the appointment of Catholic teachers and where the estate effectively controlled appointments.[36] The situation was partly resolved in the 1890s and 1900s by the importation of suitably trained and approved Catholic teachers from England. The 'thoroughly Catholic institution' of Mount Pleasant in Liverpool seems to have been heavily relied on for a supply of female primary teachers. Most, if not all, were non-Gaelic speaking but a thorough training in the role of the Catholic teacher in the promotion of the position of the parish priest, setting a good example in attendance to 'duties', dissemination of approved Catholic literature and assistance with Sunday Schools, solidalities and confraternities was more important than any proficiency in Gaelic.[37] Later, as Catholic teacher training was established in Scotland, the training of teachers for the Catholic Gaidhealtachd was through the institutions in Glasgow. The result was a Catholic Gaidhealtachd serviced and administered by priests trained in the orthodoxy of Blairs and the colleges, assisted by teachers trained in the orthodoxy of Glasgow and the west. This grounding was the making of the modern Catholic Gaidhealtachd.

In 1956 Canon MacLean was to complain that control of schools remained a problem, with no Catholic representation and the control of the education of Catholic children in the hands of men, 'unsympathetic to their needs and wholly antagonistic to their beliefs.'[38] This perceived difficulty, however, related to the Clydeside towns of the diocese where Catholics were in a minority. By the 1950s, as a result of clerical domination of the political representation of the Catholic areas, *de facto* power over schools within the Catholic Gaidhealtachd was virtually absolute. The County Education Committee made the crucial staff appointments. The scheme of religious education, the pattern of local holidays, the local management of the schools were determined at local level by the District Area Education Sub-Committee. In the predominantly Catholic areas the Church ensured that these were controlled by the clergy and 'loyal' Catholic teacher and Catholic parents representatives. The local minister, if not already a District Councillor, would be co-opted as an 'additional interest' but the overwhelming balance of the committee was firmly Catholic, with the established Church firmly relegated to minority status.

The schools were effectively run as Catholic schools. In the South Uist District Area Education Sub-Committee's official scheme for the school year, 'Church Holidays' meant *Catholic* Church holidays and the dates were those of the Catholic Holidays of Obligation. The Church of Scotland Fast Day was relegated to 'additional holiday' status. In 1944, the new headteacher at Daliburgh took this a stage further by proposing a more explicit scheme, which the committee accepted and forwarded to Inverness whereby the 'Church Holidays' were incorporated into the official school year and explicitly named. In this Catholic enclave of Scotland, the 'non-denominational' official school year now revolved around *All Saints, The Immaculate Conception, St Joseph's, Ascension Day, Corpus Christi,* and *Sts Peter and Paul.*

Despite the *de facto* control of education in the core Catholic Gaidhealtachd, elsewhere in the diocese the provision of Catholic education and the lack of Catholic schools remained an issue. In his 1954 Advent letter, Archbishop Grant reminded the diocesan faithful that 'the Catholic children of today will be the founders of the Catholic homes of tomorrow', but this depended on a grounding in Catholic education, something not readily available at secondary level where, for the great majority of diocesan pupils:

> The remainder of their school careers has to be spent in non-Catholic schools where little or no provision is made for their instruction in Catholic doctrine. Who can measure the dire effects of this miserable necessity on their character formation during the most impressionable years of their lives?

Association with non-Catholics carried the risk of defections, leading in later life to mixed or even civil marriages.[39] In South Uist, the 'danger' was guarded against by the importation of teachers with a solid background in the epicentre of Catholic educational orthodoxy, the Archdiocese of Glasgow as in the 1955 appointment as

Headteacher of Daliburgh of a Holyrood teacher with strong links to the Don Bosco Society and a background in fighting 'Communist control' in student politics.[40] By 1957 the results from Daliburgh J.S., South Uist and Castlebay J.S., Barra were appearing alongside those of St Bonaventures, Glasgow, and St Patrick's, Dumbarton, in the Scottish Catholic Observer's publication of the Catholic schools prize lists.[41] The Gaidhealtachd was gravitating towards the ghetto.

The Last Bastion of Civilisation?

In the early 1950s, the director of the *West Highland Survey*, Frank Fraser Darling, had concluded that right across the Catholic Highlands, from Banffshire to Barra:

> The Catholic Church in the Highlands and Islands is Roman in name, but the objective observer sees a liberal Catholicism which is the descendant of the Columban Church.[42]

The juxtaposition of 'Roman in name' with 'liberal' is a revealing insight into the outsider's perception of Catholicism in the immediate post-war era. To a wider Scotland itself slowly emerging from the grip of the clergy, the impression of a relaxed practice of religion and a participatory priesthood was unsurprisingly attractive, its appeal all the greater in the context of the austere, rigid Presbyterianism which prevailed elsewhere in the Highlands. Writers and cultural nationalists were drawn to this reminder of an 'alternative Scotland'. Catholic writers, mostly converts themselves, liked to portray this liberal, warm, European image of the Catholic Gaidhealtachd, none more so than the doyen of the Catholic cultural nationalist literati, Compton MacKenzie, who took up residency on Barra and extolled its virtues:

> It will be wisest to call the peculiar magic of Barra a happy mixture of the natural scene, the character of the people, and the religious atmosphere combining to produce that effect of perpetual youth which expresses as well as anything our faint human apperception of Paradise.[43]

This was the 'peculiar magic' of the Catholic west, where the responsive visitor could experience, 'the innocent freedom in which a Catholic community delights', relax and enjoy 'the customs and observances of such a community, however far they may seem to lag behind the spirit of the times.'[44]

In reality, even in the 1930s, the notion of a people who 'seem to lag behind' derived more from the customs and traditions recorded in an earlier era and first brought to public attention in the 1890s–1900s, most notably in the publication of the first and second volumes of Alexander Carmichael's *Carmina Gadelica* and in the 'Celtic twilight' variants of Kennedy-Fraser and George MacLeod.[45] The importance of *Carmina Gadelica* in the externalisation of the image of the Catholic Gaidhealtachd cannot be overstated. It became the foundation text invariably cited when the enduring continuum of a 'popular Catholicism' was being evidenced, the living testimony to the distinct Catholicism of the Gael.[46] The relationship of 'popular Catholicism' and the formal liturgy of the Church was an interest of Fr. Allan Macdonald of Eriskay, *Maighstir Ailein*. He represents that pivotal moment when the two elements in Gaelic Catholicism came closest. But what is critical to an understanding of the form of religiosity in the modern Catholic Gaidhealtachd is that the project to create a synthesis in liturgical practice did not develop beyond *Maighstir Ailein*.[47] Rather than being encouraged as an aspect of the people's Catholicism it was taken out of 'the Faith', defused and stored in the press as 'folklore', to be dusted down for an occasional airing with collectors and enthusiasts. *Carmina Gadelica* itself was a wonderful collection, but it remained just that, a revered text, a testimony to the magical-religious past, a legacy which had been superseded by the legalistic religiosity of tridentine orthodoxy which was the uniformity of Scottish Catholicism.

In the post-war era of an unresolved struggle with modernity and industrialism and a new epochal Cold War battle with socialism and Satan, the Catholic Gaidhealtachd took on a new profile as the last bastion of true religion and 'civilisation'. From his redoubt in Eigg, the ultra-reactionary convert and Catholic writer George Scott-Moncrieff fulminated against 'the incessant propaganda of an Industrialism growing shriller as it approaches its nemesis' and a left-wing 'government congenitally hostile to peasant people'. For conservative Catholics disdainful of an urban working class and predominantly Irish Catholics, the Catholic islands were the epitome of Catholic values this side of Franco's Spain, as Scott-Moncrieff found Barra on Ascension Day:

> I felt another world join with the palpable Hebridean world about me, the world of France and Italy. Here in Barra there is appreciable that

older European tradition from which we in Britain have been much cut off, first by the Reformation, then increasingly by Industrialism.[48]

However, for the Catholic writers, assessing the Catholic Gaidhealtachd from a specifically Catholic agenda, the two overarching qualities of obdurate opposition to modernity and unyielding loyalty to 'the one, true Faith' were the defining features of centuries of resistance in the face of hardship and adversity. This was what the Catholic Gaidhealtachd had come to signify to Scotland's Catholic community as it entered the post-war era. They underpinned a celebratory crucible moment of 1950s triumphalism when fideism, clericalism and historicity culminated in the final pivotal moment when the Catholic Gaidhealtachd re-created itself in a granite image on a Hebridean hillside which still casts a long, if fading, shadow over the present.

Gaels into Irish

The 1950s was a time of confident faith. The League of St Andrew offered daily prayer and Holy Communion at least once a year for the conversion of Scotland, a cause which every parish regularly and earnestly prayed for.[49] The Catholic Highlands served as a quiet, constant reminder that not everywhere was Catholicism the faith of a minority. Every Saturday, at Fort Augustus Abbey, the Litany of Our Lady was sung in open public procession.[50] A report in the Catholic press on the Glenfinnan Highland Games informed readers that there had been 'a strong representation of priests and leading lay personalities', adding with a note of quiet satisfaction: 'The event is predominantly Catholic'.[51] In the 1950s it would also have been predominantly Gaelic but to the *Scottish Catholic Observer* and its readers, a Gaelic event was an Irish event, unless it specifically said otherwise. Headlines on a new bishop being a Gaelic enthusiast referred to Clonfert not Scotland.[52] Archbishop Campbell presided at a Gaelic concert, but for the Gaelic League – of Ireland.[53] When he spoke at a church building fund concert and said he had always wanted to dedicate a church to St Brigid, the 'Mary of the Gael' it was in Toryglen to the Glasgow Irish, not in his own islands to his own native Gaels.[54] The 'Mary of the Gael' Concert was held at O'Neil's School of Irish Dancing, while St Andrew's Hall hosted the St Patrick's Ceilidh in St Andrew's Hall.[55] And under the headline 'The Shamrock in St Andrew's Cathedral', Fr. Brendan Murphy of

St Columba's, Glasgow, preached to 'we Irish', on the Celtic saints. When the papal flag flew alongside 'Mary of the Gael' as the new church foundation stone was laid in Toryglen and Archbishop Campbell spoke of Brigid and Ireland, the cub scouts of Barra were on a first visit to the city from their native island, the highlight of their mainland trip, being taken to Celtic park to meet the Celtic stars.[56] An article in the same issue on 'Columcille and the Isles' puts a firm Irish gloss on the Hebrides. The Catholic Gaidhealtachd may be Scotland's Catholic past, but it owes its presence entirely to Ireland, its continuity and the perpetuation of the memory of Columba and Bride to Irish Vincentians and Franciscans.[57] If there was a shared 'Celtic spiritual well', as was suggested to Glasgow Gaels who gathered for the re-opening of Our Lady and St Margaret, Kinning Park, then ownership and title rights lay firmly with Ireland.[58] An Edinburgh CTS (Catholic Truth Society) publication on 'Christianity in Scotland Today' acknowledged the country's debt to 'those splendid Highland Catholics' who had sustained the continuity of Catholicism in a context where 'Hatred of the Church had been bred in the bones of Scotsmen' but it was the Irish who had the 'one, unshakeable conviction', despite the sneers of virulent anti-Catholic propaganda 'that the Catholic Faith was the one reality.' Amongst Catholic Highlanders, 'this belief was held no less intensely', but the Irish had the numbers and were in the Lowlands where it mattered.[59]

In the creative reformulation of the story of modern Catholic Scotland, as Scottish history was re-worked to a purpose, the key assigned contribution of the Catholic Gaidhealtachd was not its Gaelic dimension which was always ultimately secondary and second-hand, but its fidelity. In the 1950s all Scottish history was re-presented through the prism of the struggle with 'godless Communism'. The immediate aftermath of the uprising of 1956 saw the Edinburgh CTS draw clear parallels between the struggle of Scottish Catholics since 1560 and the fate of Hungary as Scotland Catholics prepared for their National Pilgrimage to Dunfermline in honour of St Margaret:

> We pay our patroness such honour as we can, enduring with understanding the restrictions imposed upon us by our life in a non-Catholic country. At the same time we appreciate the tolerance shown to us by those who now govern and uphold the sacred places of St Margaret.

They called for more support for the pilgrimage. Scotland needed her patron saint's intercession and her pity:

St Margaret was a Hungarian Princess. We have seen what has happened to her native land. Our sympathy at the plight and distress of
Hungary is real and sincere, because our own land suffered likewise 400
years ago and again in the '45.[60]

In Edinburgh, Archbishop Gray's 1957 Pentecostal Sermon used the
coincidence of Columba's feast to proclaim 'the Roman heart of the
Celtic Church' as Celtic legacy was reduced to crude propaganda
proclaiming papal supremacy:

> Columba, said the Archbishop, was in the tradition of St Patrick, whole-
> hearted in loyalty to the Vicar of Christ, proud of the Apostolic See from
> which the power and the authority were derived. . . . if Columba had
> deviated for one moment from the Patrician tradition of fervent loyalty
> and obedience to the Vicar of Christ, then he would never have found
> his last resting place alongside the remains of St. Patrick in the Cathedral
> of Down. . . . Patrick and Ninian, Columba and Mungo apostles to whom
> we owe so much. Fearless and intrepid missionaries, who bore to this
> land the torch of the faith, a torch lighted from the quenchless flame of
> the Catholic faith; pure and radiant, first kindled at Pentecost and ever
> extinguished but ever in the safe keeping of the Papacy, bright and
> shedding its warm rays upon the world.[61]

The externalised image of a traditional, untainted 'simple faith' may
have been the cultural creation of Compton MacKenzie and other
Catholic writers, its reformulation as an essentially hierarchical tradition of 'fervent loyalty and obedience to the Vicar of Christ' the
reductive projection of the church authorities, but neither presenta-
tion met with any suggestion of disquiet from within the Catholic
Gaidhealtachd itself. On the contrary, the mantle was readily approved and accepted. Along with it came a new self-conscious
awareness, an implicit superiority.

The passive nature of quietist filial allegiance, by definition,
makes public assertions of opinion from within the laity rare. As a
rule the voice of the Catholic Gaidhealtachd was only heard through
the clergy. But a revealing glimpse into the way in which the role
assigned to Highland Catholicism was embraced and internalised is
given through the flurry of public appeals made on behalf of the *Holy
Mass Society*, a body set up from within the Catholic Gaidhealtachd
in November 1954. The declared aim of the Society was to ease the
financial burden on Argyll and the Isles by raising funds to assist in
the provision of support for priests serving the most outlying remote

mass centres.[62] But from the beginning it had a deeper, underlying purpose. In April 1955 the *Scottish Catholic Observer* carried an article which proclaimed that 'Scotland will be given back the gift of Faith through the medium of the Holy Mass Society'. According to this unattributed 'member's plea', much had happened in Scotland since Columba, with 'the Sign of the Cross', first brought the Faith, 'most of it disastrous and stemming mainly from the Reformers.' Through defeated Jacobitism, the clearances and military service to the Empire, the Gaels are presented as victims as 'disaster followed on disaster'. There is contempt for the exile network of the city émigrés, 'resplendent in new kilts' and for the 'Celtic twilight' visitors to the islands who 'wallow in the wake of Marjory Kennedy-Fraser' while the 'real Highlanders' are more to be heard in the bars of Adelaide or Durban than 'any day in Fort William or Oban.' Only the Catholic Gaidhealtachd offers a glimmer of hope in this catalogue of despair:

> However, the grim black history is shot with gleams of scarlet and gold. The Chisholms, the Macdonalds, the MacNeils kept the Faith as bravely as any people in the world 'where everyman had a dirk in his stocking and a history at his back'. Strathglass and Moidart, Lochaber and Morar, Mingulay to Benbecula – the very names ring like bugle notes in the true history of Scotland.

Little known names from the Jacobite era and penal times are cited as heroes to be remembered for:

> These and others kept Scotland in alignment with the Church of the great Franciscans – Assisi, Sales, Xavier and Borgia. They kept for us the heritage of Aquinas, Augustine and a Kempis.

The plea for support ends by declaring that Scotland will be given back the gift of Faith as her sons go forth in ever greater number to the foreign missions but their vocations can only be secured by the intense cultivation of the ground at home, which meant the heartland of the Catholic Gaidhealtachd where the Holy Mass Society took its place in the ranks under the banner of St Columba.[63] The appeals were tinged with messianic zeal. When a mass centre in Benderloch closed, the Society secretary wrote to *the Scottish Catholic Observer* warning that 'this Highland surrender must be the last':

> Even as the old folk of Ailort to the sea were to recall, 'There was never a minister's sermon in Morar till the railway came.' . . . There is an alien faith in Iona now, and the work of St Columba's missioners is still there,

to be done all over again. The Holy Mass Society was founded to maintain these little strongholds of the Faith, in the fastnesses of the North.... Recently one outpost was abandoned. The Redemptorists had to withdraw from Benderloch. That must be the last surrender.[64]

The Diocese of Argyll and the Isles had 'a list of saints in the calendar surpassing that of any other Bishopric in the world, excepting Rome itself' and 'all Scotland is doubly in debt to the Braes of Lochaber and the Sands of Morar, where down the years they kept the Faith 'for the men they gave to the hierarchy of Scotland. Now they needed a Centurion tank for the priest serving Dalavich, a helicopter for Benbecula, a half-track for Taynuilt while the Mam Barrisdale track to Fr. Gillies in Knoydart would be a trial for any reader.[65] If sufficient funds came to the Society treasurer in Spean Bridge, then all of the Highlands were recoverable for Catholicism, even the most unlikely corners:

> Lewis held the Faith for upwards of 80 years after the Reformation only to lose it because of the lack of priests. Now it will be quite the most difficult part of Scotland to win back. The prejudice of all things Catholic is traditional, and all the more saddening, as the Lewismen are a staunch, stalwart and a kindly people. Mass in the town of Stornoway is the story of the Catecombs all over again. The mere handful of Catholics are all 'incomers', local government officers and civil servants, which is all the more reason why this most isolated Mass centre must be zealously guarded and maintained.[66]

The Holy Mass Society was a small and seemingly short-lived venture, important for an insight into thinking within the Catholic Gaidhealtachd rather than as an organisation in itself. A more established body was the Caledonian Catholic Association centred on Glasgow. Unlike the Catholics of the North East, the Catholic Gaels retained an identity in exile and by the 1950s the Gaelic Catholic exile community in Glasgow was a firmly established and recognised feature of Catholic life in the city, with occasional reports on their social activities appearing in the Scottish Catholic press.[67] The CCA was heavily dominated by exile Gaels, Gaelic figured prominently in its social activities, and it held an annual Gaelic service, initially in St Andrew's Cathedral, latterly in Our Lady and St Margaret's, Kinning Park, the focal parish for Highland and Island Gaelic exiles.[68] Indeed, as support fluctuated, a not infrequent cause of concern was that the Association was perceived by others to be essentially a Gaelic body.[69] It served as a focal point for an emergent and growing Gaelic professional middle class in the city, an important link between an obedient laity and the clergy. Not surprisingly, as an exile Catholic Gael himself, Archbishop Campbell appears to have been particularly supportive. At the Association's 1957 annual dinner, J.J. Campbell JP proposed the toast to the hierarchy on behalf of the Association in fulsome and reactionary terms. In reply Archbishop Campbell called his namesake 'a most distinguished gentleman, and a zealous, loyal and fearless Catholic' and said of the CCA, 'We are proud of you – grateful for your spirit of loyalty and co-operation.' Fr. Agnellus Andrew OFM assured them that the CCA's work was held in high esteem by the hierarchy for their care for Catholics coming from the Highlands and for the way in which they had shown themselves willing to espouse any good cause commended to them by the Bishops. It was felt by some that Caledonian and Catholic did not mix and an impression was abroad that Scotland was altogether a Protestant land. Yet, he maintained, they were never as Catholic as they were today, which was why the Association was so important.[70]

The diocesan hub of Argyll and the Isles was Oban, the centre for educational control in the core Gaidhealtachd was Inverness but what the activities of the CCA underlined was that the crucial alignment of the core Gaidhealtachd was emphatically with Glasgow and that there was developing a seamless web of Catholic identity which incorporated the Gaidhealtachd into the robe of Glasgow Catholicism. The fact that Archbishop Donald Campbell was not only a Gael, but had been a parish priest in the islands, as well as Bishop of Argyll and the Isles before being translated to Glasgow helped in translocating the intimacy of the Gaidhealtachd to the metropolis no less so than the social hubris around the Paisley Road and Kinning Park.[71]

The declaration of 1954 as Marian Year triggered off a series of Marian commemorations across Scotland. At Celtic Park a huge crowd gathered for a Marian rally under Archbishop Campbell, singing 'God Bless the Pope' to the playing of the St Patrick's (Shotts) Band, as the papal flag and the St Andrew's cross flew side by side.[72] On the cricket pitch of Fort Augustus Abbey School, a more sedate gathering of over two thousand, the biggest Marian commemoration in the Highlands since the Reformation, honoured 'Our Lady of Aberdeen'.[73] In July, the first Argyll and the Isles pilgrimage to Lourdes included contingents from Barra and South Uist.[74] With reports coming in from across the world of plans for statues being erected at coastal and island sites[75] it was announced that a 24ft statue was to be built on South Uist to be unveiled in 1956,[76] while from Barra it was reported that one was to be erected specifically to commemorate the Marion Year. Before a crowd of over a thousand with banners and flowers, illuminated against the evening darkness, it was unveiled on a hill overlooking Castlebay on 15 August.[77] On South Uist the first of 12 roadside shrines to Our Lady was also unveiled in a ceremony described as unique in the history of the Outer Hebrides. *Failte, Reul na Mara* was sung as Fr. Ninian Macdonald OSB conducted the ceremony, but this was no 'popular Madonna' ritual of ethnic Gaelic Catholicism. On the contrary:

> Devotion to Our Lady has always been a feature of the Catholic life of these islands. Hitherto it has been confined to our churches and our homes. Now, however, it is felt that the time has come to fall in line with the Catholic countries of Europe for example, the Rhineland of Germany, Bavaria, the Austrian Tyrol, Poland, Carinthia, Belgium, France and Italy, where wayside shrines are a striking characteristic of the Catholic life of the people. Even as the Feast of the Assumption is a red-letter day in the calendar of the Church, so this should prove a red-letter day in the Outer Isles.[78]

In reality, the Catholic Gaidhealtachd had always 'been in line' in all its devotional practice, not least its Marian homage. The language and settings were markedly different, but the 40,000 at a Coatbridge Rosary Rally a fortnight later, building shrines around tenement lamp-posts, displayed the same essential Marian devotional format.[79] Indeed the dedication of the South Uist 'Our Lady of the Isles', was held back from 1956 to 1958 in order to mark another official Marian year, the Lourdes Centenary. The *Scottish Catholic Observer* presaged the event with a lengthy homily on 'Bright Mary of the Isles' which located Lourdes and the Immaculate Conception firmly in the 'glory of Scotland' which was 'the living devotion to Mary in the Western Isles'.[80]

Over the intervening period the plans for a major 'rocket range' development on the island had been announced and Catholic writers and the Catholic press had joined the parish priest, Fr. 'Rocket' (Fr. Morrison) in expressing their protest over its threat to the Gaelic culture of the island and the implicit threat of dilution to the Catholic identity of this core within the core of the Catholic Gaidhealtachd.[81] A scheme was even floated to import a northern Irish Catholic workforce to ensure the Catholic identity would be protected.[82]

Conclusion: into the Ghetto?

> In Tir-nan-Og, the Celtic Paradise, it is always sunlight with a sheen on the sands. There is an ultimate thule, the fairest island in the West and the land of heart's desire. For the young there is all the good they ever knew and for the old all the good that ever was. There too is Mary gentle, Bright Mary, Mary guileless and Mary fragrant, a lady-lord clothed in white, Our Lady of the Western Isles.[83]

The dedication of 'Our Lady of the Isles' in 1958 was important. It marked the epitome of all that the Catholic Gaidhealtachd had come to represent. It was a confident, assertive moment, clothed in the 'magic' of 'an unbroken tradition'. Yet in reality it was an elegiac watershed, the moment when 'the long nineteenth century' of Highland Catholicism finally began to draw to a close. A few years ahead lay the realisation of the 'rocket range' in the Uists, the rapid transformation of the social fabric of the entire Catholic Gaidhealtachd area and even more dramatic shrinkage. Badenoch, Knoydart, Canna, Eigg were effectively eclipsed, Moidart drastically thinned and in 1974 the Catholic Hebrides were re-aligned as the 'Southern Isles' appendage to a new administrative structure dominated by old-style fundamentalist Presbyterianism unaccustomed to co-habitation. Electricity – and thereby the cultural impact of television – reached most areas by the 1960s and even the most isolated pockets by the 1980s. Improved communications, social mobility, educational opportunities and greater fluidity in employment patterns intensified the assimilative association with Glasgow.

Significantly it has been the social transformation of the area which has altered the religiosity of Catholic Gaidhealtachd more than the consequences of Vatican II. For while the latter brought a Gaelic liturgy, it was a change in the medium, not the message. There was no evolution of a popular-cultural Catholicism of the Gael, no 'liberated' Mariology building on the protecting Mary of Celtic tradition, no hermeneutical Christology deriving from the presence in the oral legacy of the 'unbroken tradition'.[84] Exploration of the spirituality within Celtic Christianity develops across the globe and the world wide web, but not in the Catholic Gaidhealtachd of Scotland.

Yet while in appearance the fideism and clericalism of the early modern Catholic Gaidhealtachd remains, it is a superficial impression and in reality the transformation is no less dramatic than elsewhere. As with the close of Ireland's 'long nineteenth century', the monolithic

power of the Church has fragmented, its holistic, overarching authority has fragmented and the parallel in the consequence is striking. In
a close community, *maighstir* may remain the term of address for the
parish priest but now with more a sense of affection amongst equals
than deference to authority. The days of *maighstireachd*, of unques-
tioned moral power, of superiority and the habit of assuming authority are over and as elsewhere the awe, reverence and obedience which
the priest enjoyed well into the early modern era of the Catholic
Gaidhealtachd 'have begun to dissipate into general disregard if not
public cynicism.'[85] The otherworld Catholic Gaidhealtachd, extolled
on a hillside of South Uist in 1958, lingered well into the 1980s, but
today it is as distant and ethereal as the 'land of heart's desire' evoked
in Fr. Keenan's Celtic prose. The youth of today's Catholic Gaidhealtachd reflect values and attitudes which differ little from those of their
non-Catholic Gaelic counterparts and which are essentially indistin-
guishable from those of their city Catholic cousins.[86] Indeed, such is
the extent of assimilation to the dominant Catholic community of
Glasgow that within the translocated surrogate ghetto of the Catholic
islands, the familiar hoops of Glasgow Celtic are the colours of Catholic identity and the incantations of Celtic Park more familiar than the
lost obscurities of *Carmina Gadelica*, the title itself more likely to be
mistaken for the name of the latest continental signing. This absorption process, however, is not at the expense of a diminished local,
Gaelic or Scottish national, even nationalist, identity.

It has been argued, in relation to Catholic identity in modern
Scotland and Glasgow Celtic FC, that:

> Celtic provides the platform on which many Catholics relate to their
> ethnic-religious identity and the community to which they belong and,
> just as importantly, the one to which they do not.[87]

The ethnie, of course, is Irish, the ascriptive identity of those who
support Celtic being emphatically 'non-Scots' – more in tune to the
harp than the bagpipe.[88] Yet this simply does not match up with
the felt experience of identity within the Catholic Gaidhealtachd,
the actuality of Scottish Catholic as opposed to *Irish* Catholic reality. The Catholic Gaidhealtachd's cultural absorption into the
greater Glasgow ghetto may reveal inherent weaknesses, a situation, as I have sought to suggest, largely attributable to the
Church. At the same time it also highlights the continuing hegem-
ony of the Irish Catholic urban West as the dominant cultural bloc
within Catholic Scotland and the continuing insistence that the

'basic background' to understanding modern Scottish Catholicism remains the historical experience of this constituency.[89] There is a profound irony in the fact that the obstacle to a further understanding of the nature of the contemporary Scottish community is not the 'usual suspect' of an overarching anglocentrism but the denial of parity of esteem by an overbearing hibernocentrism.

NOTES

1. Fr. A. Keenan OFM, 'Bright Mary of the Western Isles, *Scottish Catholic Observer*, 3 January 1958.
2. I use the term 'Catholic Gaidhealtachd' to distinguish the focus of this essay from the present Catholic community scattered throughout the Highlands and Islands as generally defined in administrative terms. It implicitly has an organic relationship to the survival of the 'old' Catholic Gaidhealtachd as defined in an ethnic or cultural sense and is more specifically traced within the linguistic retreat of Gaelic, see C. W. J. Withers, *Gaelic Scotland: the transformation of a culture region* (London, 1988). The emergence of a 'new' Catholic Highlands, particularly the development of Catholic communities within traditional Presbyterian areas, is a subject which merits a study in itself.
3. I have borrowed the phrase from T. Inglis, *Moral Monopoly: The Catholic Church in Modern Irish Society* (Dublin, 1987), p. 224.
4. Studies of modern Scottish Catholicism are, in fact, either explicitly or implicitly studies of the west of Scotland Irish Catholic community and the wider modern community, not least the North East and the Highlands and Islands, have yet to receive scholarly attention although there has been a steady stream of important studies on the historical Catholic Gaidhealtachd, notably the work of J.L. Campbell, M. Dilworth, R. Macdonald, A. MacWilliam and A. Roberts. This preliminary essay draws on 'work in progress' to outline a tentative approach to the formation of the modern Catholic Gaidhealtachd. Only when this 'benchmark' formative outline of the modern has been established can the more recent and not unimportant developments of the last 25 years be put in context.
5. 'Particular condescendance of some grievances from the encreasce of poperie, and the Insolence of popish priests & Jesuits', 29 May 1714, transcribed in N. M. Wilby, 'The "Encreasce of Popery" in the Highlands 1714–1747', *The Innes Review*, XVII, 1967, p. 93.
6. An inadequate but sole map of this area is contained in O. Blundell, *Catholic Highlands of Scotland*, I (London, 1909), facing, p. 17.
7. For the prior administration of the Gaidhealtachd and the background to the restoration see P.F. Anson, *Underground Catholicism in Scotland 1622–1878* (Montrose, 1970); C. Johnson, *Developments in the Roman Catholic Church in Scotland, 1789–1829* (Edinburgh, 1983). The Gaidhealtachd was not alone in suffering from Church authorities indifferent to cultural and ethnic identity. In 1861 the Congregation de Propaganda Fide transferred Caithness, Orkney and Shetland to a

short-lived Arctic Mission, alongside Lapland, the Faroes, Iceland, Greenland and part of northern Canada, see P.F. Anson, *op. cit.*, pp. 306–7.

8. This was recognised by Canon Duncan MacLean in his official review of the diocese in 1956 when he acknowledged that as a result of 'a difference in language and forebears', Argyll and Bute had little in common with 'the Rough Bounds, Lochaber and the Isles'. See D. MacLean, 'Argyll and the Isles', in Br. Clare, (ed.), *1878–1955 Glasgow Observer and Scottish Catholic Herald Scottish Survey*, *The Scottish Catholic Observer*, 10 February 1956.

9. For an insight into the 'abandoned' areas see O. Blundell, *op. cit.*, and *Catholic Highlands of Scotland*, II (London, 1917). For more specific historical backgrounds see also A. Roberts, 'Catholic Kintail: A Marginal Community', *Transactions of the Gaelic Society of Inverness*, LVIII 1993–4, pp. 133–135; A. MacWilliam, 'The Jesuit Mission in Upper Deeside 1671–1737', *The Innes Review*, XXIII, 1972, pp. 22–39; A. MacWilliam, 'A Highland Mission: Strathglass, 1671–1777', *The Innes Review*, XXIV, 1974, pp. 75–102.

10. For further discussion of this concept see Yves Congar, *Lay People in the Church* (Westminster, 1965). See also the discussion of the key category of *potestas* in L. Boff, *Church, Charisma & Power: Liberation Theology and the Institutional Church* (London, 1985).

11. See E. De Smedt's speech in *Acta Concilii Vaticani II*, I, pt. 4 (Vatican City, 1971).

12. It is difficult to see to what extent it differed – if at all – from the urban situation, not least in the leading role of the parish priest and the supportive role fulfilled by women, whereby, 'nuns, female teachers, mothers and devotion to the Virgin Mother of God were central to the continuation of the Church'. See B. Aspinall, ' "Children of the Dead End": the formation of the Archdiocese of Glasgow', *The Innes Review*, XLIII, 1992, p. 139.

13. For examples of the influence, the aristocratic patrons sought to exercise see R. Macdonald, 'The Catholic Gaidhealtachd', *The Innes Review*, XXIX, 1978, pp. 56–72.

14. The sequence of dedications, all notably non-Celtic was: 1884 Benbecula, *St Mary's*; 1886 Knoydart, *St Agatha's*; 1888 Castlebay, *Our Lady Star of the Sea*; 1889 Morar, *Our Lady of Perpetual Succour and St Cumin*; 1894 Portree, *Our Lady of the Assumption*; 1902, Howbeg, *St Joseph's*; 1902 Taynuilt, *The Visitation*; 1913 Vatersay, *Our Lady of the Waves and St John*. The only Celtic exception, an obscure one, was 1909 Glencoe, *St Mun's*. For a discussion of the 'official' metacult of Mary and the potential for ethnic, cultural 'splintering' of Marian cults see M. P. Carroll, *Madonnas that Maim: Popular Catholicism in Italy since the Fifteenth Century* (Baltimore, 1992).

15. The detailed account from *The Tablet* 11 May 1889 is given in P. Galbraith, *Blessed Morar (Morair Bheannaichte)* (Morar, 1989), pp. 346.

16. The important role Fort Augustus Abbey has played in the Catholic Highlands has yet to be assessed, not least its contribution to Gaelic

scholarship and Highland historiography. For a brief account of its foundation see P. F. Anson, *op. cit.*, pp. 321–5.

17. *Scottish Catholic Observer*, 19 March 1954.
18. *Ibid*.
19. See J. L. Campbell, *Fr Allan McDonald of Eriskay, 1859–1905, priest, poet, and folklorist* (Edinburgh, 1954), p. 7.
20. *Leanmhuin Chriost* (Edinburgh, 1826); *An Cath Spioradail* (Perth, 1835); *Cràbhadh do'n Tighearna Iosa* (Liverpool, 1879); *Iùl a' Chriosdaidh* (Perth, 1834, Antigonish, 1901); *Lòchran an Anma* (Edinburgh, 1906). These still feature as current Gaelic Catholic religious resources. Gaelic Catholic literature remains, as the Gaelic catechism *Aithghearradh Teagasg Chriosda* (Oban, 1902), firmly based in the Council of Trent, resolutely conservative. See J.A. Galbraith, *Catholic Church, Western Isles, Scotland: Gaelic Religious Resources* (http: dspace.dial.pipex.com/town /avenue/pa44/webdoc8.htm, 1997).
21. A. Ross, *The root of the matter: boyhood, manhood and God* (Edinburgh, 1989), p. 133. A significant reflection on the conservatism of the Catholic Gaidhealtachd is that in the 1930s, in Morar, as in Beauly, the people went to Confession and Communion only about once a year, *op. cit.*, p. 131.
22. W. Bradley, 'The Changes in Parochial Life', in Br. Clare, *op. cit.*.
23. B. Aspinall, *op. cit.*, p. 136
24. Donald Martin (1919–1938) was a third cousin to both his successors, Donald Campbell (1938–1945) and Kenneth Grant (1945–1959) and Campbell and Grant were second cousins. See J. Darragh, *The Catholic Hierarchy of Scotland* (Edinburgh, 1986), pp. 38–40.
25. Darragh, *ibid*.
26. D. MacLean, *op. cit.* In 1878 there were 13 priests for a diocese of 12,000 and by 1956 it had 30 priests and 40 churches with the number of Catholics remaining static at *c.* 12,000, *ibid*.
27. Apart from key senior figures such as Archbishop Donald Campbell and Canon Duncan MacLean, Fr. John MacMillan of Barra merits particular attention for his role in the externalisation of the image of the Catholic Gaidhealtachd, both in his own activities and particularly through his influence on Compton MacKenzie and Fionn MacColla. See obituary notice, *Scottish Catholic Directory* (Glasgow, 1952), pp. 320–3.
28. James Galbraith was in Mingarry (Moidart), 1941–51, succeeded by Joseph Campbell, 1951–62; John MacNeill (1900) was in Arisaig, 1933–64; John MacNeill (1903) was in Morar, 1923–58.
29. The parishes varied in size. Although the areas were extensive, the numbers were small. Most were *c.* 350–750 although Daliburgh and Castlebay were each over 1000, while scattered Moidart was just over 200 and Eigg only 65.
30. [S]cottish [C]atholic [A]rchive, DA42/132/4. D. MacLean to Bp. Campbell, 12 February 1940.
31. A. Ross OP, 'The Development of the Scottish Catholic Community 1878–1978' *The Innes Review*, XXIX, 1978, pp. 30–55.

32. SCA DA42/132/10, D. MacLean to Bp. Campbell, 23 May 1941.
33. P. Galbraith, *op. cit.*, p. 41.
34. A. E. MacInnes, *Eriskay Where I Was Born* (Edinburgh, 1997), pp. 49–50.
35. F. Fraser Darling, *West Highland Survey* (Oxford, 1955), pp. 314–6.
36. See F. G. Rea, *A school in South Uist: reminiscences of a Hebridean school-master, 1890–1913* (London, 1964.
37. The influence of Mount Pleasant was felt in Barra, South Uist, Ben-becula, Moidart, Lochaber, Badenoch and Strathglass. See B. Aspinall, 'Catholic teachers for Scotland: the Liverpool connection', *The Innes Review*, XLV, 1994, pp. 64–70.
38. Duncan MacLean, *op. cit.*.
39. *Scottish Catholic Observer*, 3 December 1954.
40. *Scottish Catholic Observer*, 2 December 1955.
41. *Scottish Catholic Observer*, 12 July 1957.
42. F. Fraser Darling, *op. cit.*, p. 316.
43. C. Mackenzie, 'Catholic Barra' in J. L. Campbell, *The book of Barra* (London, 1936), p. 5.
44. *Ibid.*, p. 28.
45. A. Carmichael, *Carmina Gadelica, Ortha nan Gaidheal*, I–VI (Edinburgh, 1900, 1928, 1940, 1941, 1954, 1971). See also the important Preface by John MacInnes in the compendium edition, (Edinburgh, 1992), pp. 7–18; G. MacLeod, *The Road to the Isles*, (London, 1943).
46. D. MacLean, 'Catholicism in the Highlands and Isles 1560–1680', *The Innes Review*, III, 1952, p. 7; R. Macdonald, *op. cit.*, pp. 68–70.
47. The extent and nature of Gaelic 'popular Christianity' is a complex issue in itself. The late Calum MacLean, a major collector in the field in the late 1940s and 1950s, a convert to Catholicism from a Free Presbyterian Raasay upbringing, consistently argued that the vestigial Celtic 'popular Christianity' of Gael was to be found in all Gaelic communities, not just the Catholic Gaidhealtachd. See C. MacLean, *The Highlands* (London, 1959), pp. 1203–4. Fr. Allan seems to have confined his experiments to the liturgy, particularly hymnology. Devotional practices based on an older popular Celtic 'Catholicism' do not seem to have been developed. The focus was on the translation into Gaelic of orthodox devotional practices. A valuable starting point would be J. L. Campbell, 'The Sources of the Gaelic Hymnal, 1893', *The Innes Review*, VII, 1956, pp. 101–11.
48. G. Scott-Moncreiff, *The Scottish Islands*, (London, 1952), pp. 51, 97.
49. *Scottish Catholic Observer*, 4 January 1957.
50. *Ibid.*
51. *Scottish Catholic Observer*, 27 August 1957.
52. *Scottish Catholic Observer*, 1 January 1954.
53. *Scottish Catholic Observer*, 12 February 1954.
54. *Scottish Catholic Observer*, 18 January 1957.
55. *Scottish Catholic Observer*, 11 January 1957.
56. *Scottish Catholic Observer*, 3 May 1957.
57. Nablia di Dubhcean, 'Columcille and the Isles', *Scottish Catholic Observer*, 3 May 1957.

58. *Scottish Catholic Observer*, 20 December 1957.
59. *Scottish Catholic Observer*, 20 November 1957.
60. *Scottish Catholic Observer*, 7 June 1957.
61. *Scottish Catholic Observer*, 14 June 1957.
62. *Scottish Catholic Observer*, 3 December 1954. The three founding members were, J Farrel, the Procurator-Fiscal for Shetland and the Outer Hebrides, T. MacKenzie, Lochaber and Hugh Macdonald, Morar.
63. *Scottish Catholic Observer*, 15 April 1955.
64. *Scottish Catholic Observer*, 29 April 1955.
65. *Scottish Catholic Observer*, 27 May 1955.
66. *Ibid.*
67. *Scottish Catholic Observer*, 22 January 1954. The focal point was Paisley Road, the principal parish was Kinning Park.
68. *Scottish Catholic Observer*, 4 January 1957. The service was initially held in St Andrew's Cathedral but, with falling numbers, transferred latterly to Our Lady and St Margaret's, Kinning Park.
69. When the CCA advertised a Gaelic concert it had to be specified as a *Scottish* Gaelic Concert.
70. *Scottish Catholic Observer*, 6 December 1957.
71. Donald Campbell's predecessor, Donald Mackintosh was also a Gael and his uncle, also Donald Mackintosh, also from Brae Lochaber had been co-adjutor-archbishop and a parish priest at St Margaret's, Kinning Park. See J. Darragh, *op. cit.*, pp. 53–6.
72. *Scottish Catholic Observer*, 4 June 1954.
73. *Scottish Catholic Observer*, 4 June 1957.
74. *Scottish Catholic Observer*, 30 April 1954.
75. *Scottish Catholic Observer*, 13 January 1954.
76. *Scottish Catholic Observer*, 26 February 1954.
77. *Scottish Catholic Observer*, 6 August 1954.
78. *Scottish Catholic Observer*, 27 August 1954.
79. *Scottish Catholic Observer*, 10 September 1954.
80. *Scottish Catholic Observer*, 3 January 1958.
81. *Scottish Catholic Observer*, 3 December 1954. When it was revealed that the range site was to be in close proximity to the proposed statue site and there was a report that the Government wanted the statue moved, the *SCO* carried the banner headline story: 'Now they are afraid of spies disguised as pilgrims – Rocket Range Close by Queen of the Isles Headland – Oh, What an outcry if Iona had been site of weapon project', *Scottish Catholic Observer*, 19 August 1955.
82. *Scottish Catholic Observer*, 6 September 1957. The scheme fell through when its advocate, Patrick Byrne, an Irish journalist and Gaelic enthusiast, died suddenly, *Scottish Catholic Observer*, 13 September 1957.
83. Fr. Keenan, *op. cit.*
84. For an examination of such a 'popular Mariology' with Mary as the patroness of the people, a 'projection' of the suffering of the people, see I. Gabara, M.C. Singemar, *Mary, Mother of God, Mother of the Poor* (London, 1989).
85. T. Inglis, *op. cit.*, p. 225.

86. Survey of religious attitudes of senior Uist school pupils, 1994, in private possession.
87. J. Bradley, 'Religious Cleavage and Aspects of Catholic Identity in Modern Scotland', *Records of the Scottish Church History Society*, XXV (1995), p. 452.
88. *Ibid*.
89. J. F. MacCaffrey, 'Roman Catholics in Scotland in the 19th and 20th centuries', *Records of the Scottish Church History Society*, XXI (1991), p. 275 fn.1.

9

CONCLUSION: THE FUTURE OF CATHOLIC SCOTLAND

Raymond Boyle and Peter Lynch

The Scottish Parliament

The attitudes of the Catholic Church towards a devolved Scottish parliament have been difficult to discern. Though the issue of constitutional change rose on the political agenda over the last decade, culminating in the double Yes vote at the referendum on 11th September 1997, the Church's position has been one of ambivalence. In contrast to the Church of Scotland, the Catholic Church did not adopt a position on the constitutional issue, though its membership was supportive of both devolution and independence as demonstrated earlier in this book (see chapter 4). Though the Church may have eschewed developing a position on constitutional change, the establishment of a Scottish parliament has a substantial impact on the Church in areas such as education.

Devolution is a challenge to the Catholic Church because it involves change and uncertainty, though also some opportunities as will be argued below. The fact that the Scottish parliament will be responsible for education will bring a new openness to educational debate which will clearly impact on Catholic education: old debates will be reopened and new ones shall emerge. Instead of the Church, local authorities and the Scottish Office being responsible for Catholic schooling through internal mechanisms that have developed since 1918, there will be greater public debate about the role and existence of Catholic schools and the entry into educational policy-making of an interventionist Scottish parliament. The new political context of devolution will doubtless throw up some of the usual demands to end the 'segregated' schooling system, and the Church might find itself on the defensive in areas such as school mergers in an era of falling pupil rolls and school closures. It might also find aspects of the post-1918 educational settlement discussed in terms which it finds damage its interests, such as the Church's role in approving teachers and its right of appeal to the Secretary of State for Scotland in the event of proposals to close a Catholic school, which might be challenged by the effect of the devolution process on the Scottish Secretary's position anyway. In addition, it might be that the parliament adopts a more active role in education which usurps the traditional role of the local authorities and undermines the role of Church representatives on local education authorities.

Whatever developments occur, it will be vital that the Church, along with many other pressure groups, seeks strong links with the parliament and individual parliamentarians in a spirit of co-operation and constructive engagement rather than one of conflict. Unfortunately, the recent activism of the Church in education such as demanding that teachers of home economics and modern studies in Catholic schools are Catholics; the demand for the extension of the 1918 educational settlement to include nursery schools; and the various right to life conflicts such as Cardinal Winning's dispute with Labour discussed in chapter 3, all indicated a Church prone to adopting a conflictual approach to difficult issues which made it frequently appear on the defensive. The nature of the Bishop Wright sex scandal, the need to prevent school closures and the disputes of sexual and non-sexual abuse involving individual priests as well as Catholic children's homes, have all presented the Church with difficult issues. However, on occasions the Church's response has been damaging, though dealing with such no-win situations would always have been problematic.

Three points are worth making about the Church's position in the New Scotland. First, the Church has a mission to explain its role in, and to, Scottish society. Clearly, and for the hundredth time no doubt, it will have to justify the continued existence of the Catholic education system. However, in doing so, the Church needs to focus its campaigning efforts on ordinary Scots, not just the government, local authorities and grassroots Catholics. Most Scots have no experience of Catholic schools and little awareness of what makes them different besides religious education. They will have little awareness of the role of parents in Catholic education, the functioning of the Church-school-family triangle within Catholic schooling, and the pastoral work of the teachers.[1] These are the social aspects of Catholic education that are not widely known amongst the Scottish public and it is ironic that in an era of parental rights and involvement, in which governments and parents have been concerned with standards, discipline and schools performance, that the benefits of Catholic schools in these areas have been overlooked. Therefore the Church needs to get away from a simple defensive stance on Catholic schools to make a broader case about the benefits of the system to pupils and to wider Scottish society. And when it comes to whether the schools actually perform well in their basic educational functions, it probably has the league tables to do it.[2]

Second, the Church needs to take account of the social agenda of the new Labour government. On occasions, in areas such as homelessness, poverty, etc., the Church will clearly come into dispute with Labour given the latter's commitment to stringent expenditure constraints. However, it can be argued that the government's concern for stakeholding, rights and duties and community has a substantial resonance in the social teaching of the Church. Indeed, one academic has argued that the language and attitudes of the new communitarianism can be understood as 'old communion wine in new bottles.'[3] The fact that the intellectual mood has shifted somewhat towards community and society and away from the individualist attitudes of the 1980s can be seen as a useful background for the Church to develop its own social message. The new moralism or Puritanism of the Labour government can also be seen as an area of common ground rather than conflict, with opportunities to influence public debate and the broad outlines of government policy.

Finally, the Church needs to escape its defensive posture, which all too often dominates its media profile and to recognise that its role and position in Scottish society have changed. It might like to think of itself on occasion as an institution under attack in Scotland – which has certainly come across in some of its pronouncements and activities – but it is in fact a well-established Scottish institution with a key role, if it wants it, in the development of a more pluralist Scotland. Though the old fear of devolution or independence leading to a quasi-Orange Scottish state on Northern Irish lines has disappeared, the Church does not seem to have replaced it with a positive agenda. The Church therefore needs to approach the New Scotland with the firm intention to play a role in a multi-cultural society with an increasingly ecumenical religious environment not through acting solely to defend Catholic education, which tends to dominate media coverage, but through presenting its case for a socially just Scotland which cares for the poor and disadvantaged at home and abroad: the type of message which seems to gel with the view of Scotland as a collectivist, egalitarian society.

Of course, devolution does not apply to everything and its impact is limited. The Scotland Act 1998 devolved a range of matters to the new Scottish parliament. However, significantly, it did not devolve policy areas such as overseas aid and development; immigration and nationality; human fertilisation and embryology; abortion; and human genetics:[4] all areas in which the Church has shown a keen interest. Therefore, similar to other institutions and pressure groups, the Church may find its political attention and concerns divided between Edinburgh and Westminster, which will shape the Church's media image in Scotland as the Scottish media focuses on the Scottish parliamentary concerns of the Church in education and housing and ignores its other efforts. Thus it is clear that the Church's media image in Scotland is likely to continue to revolve around the issue of Catholic schools and the defence of the status quo in education, reinforcing the Church's defensive image. However, while there are possible problems associated with the new context of devolution, there are also opportunities.

No-one really knows how the new terrain of Scottish political autonomy will impact upon the related cultural and social areas of civil society in Scotland. For examples, Schlesinger noted that the devolution referendum of 11th September 1997:

> implicitly identified the Scots as a civic nation, as voting was open only to residents of Scotland, irrespective of their ethnic background or places of birth. Ethnic Scots outside the country had no voting rights. This is an important benchmark, though still little appreciated, for future political discourse about 'the nation' in Scotland.[5]

There is little evidence to suggest that the role played by the various churches in Scotland will be diminished by the new devolution arrangements. As noted earlier, the increased media focus on Holyrood rather than Westminster as the political centre of Scottish life may actually serve to strengthen, at least in the short-term, the interventions made by all churches in public discussions over political decisions that impact on Scottish society.

Devolution is, of course, not the only challenge facing the Catholic Church. The Church must face up to its own internal debates and problems such as celibacy, the role of women and ordinary members in the Church and a gap between the Church and its adherents over social and moral issues. It also has to deal with a Catholic community which will continue to experience social change as Scottish society continues to develop, changes which make Catholics less distinctive, more integrated into Scottish society and perhaps also more secular.

Sectarianism and 'Civic' Scotland

One of the issues often surrounding the Catholic experience in Scottish society is that of sectarianism. However, as is clear from some of the previous chapters, there is a certain level of debate, and indeed dispute, about the existence or otherwise of this phenomenon in contemporary society. To some, sectarianism, or discrimination against Catholics, does not exist because it cannot be statistically or materially proven and is in part generated by sections of the media or academics who have focused research on the 'Old Firm' rivalry. Perhaps part of the problem lies in the usage of the word sectarianism, carrying as it does many connotations associated with the Northern Ireland conflict. Despite the continual existence of religious labelling in some parts of Scottish society, Scotland is not Northern Ireland, and to simply transplant a framework for analysis which fails to take into account the specific economic, cultural and political development of Scotland is likely to be of limited use.

Rather than the emotive use of sectarianism with all its historical baggage, the simple terms of prejudice, bigotry, dislike and at certain times discrimination would be perhaps a more useful lexicon in dealing with differences which exist along the lines of ethnicity, race, geography or gender. While there may not any longer be systematic discrimination against Catholics in Scottish society, that does not mean that in certain social circumstances, particularly in the west of Scotland, there are situations in which Catholics can be made to feel uncomfortable simply because that creed is viewed with suspicion or simple dislike. When similar attitudes are applied to ethnic minorities, we quite correctly label this racist. In other words, one of the issues that Scottish society has to face up to is tackling prejudice and discrimination at all levels and against any citizen.

A Research Agenda

Whilst this book has dealt with a range of issues relevant to the Catholic community, there are numerous issues which have been neglected in our own work and in studies of Scottish society in general. On the one hand, there needs to be greater emphasis on examining and re-examining the past to determine questions such as the changing employment practices in Scotland which saw the easing of sectarian divisions in the job market and enabled Catholics to have a wider range of job opportunities. Similarly, the way in which the Catholic Church, the state and local authorities have managed education and the schools issue is a major area requiring historical attention and analysis. On the other hand, more contemporary studies need to address the political role of the Church; the growth of inter-Church links in an increasingly ecumenical climate; and the grassroots involvement of individual members of the Church. In addition, very little is known about the Catholic community outside the central belt.

It is ironic that at a time in the Academy, and particularly within areas such as sociology, cultural and media studies, when issues relating to the constitution and reconstitution of cultural and national identities are very much on the agenda, that a more vigorous research culture around Catholicism and contemporary identity formation has not developed. This is not about 'Ghetto Studies', as any worthwhile examination of Catholicism in Scotland must be about shedding light on wider aspects of modern Scottish culture and society and not one particular group within that country. Of course we would also argue that much work remains to be done in developing a body of work focused on examining the contemporary Scottish experience within the wider domain of the social sciences, which still remains heavily centred on what is actually the English experiences of youth and popular culture. This is another area where, despite groundbreaking work by David McCrone,[6] much more needs to be done to examine Scottish society through the lens of the social sciences. However that remains an argument for another day.

Conclusion

One hopes that a period of increasing Scottish political self-expression and confidence will see the country involve itself in both an examination of internal divisions and prejudices, while also witnessing an outward-looking gaze to Europe and beyond which seeks to embrace cultural difference, confident of its own ever-changing and dynamic identity. That need to change, adapt and remain relevant is also a challenge faced by the Catholic Church, not simply in Scotland but across the globe. While we are often told we live in a global media community and are subject to the whims of a global economy, the local and the national remain important. What remains fundamental to understanding contemporary experience is the interaction between these international and increasingly European forces and more rooted and localised concerns, identities and communities. What we have seen in Scotland is the extent to which a universal Catholic Church can help shape, and be shaped by the specific political, economic and cultural contours which have characterised Scotland, the Scots and Scottish identity over the last few centuries. What is required of the Catholic Church now is the confidence, the honesty and the openness to remain part of this process as we enter the next century.

NOTES

1. B. McGettrick, 'Information Paper 14: Catholic Education in Scotland – An Overview of Current Practice', *Scottish Educational Review*, Vol. 16, No. 2, 1984, p. 135.
2. Tom Little, 'Money plus religion equals top marks – right or wrong?', *The Scotsman*, 4 February 1998.
3. Daragh Minogue, 'Etzioni's Communitarianism: Old Communion Wine in New Bottles', *Politics*, Vol. 17, No. 3, 1997, pp. 161–8.
4. Head 9 – Health and Medicine, Schedule 5, reserved matters, Scotland bill 1997.
5. P. Schlesinger, 'Scotland's Parliament: Devolution, the Media and Politics Culture', in J. Seaton (ed), 'The Media and Politics', special issue of *Political Quarterly*, 1998, p. 4.
6. David McCrone, *Understanding Scotland: The Sociology of a Stateless Nation* (London, 1992).

INDEX